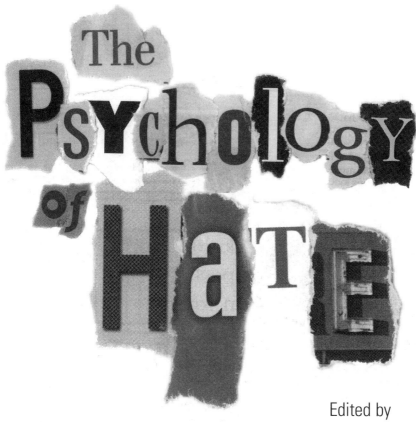

The Psychology of Hate

Edited by

ROBERT J. STERNBERG

American Psychological Association • Washington, DC

Second Printing October 2005

Published by
American Psychological Association
750 First Street, NE
Washington, DC 20002
www.apa.org

To order
APA Order Department
P.O. Box 92984
Washington, DC 20090-2984
Tel: (800) 374-2721; Direct: (202) 336-5510
Fax: (202) 336-5502; TDD/TTY: (202) 336-6123
Online: www.apa.org/books/
E-mail: order@apa.org

In the U.K., Europe, Africa, and the Middle East, copies may be ordered from
American Psychological Association
3 Henrietta Street
Covent Garden, London
WC2E 8LU England

Typeset in Goudy by Page Grafx, Inc., St. Simons Island, GA

Printer: Sheridan Books, Ann Arbor, MI
Cover Designer: Naylor Design, Washington, DC
Technical/Production Editor: Emily Leonard

The opinions and statements published are the responsibility of the authors, and such opinions and statements do not necessarily represent the policies of the American Psychological Association.

Library of Congress Cataloging-in-Publication Data

The psychology of hate / edited by Robert J. Sternberg.— 1st ed.
    p. cm.
Includes bibliographical references and index.
ISBN 1-59147-184-2
1. Hate. I. Sternberg, Robert J.
BF575.H3P74 2004
152.4—dc22

2004012194

British Library Cataloguing-in-Publication Data
A CIP record is available from the British Library.

Printed in the United States of America
First Edition

CONTENTS

Contributors . . . .   *vii*

Preface . . . .   *ix*

Chapter 1.　From Plato to Putnam: Four Ways to Think
　　　　　　About Hate   3
　　　　　　Edward B. Royzman, Clark McCauley, and Paul Rozin

Chapter 2.　Understanding and Combating Hate   37
　　　　　　Robert J. Sternberg

Chapter 3.　The Origins and Evolution of Hate, With Notes
　　　　　　on Prevention   51
　　　　　　Ervin Staub

Chapter 4.　A Cognitive Perspective on Hate and Violence   67
　　　　　　Aaron T. Beck and James Pretzer

Chapter 5.　Roots of Hate, Violence, and Evil   87
　　　　　　Roy F. Baumeister and David A. Butz

Chapter 6.　The Diminution of Hate Through the Promotion
　　　　　　of Positive Individual–Context Relations   103
　　　　　　Richard M. Lerner, Aida Bilalbegović Balsano,
　　　　　　Rumeli Banik, and Sophie Naudeau

Chapter 7.　Hate, Conflict, and Moral Exclusion   121
　　　　　　Susan Opotow

Chapter 8.　On Hate and Its Determinants: Some Affective
　　　　　　and Cognitive Influences   155
　　　　　　Leonard Berkowitz

Chapter 9.   Genocidal Hatred: Now You See It,
              Now You Don't 185
              David Moshman

Chapter 10.   On the Nature of Prejudice: The Psychological
              Foundations of Hate 211
              *John F. Dovidio, Samuel L. Gaertner, and
              Adam R. Pearson*

Chapter 11.   Hate Is the Imitation of Love 235
              C. Fred Alford

Index 255

About the Editor 263

CONTRIBUTORS

C. Fred Alford, PhD, Professor of Government and Distinguished Scholar-Teacher, University of Maryland, College Park

Aida Bilalbegović Balsano, MA, Eliot-Pearson Department of Child Development, Tufts University, Medford, MA

Rumeli Banik, MA, Eliot-Pearson Department of Child Development, Tufts University, Medford, MA

Roy F. Baumeister, PhD, Department of Psychology, Florida State University, Tallahassee

Aaron T. Beck, MD, Professor of Psychiatry, University of Pennsylvania Medical Center, Philadelphia; President, Beck Institute for Cognitive Therapy, Bala Cynwyd, PA

Leonard Berkowitz, PhD, Vilas Research Professor Emeritus, University of Wisconsin—Madison

David A. Butz, MS, Department of Psychology, Florida State University, Tallahassee

John F. Dovidio, PhD, Department of Psychology, Colgate University, Hamilton, NY, and University of Connecticut, Storrs

Samuel L. Gaertner, PhD, Professor, Department of Psychology, University of Delaware, Newark

Richard M. Lerner, PhD, Bergstrom Chair in Applied Developmental Science and Director, Institute for Applied Research in Youth Development, Eliot-Pearson Department of Child Development, Tufts University, Medford, MA

Clark McCauley, PhD, Professor, Department of Psychology, Bryn Mawr College, Bryn Mawr, PA; Director, Solomon Asch Center for Study of Ethnopolitical Conflict, University of Pennsylvania, Philadelphia

David Moshman, PhD, Professor of Educational Psychology, University of Nebraska—Lincoln

Sophie Naudeau, MA, Eliot-Pearson Department of Child Development, Tufts University, Medford, MA

Susan Opotow, PhD, Professor, Graduate Program in Dispute Resolution, College of Public and Community Service, University of Massachusetts Boston

Adam R. Pearson, doctoral student, Department of Psychology, University of Connecticut, Storrs

James Pretzer, PhD, Director, Cleveland Center for Cognitive Therapy; Clinical Assistant Professor of Psychology, Department of Psychiatry, Case Western Reserve University School of Medicine, Cleveland, OH

Edward B. Royzman, MA, doctoral student, Department of Psychology, and Research Fellow, Solomon Asch Center for Study of Ethnopolitical Conflict, University of Pennsylvania, Philadelphia

Paul Rozin, PhD, Edmund J. and Louise W. Kahn Professor of Psychology, Department of Psychology and Associate Director, Solomon Asch Center for Study of Ethnopolitical Conflict, University of Pennsylvania, Philadelphia

Ervin Staub, PhD, Professor, Department of Psychology, Director of PhD Concentration in the Psychology of Peace and the Prevention of Violence, University of Massachusetts Amherst

Robert J. Sternberg, PhD, IBM Professor of Psychology and Education, Department of Psychology, Yale University, New Haven, CT

PREFACE

The goal of this book is to present alternative perspectives on the psychology of hate. After the genocide perpetrated by the Nazis in World War II, the expression "never again" became a familiar refrain. Perhaps there were aspects of the Nazi horrors that would not be repeated, but the massacres and genocides inspired and committed by the Nazis were far from the last the world was to see. The last decade of the 20th century saw massacres and genocides in record numbers, and indeed, the last half of the 20th century witnessed a staggering number of massacres and genocides. The beginning of the 21st century has seen fresh waves of terrorism, such as those culminating in the events of September 11, 2001. These were not random killings or sudden bursts of irrationality on the part of crowds. Rather, they were carefully planned and orchestrated killings that, at times, approached the efficiency of the Nazi death machine in the sheer number of deaths produced. In many cases, although certainly not all, one of the underlying causes was one of the most powerful of human emotions: hate.

The dictionary definition of *hate* is "1. to have strong dislike or ill will for; loathe; despise. 2. to dislike or wish to avoid; shrink from" (Neufeldt & Guralnik, 1997, p. 617). Although this definition serves as a starting point for an understanding of hate, it is not sufficiently detailed to serve as an ending point. Psychologists who study hate, therefore, seek to expand on this definition and similar ones.

Psychologists have not generated a lot of theories of hate, certainly fewer than theories of love. A survey of some recent introductory social psychology texts revealed *love* as an index term in all of them but *hate* as an index term in none of them. The goal of this book is to help redress an imbalance—to propose a number of different theories that answer questions about hate in related, but different, ways. The theories proposed in this book cover the gamut, including clinical, cognitive, social, and eclectic emphases on understanding hate.

Authors have been asked to address a common set of questions to ensure unity of their contributions:

1. How do you conceptualize hate?
2. What evidence is there for this conceptualization?
3. How does your view relate to other views?
4. What do you see as the role of hate in terrorism, massacres, and genocides?
5. How, if at all, can hate be assessed?
6. How, if at all, can hate be combated?

This book is addressed to anyone who has an interest in hate, whether a psychologist or not. Chapters are written at a level that should be comprehensible to any intelligent layperson.

I am grateful to Cheri Stahl for her help in the preparation of the manuscript and to the American Psychological Association for taking an interest in publishing this book.

REFERENCE

Neufeldt, V., & Guralnik, D. B. (1997). *Webster's new world college dictionary* (3rd ed.). New York: Macmillan.

1

FROM PLATO TO PUTNAM:
FOUR WAYS TO THINK ABOUT HATE

EDWARD B. ROYZMAN, CLARK MCCAULEY, AND PAUL ROZIN

The English word *hate* signifies a domain of dizzying versatility and breadth. Consider: A child hates a bully, a woman hates her estranged husband, a bigot hates the "inferior race," a fighter for human rights hates injustice, an anorexic hates her calves, a widower hates long weekends, some Jews hate Germans, Sallieri hates Mozart, Mozart hates bogus art, millions hate Saddam Hussein, little Jimmy hates his broccoli. People act out of hate, feel overcome by hate ("I really hated her at that moment!"), endure it as a life-long affliction ("Unfortunately, I hate Aunt Margie, always have, always will . . ."), or elevate it into a virtue ("I hate hypocrisy").

In spite of scores of books, topical discussions, stirring editorials, and hate-fighting initiatives, there is no single, commonly accepted definition of *hate*. What is it precisely that people are discussing, fighting against, or trying not to let into their hearts? In this chapter we review major conceptions of hate, both classic and modern. Finding no consensus, we discern in the welter of proposals four ways of asserting an understanding of hate: categorical

We thank James Russell and John Sabini for their comments on drafts of this chapter.

meta-description, (paradigm-based) causal explanation, stipulation, and Platonic insight. Each of these offers a distinctive basis for defining hate and for evaluating that definition. We conclude that a clearer understanding of hate, its origins, and its consequences will be advanced by paying more explicit attention to the different roles that different authors ascribe to their conceptions of hate.

CONCEPTIONS OF HATE: OLD AND NEW

Classic Definitions of Hate

The classic formulations of hate, those by Aristotle, Descartes, Spinoza, Hume, and Darwin, are notable for their contradictions. For Descartes (1694/1989), hate was an awareness of an object as something bad and an urge to withdraw from it. For Spinoza (1677/1985), it was a case of pain (sadness) accompanied by a perception of some external cause. For Aristotle (trans. 1954), the distinguishing phenomenological fact about hate was that it is pain-free (in addition to being incurable by time and striving for the annihilation of its object). Hume (1739–1740/1980) argued that neither love nor hate can be defined at all, because both are irreducible feelings with the introspective immediacy of sensory impressions. Darwin (1872/1998) also saw hate as a special feeling, one that lacks a distinct facial sign and manifests itself as rage.

The contradictions in these definitions have to do with the weighting of feeling and (affect-free) judgment, with some authors emphasizing a negative feeling toward the object of hatred (Spinoza, Hume, and Darwin) and others emphasizing a negative judgment about that object (Descartes and Aristotle). Aristotle's qualification that hatred does not change with time suggests, in particular, a negative judgment about the character or essence of that which is hated, rather than a reaction to a specific negative trait or action. Another source of contradiction involves the behavioral tendency associated with hatred: Descartes suggested withdrawal, whereas Aristotle suggested attack. Darwin's understanding of hatred also suggests attack, insofar as hatred is manifested as rage, but Descartes made hatred more like fear (or disgust) in its link to withdrawal. In these classic treatments of hatred, then, is already apparent the outline of current contentions about the beliefs, feelings, and behaviors associated with hate and about the relation of hate to emotions such as anger and fear.

Emotion or Disposition?

Recent research understands *emotion* as a set of "multicomponent response tendencies that unfold over relatively short time spans" (Fredrickson

& Branigan, 2001, p. 125). That is, emotion is understood as episodic rather than dispositional, and any particular emotion is experienced as a pattern of specific cognitions, subjective experiences, and physiological reactions. Such garden-variety emotions should be distinguished from *episodic dispositions* (Averill, 1991; Ryle, 1949), or relatively long-term tendencies to emote (in the sense of displaying a distinct episodic emotion) about an object, event, or person, or a category of objects, events, or persons.

A very similar distinction between emotional experience and the disposition to experience emotion was offered in Shand's (1920) far earlier and much-neglected treatment of hate. For Shand, hate was the perfect antimony of love: Love involves a positive alignment between the emotions of the lover and the fortunes of the beloved, whereas hate involves a negative alignment:

> The health and prosperity of the loved object are causes of joy: in hatred, they are causes of bitter sorrow. In place of the delight of being again with one we love, is a peculiar mixture of repugnance and anger when we find ourselves again in the presence of one we hate; the one impelling us to avoid the person, the other to attack him . . . The joy of hate is the opposite of the joy of love, being caused by the suffering, loss of power and reputation of the hated person; and the sorrow of hate is opposite to the sorrow of love, and is caused by his power, reputation, and happiness. (p. 59)

Shand (1920) described hate as a *syndrome*, or a bundle of episodic dispositions united by a common emotional object or a common category of such objects. The key feature of such a syndrome is that a person may be legitimately characterized as having it without being imputed any corresponding episodic state.

Patriotism is a case in point. The term has a dual meaning—it refers both to an ideological stance and an affective syndrome that goes with such a stance; people commonly speak of feeling more or less patriotic at different periods of their lives. What are these feelings like? The obvious answer is that no such feelings need to exist, at least not apart from a person's tendency to experience other kinds of feelings (pride, sorrow, shame) in which his or her affective life appears to be aligned with the fortunes of his or her nation (cf. Ryle, 1949; Sabini & Silver, 1998). Thus, a patriotic person would be expected to feel joy and pride when his or her nation is victorious, sorrow and sympathy when it is facing a crisis, anger when it is unjustly slighted, and despair when it suffers a humiliating defeat. Yet carefully as one may inspect a patriotic person's interior life and daily habits, one will never find in it a trace of the special feeling called "patriotism" that exists apart from all of the above. In fact, in our view, the very expectation of such a discovery should automatically attract the suspicion of the so-called category mistake (Ryle, 1949), the mistake of imagining that a given higher order phenomenon exists as something separate and independent of its basic constituents. (Ryle's own famous example is that of a foreigner who, after being shown the various lecture halls, libraries, lanes, and gardens comprising the Oxford University, asks, "Yes, all of these are fine, indeed, but where is the Oxford itself?").

The syndrome that Shand (1920) identified with "love" has also been described as *positive identification* (McCauley, 2001), or a tendency to track and react congruently to the fortunes of another person or group. Similarly, "hate" would qualify as the perfectly symmetrical syndrome of *negative identification*. In this view, hate is neither a special emotion nor a blend of emotions, but rather a tendency to emote in a number of ways to a number of situations involving the object of hatred.

Modern Conceptions of Hate

In the modern literature on emotions, Ekman (1992) has advanced a view of hate similar to Shand's (1920) idea of hate as syndrome. Ekman argued that hate is not an emotion but an "emotional attitude," the term he reserved for affective phenomena that are "more sustained [than a garden-variety emotion] and typically involve more than one emotion" (p. 194). That is, Ekman saw hatred as more an episodic disposition than a particular emotional experience. In contrast, Elster (1999) argued that hate is an emotion after all, one that is caused by a judgment that another is evil: "Negative emotions triggered by beliefs about another's character. (Contempt is induced by the thought that another is inferior; hatred by the thought that he is evil)" (p. 21).

Although Elster saw hate as separable from contempt, Sternberg (2003) recently proposed that both disgust and contempt are special kinds of hate, "cold hate" and "cool hate," respectively (see also Oatley & Johnson-Laird, 1987, for a claim that hate is a derivative of disgust). Sternberg's proposal is part of a broad theoretical typology based on the principle that, like love, hate can be characterized in terms of three action–feelings components: (a) intimacy (more precisely, the negation thereof), (b) passion, and (c) commitment. The feelings and actions associated with the first (negation of intimacy) component include revulsion–disgust and distancing, respectively. Fight-or-flight is the action pattern, and anger–fear are the feelings attending the passion element. The last (commitment) component involves an attempt to devalue the target of hatred through contempt. On the basis of this triangular structure, Sternberg posited a variety of hates. There is, for example, the already mentioned "cool hate," composed solely of disgust, and "hot hate," composed solely of the anger–fear combination. There are also "cold hate" (devaluation through contempt alone), "boiling hate" (disgust + anger–fear), "simmering hate" (disgust + contempt), "seething hate" (passion + commitment; also called "revilement"), and, finally, "burning hate," which includes all three action–feelings components.

Although Sternberg linked hate to negation of intimacy and judgments of inferiority (devaluation), Solomon (1977) argued that to associate hate with malice, viciousness, and denigration of one's opponent is to confuse it with another emotion: resentment. He maintained that, unlike other hostile responses, "hatred is an emotion that treats the other on an equal footing, neither degrading him as 'subhuman' (as in contempt) nor treating him with the lack of respect due to a moral inferior (as in indignation) nor humbling oneself before (or away from) him with the self-righteous impotence of resentment" (p. 324). True hate, he argued, is an emotion of intimacy, respect, and strength—"There can be no hatred in weakness" (Solomon, 1977, p. 326); he saw this equality of power as part of hate's special mythology, ensuring that the antagonism involves an element of "mutual respect." Though Solomon referred to hate as an emotion, the general affective construct that appears to fit best his own characterization of hate dynamics is that of a syndrome.

Another recently popular approach has been to view hate as a kind of "personalized," "generalized," or "globalized" anger. For example, Frijda's (1986) analysis of hate distinguishes between emotions that "involve attaching positive or negative valence to a person or object" (p. 212) and those that ascribe valence to an action or event. This distinction led him to describe hate as "emotion that contains the component of object evaluation" (p. 212) or a highly personalized version of anger (see also Kolnai, 1998). Power and Dalgleish (1997) described hate as "generalized anger." It is anger that ceased to be "about one event or one thwarted goal and has broadened to embrace parts of, or indeed all, aspects of the person or object" (p. 334). The generalized evalution involved in hate has also been stressed by Ben-Ze'ev (2000).

One of us previously proposed that hate could be viewed as a compound of anger and fear (e.g., McCauley, 2002); the object of hate not only is blamed for some past maltreatment of oneself or someone one cares about but also is recognized as a source of future threat. For Beck (1999), hate is also defined, in part, by the belief that the source of the threat lies in some stable (although not necessarily global) feature of the hated person (Beck's examples suggest that he thinks of hate as capable of being both an episodic disposition and an episodic emotion): "Assigning responsibility to another for unjustly 'causing' an unpleasant feeling is a prelude to feeling angry. The persistence of a sense of threat and the fixed image of a malicious person leads to at least a temporary feeling of hate" (Beck, 1999, p. 44, see also the example on p. 11).

In a book-length treatise on hate, Dozier (2002) suggested that hate is a sort of adaptively antiquated anger, "anger phobia" as he calls it. In this view, the primary feature that distinguishes hate from anger is not its abidingness or its global focus, but its irrationality. However, in a dictionary of psychological lexicon, Reber and Reber (2002) defined *hate* as a "deep, enduring, intense emotion expressing animosity, anger and hostility towards a person, group or object" (p. 315). The stress here is on the intensity and depth, rather than irrationality.

Gaylin (2003) proposed that real hate is a mental abnormality (p. 14) that exhibits obsessive–paranoid ideation and whose emotional core is rage (p. 34): "Hatred is a neurotic attachment to a self-created enemy that has been designed to rationalize the anxiety and torment of a demeaning existence" (p. 240). Gaylin also suggested that "the hate-driven people live in a distorted world of their own perceptions" (p. 202). Another psychoanalytic author (Blum, 1995) also has viewed hate as having pathological overtones:

> [Following Freud], hate is an ego attitude with the intent of destructive aggression. Hatred may be mobilized by need, fear, and frustration and by all unpleasant and noxious experiences. Transient or enduring, it tends to be closely linked to disturbance in psychic structure. (p. 20)

Ostensive Definitions of Hate

All the definitions of hate considered thus far, classic or contemporary, may be considered "direct" in that they handle their definiens as well as their definiendum (hate) in rather explicit terms. Such explicitness, however, is not necessarily essential to the practice of defining things. Philosophers also recognize a form of definition in which a definiens is communicated by either literally pointing to or otherwise indexing a case in which the definiendum is thought to be in evidence. Such definitions "by example" are called "ostensive" (Audi, 1995). Thus, one may give an ostensive definition of "pain" by pointing to a person in the throes of a toothache and saying "This is pain" or "This is what pain is like" (the more fine-tuned definition would entail the use of either statement right after stepping on someone's toe or poking him with a sharp stick).

Affirming the legitimacy of ostensive definitions is important because such definitions appear to be the staple for a number of recent political treatises on hate (e.g., Kaufman, 2001; Kressel, 2002). What may be initially confusing about such volumes is that, notwithstanding the word *hate* or *hatred* crisply displayed in their titles, they fail to offer anything like an explicit formulation of the very phenomenon they seem poised to elucidate. A careful reading, however, will indicate that what may at first pass for the absence of a definition is more generously interpreted as an ostensive definition.

Thus, though Kressel's (2002) "mass hate" does not openly define hate, it gives numerous instances of what hate is supposed to look like. The formulation of hate derivable from such instances is that hate is the motivational force that is responsible for acts of ethnic violence from the Holocaust to Rwanda, barring all those instances in which the violence is merely the result of conformity, blind obedience, or pure profit motive. The advantage of such a formulation is that it pinpoints a set of real problems (ethnic discrimination, ethnic rioting, genocide) that make the study of hate, whatever it may be, genuinely worthwhile (see Sternberg, 2003, for a deft argument regarding the importance of psychological study of ethnic violence). This delineation of hate, however, leaves no room for doubt as to whether hate is, indeed, responsible for ethnic violence. Granted that *being driven to commit acts of ethnic violence* is an integral part of what it means to *hate*, any claim concerning the link between hate and ethnic violence enjoys all the certainty of a tautology. Furthermore, as long as one acquiesces to define hate in terms of whatever is happening in some presumed paradigmatic instance of hate, one should also be ready to accept that whatever is going on in such instances may turn out to be radically different from one's a priori conceptions of hate.

Hate as a Normative Judgment

A special case of ostensive formulation might be found in the concept of the so-called hate crime. Hate crimes are commonly characterized as "criminal actions intended to harm or intimidate people because of their race, ethnicity, sexual orientation, religion, or other minority group status" (Herek, Gillis, & Cogan, 1999, p. 945; Levin & McDevitt, 1993). In this context, hate means roughly that which motivates a deliberate act of physical violence or intimidation against a member of a minority group by virtue of him or her being a member of that group. In this view, classifying a criminal deed as one of "hate" is compatible with a wide range of psychological states, anything from anger to boredom to fear. Why not speak of, say, "anger crimes," then?

One reason, we think, is that describing a hate criminal as acting out of anger carries some unwelcome normative implications (in this context, *normative* should be taken to mean a statement reflective of the generally accepted norms and values, as in "blackmail is morally wrong"). There has been a strong and honorable tradition in both philosophy and psychology of linking anger to a legitimate defense of one's rights (Aristotle, trans. 1954; Averill, 1982; Baumeister, Stillwell, & Wotman, 1990; Hall, 1898; Rozin, Lowery, Imada, & Haidt, 1999; Scherer, 1997). Thus, citing "anger" as a motive of someone's aggressive action may carry a built-in implication of legitimacy-ascription and evaluative approval that is unwelcome in the context of criminal attacks based on race or sexual orientation. Thus, lurking behind the concept of "hate crime," there seems to be yet another cultural meaning of hate as that which motivates acts of senseless (normatively unjustifiable) violence. Of course, what seems senseless to one person may seem like a justifiable act of force to another. In light of Baumeister's (1997) argument that an attack will generally seem more gratuitous to the victim than it does to the perpetrator, insistence on the use of *hate* in a particular situation may be less a matter of descriptive characterization than a reflection of normative commitment to identify with the plights of the victims while distancing from the viewpoints of the perpetrators.

The recognition of the normative or evaluative aspect of folk concepts is important because it may indicate the possibility that a disagreement over whether a certain folk psychological concept is applicable in a particular case may really be a disagreement about whether the evaluative meaning of that concept should dominate its descriptive (psychological) meaning or vice versa. A quick illustration will suffice. As Rachman (1978) pointed out, the folk concept of courage maps onto at least two psychological phenomena, including a capacity to remain fearless (with or without autonomic signs of fear) while in an objectively dangerous situation and a capacity or willingness to press on (with or without the associated autonomic arousal) in the face of fear. An ability to press on while being both subjectively and autonomically afraid seems to come closest to the ordinary conception of courage.

Yet few would describe a home burglary as an act of courage, even though each burglary may require the perpetrator to confront afresh and carry on in the face of a very real risk of capture, injury, or even immediate death at the hands of a disgruntled homeowner—as such, a burglar appears to perfectly fit the profile of someone capable and willing to uncouple the behavioral and the subjective–autonomic aspects of fear. The reason that home burglary is not thought to be an act of courage is that the ordinary conception of courage is not exhausted by a description of a certain psychological state, but it also entails a normative message to the effect that the action prompted by that state was a worthy one and that all good people should do likewise (Walton, 1986).

This normative aspect of courage was brought home spectacularly by the public outcry over comedian Bill Mahr's assertions that the 9/11 terrorists were not cowards and, by implication, were men of courage. If people's everyday notion of a courageous act were purely psychological, describing, as Rachman (1978) had it, a willingness or capacity to uncouple the behavioral and the mental elements of fear in the name of what the actor considers to be a worthy cause, then terrorists' suicidal assaults would be considered a paragon of courage.

The depiction of the 9/11 hijackers in terms of hate rather than anger or despair could also be interpreted as not so much a descriptive characterization of their psychological states as a normative avowal that the attack was an act of senseless aggression (essentially a "hate crime," albeit one of gigantic proportions) and that the terrorists' actions were deeply, monstrously immoral. We are confident that had some public figure stated that the terrorists "acted out of anger," the ardor of the ensuing controversy would have approximated (or even eclipsed) that occasioned by Mahr's incendiary comment.

To sum up, despite much recent attention to hate as a topic of discussion and intervention, there currently exists no generally accepted definition of hate. More grievously, there is nothing approaching a consensus on how to delimit the domain within which such a definition would fall. Meanings of hate differ both across and within contexts. Thus, it remains unclear if different authors are indeed discussing or intervening against the same thing.

The situation raises a number of questions: Why this cornucopia of meaning? How are psychologists to characterize the underlying disagreements? How are they to decide which disagreements are substantive and which are purely semantic? How are people to decide who is right and who is wrong? What would it mean to be right or wrong in this context? These are trying questions, to which we turn in the next section.

MAKING SENSE OF DIFFERENT CONCEPTIONS OF HATE

What is hate? In the preceding pages, we reviewed attempts to provide a single, nonarbitrary answer. In this section, we dissect the question itself. This question, we argue, lends itself to four distinct interpretations, each equipped with its own logic and its own evidentiary standard, corresponding to four different types of claims concerning the meaning of hate.

(Categorical) Meta-Description

Imagine opening a book and reading, "Hatred is a self-destructive impulse turned outwards." What would you make of this? One natural interpretation is that the author's aim is to offer a window on his or her own psyche. In this view, the author's purpose is to inform readers about a knowledge structure that the word *hate* prompts in his or her own mind ("Just letting you know what comes to my mind when you say . . ."), irrespective of whether he or she thinks that this opinion is in tune with the consensus of the field or if an analogous knowledge structure would be prompted in the mind of a representative layperson. Though self-descriptions may be aplenty in everyday conversation and memoirs, they may not be a very generous way to read a scholarly text.

A more charitable interpretation is that the author is offering a (categorical) meta-description, a claim that is part of what Russell and colleagues (e.g., Fehr & Russell, 1991; Russell, 1991) called "descriptive analysis" (see Wittgenstein, 1953). To interpret the statement "Hate is a self-destructive impulse turned outwards" in this manner is to assume that the author is not merely describing the pertinent knowledge structure in his or her own mind; rather, the author is offering a meta-description, a tidied-up summary description of what *hate* means to a particular culture, community, or group. For example, statements such as "In my opinion, most ordinary English-speaking people would agree: Hate is a self-destructive impulse turned outwards" or "Based on my discussions with many persons, there is a consensus emerging within our field: Hate is a self-destructive impulse turned outwards" could be rightfully understood as summative or hypothetical claims regarding the lay and academic meanings of hate, respectively. The validity of the former claim could be established by investigating the meaning of hate within the designated segment of the lay community; the validity of the latter claim could be established via a comprehensive literature review. (One point of contrast for a categorical meta-description is a self-description, another is a meta-description that targets particular individuals; a historian may show an avid interest in what hate meant to Aristotle qua Aristotle, not qua an average Athenian or Macedonian).

Insofar as meta-descriptive claims concern categories ("English-speaking lay people"; "most emotion theorists") rather than individuals, they demand the same background assumptions as self-descriptive claims, plus the assumption that members of the designated category can show some level of consensus on what does or does not constitute hate. The question of whether such a consensus exists is orthogonal to the question of how the concept of hate is organized within the minds of the members of the target category. For example, most of the existing expert conceptualizations of hate seem to be marked by a clear set of defining features. However, given the lack of consensus among various emotion theorists as to what these defining features are, any single meta-descriptive claim intended as a representation of the prevailing psychological understanding of hate is bound to be inaccurate.

The basis for classifying a claim as self-descriptive or (categorically) meta-descriptive is its intent, not its source. For all we know, either claim may begin with a person asking him- or herself, "What sort of image (idea, set of defining or prototypic features) does 'hate' bring up in my mind?" The answer may then be served either as a self-description ("My personal intuition is . . .") or, assuming the person sees him- or herself as a good proxy for some target category, as a meta-description intent on capturing the mentality of that category ("All clear-thinking people will agree . . ."). Of course, meta-descriptions may have an altogether different source: results of direct surveys of those whose mentality one wishes to illuminate.

Meta-descriptive claims are clearly present in at least some analyses of love and hate. For example, Shand (1920) prefaced many of his statements regarding love, hate, and anger with the pronoun *we*. Considering Shand's skepticism about the emotion theories of his day, the most plausible interpretation of this practice is that *we* stands for the collective of theoretically neutral laypersons and that his analysis is to be taken as disclosing the everyday meaning of hate (love, anger), irrespective of the prevailing expert opinion. Likewise, Beck (1999), Ben-Ze'ev (2000), and Power and Dalgleish (1997) appeared to write as if intent on capturing the meaning of hate as everyone understands and uses it. As indicated earlier, the standard for judging the truth or falsity of meta-descriptive claims resides in how well they pan out when assayed by empirical means vis-à-vis the target category specified by the claim. What follows is an outline of one meta-descriptive conception of hate that emerges from a number of survey- and interview-based studies tapping the perspective of a run-of-the mill, linguistically competent layperson. Spanning 5 decades and three continents, these studies show a remarkable degree of convergence regarding the much-discussed link between "hate" and "anger" and the evaluative feature that sets these two apart.

The traditional view holds that hate entails an intense desire for the annihilation of its object (e.g., see Aristotle, trans. 1954; Kolnai, 1998; Ben Ze'ev, 2000), but hate seems also consistent with a wish that the hated person experience sufferings whose nature and magnitude are roughly proportionate to one's own. Of course, the two wishes may be confounded, as when someone expresses a desire that his or her enemies "rot in hell." But, in principle, the desire for the hated one's distress may also appear in isolation from and even outweigh the impetus toward his or her destruction.

This idea is bolstered by what appears to be the earliest empirical investigation of hate. In 1950, McKellar carried out a series of semistructured 1-hour interviews whose stated purpose was to examine the nature of "hostile attitudes" (dislike, contempt, hate). Each interviewee was asked to think of an incident involving him- or herself and the hated or otherwise disliked person. The participant was then asked to imagine the "ideal resolution" of the incident and describe both his or her current feelings toward the "object of hostility" and how he or she would expect to feel and act toward this person upon encountering him or her in the vicinity of the interview room.

In tallying his results, McKellar (1950) described a participant who admitted to having "suffered prolonged physical pain as a result of the actions of the person whom he now hated . . . [and who was now filled with] malevolence towards the object of hate, [wanting] the other person [to experience] exactly the same amount of pain, no more and no less, that he had himself experienced" (p. 110). McKellar cited other cases that testify to what, in his opinion, is the main wish associated with hate, that is, giving the hated person "a dose of his own medicine." As one female participant put it, "I'd like to hear her cry the way she's heard me. I would still carry on . . ." Yet another participant said, "[I] would like to torment her; have her crawling to me for mercy. If she died it would be a pity . . ." (McKellar, 1950, p. 110).

To complicate the story somewhat, hate seems also consistent with an urge to altogether avoid the hated person. Of course, avoidance is consistent with the desire to punish another if one believes that the other will find one's absence distressing, especially if the reason one "hates" or "is angry" with another is that one has been previously the object of another's neglect. For example, in Fitness and Fletcher's (1993, Study 1) examination of real-life incidents of hate in the context of marital relationships, the participants described *leaving the situation* and *acting coldly toward the partner* as the urges and behaviors most typical of hate. One possible interpretation for the discrepancy between these results and those reported in McKellar (1950) is that the range of hostile reactions is inherently greater when the object of hatred is a relative stranger rather than an intimate. It could also be that reports of hate in close relationships are more sensitive to social desirability concerns. Indeed, Fitness and Fletcher (1993, Study 2; see also Davitz, 1969) discovered that references to verbal and physical attack increased markedly when the participants were asked to think of an exemplary hypothetical instance of hate rather than to recall a real-life incident. In other respects, the simulated and the remembered incident were strikingly alike. On the basis of some further work, Fitness and Fletcher concluded that the results of the initial recall study could not have been due entirely to social desirability concerns and that avoidance reflected a real hate-associated action tendency, one that separated hate from anger. This link between hate and avoidance was further corroborated by a recent examination (Fitness, 2000) of hate and anger in the workplace; this study suggests that revenge and avoidance may both be part of an all-inclusive hate script.

Also, it is important to recall that self-reports offered by McKellar's participants represent what these individuals felt like doing under idealized conditions, not what they in fact did. Only 2% of Fitness and Fletcher's (1993) participants recalling episodes of hate did anything to hurt their spouses, a rate not much higher than the 0% for participants recalling episodes of anger. However, the anger-driven participants were significantly more likely to engage in what could be described as acts of verbal abuse and instrumental intimidation. It may be that vengeful fantasies are insensitive (perhaps precisely what makes them so "sweet") to the social constraints that limit people's urges as well as their actions in a real hostile episode. It could also be that the prototypic behavioral urges associated with hate are poised to be less extreme when a close relationship is at stake.

These findings intimate that, in the mind of many a layperson, hate is associated with a set of action tendencies that may vary with the context and are largely contradictory to the urge for destruction. Destroying a person stands in the way of making him or her suffer; conversely, making a person suffer depends on keeping him or her alive ("If she died it would be a pity" [McKellar, 1950, p. 110]). And getting away from a person seems to be something else altogether, despite occurring in many recollections of hate episodes.

Another early investigation into laypeople's phenomenological accounts of hate is that of Davitz (1969), who sought to produce "a dictionary of emotional meaning" whose authority would derive from the validated consensus of contemporary laypersons of various ages and backgrounds. Toward this goal, Davitz created a 556-item checklist describing the presumed experiential properties of 50 emotional experiences, including those of anger and hate. The checklist was submitted to a sample of

50 people, "25 men and 25 women, all volunteers, ranging in age from 20 to 50, and including both White and Negro subjects" (Davitz, 1969, p. 8). These 50 individuals were instructed to think of a specific instance when each of them experienced a given emotional state. The participants were then asked to give a brief description of the situation that triggered that state and mark any statement in the checklist that described his or her experiences while in that state. The results of the survey were subsequently analyzed for response frequency.

Davitz's (1969) decision, a decision that he acknowledged being somewhat arbitrary but reasonable, was "to include on the definition of a term every statement that was checked by over one-third of the subjects in their descriptions of the emotional experiences labeled by that term" (pp. 12–13). As a further check on the robustness of his findings, Davitz asked a number of independent judges to rate the adequacy of each newly created definition (with 1 and 4 denoting most and least adequacy, respectively) based on their own emotional experiences. Thus, a 50-item dictionary of emotional meanings was born.

For our purposes, the two most noteworthy items are anger and hate. Considering the profiles of hate and anger side by side indicates that the participants understood them as largely overlapping, if not analogous, phenomena. Both anger and hate were characterized by a pattern of muscle tension, gastrointestinal discomfort, quickening pulse and high blood pressure, feelings of being "overcharged," an impulse "to strike out . . . kick, or bite" (pp. 35, 65), a sense of being overwhelmed or gripped by the situation, the experience of having one's attention fixed on one thing, and thoughts of revenge (see also McKellar, 1950). On the whole, hate looked remarkably similar to anger. This fits well with Russell and Fehr's (1994) more recent report that people view hate as one of the more prototypic subcategories of anger.

Davitz's pattern of findings is also largely consistent with Fitness and Fletcher's (1993) more recent research on emotions in close relationships. In Fitness and Fletcher's Study 1, a group of 160 married participants were asked to recall the various details of a recent episode of hate, love, anger, or jealousy toward their partner (20 men and 20 women were randomly assigned to each emotion); the participants also answered a series of follow-up questions that probed the physiological symptoms that went with these experiences and the remembered evaluations of the triggering events on a variety of dimensions (e.g., pleasantness, predictability, number of perceived obstacles associated with each event, perceived control). The participants' responses for hate and anger revealed considerable overlap, but there were consistent differences as well. For example, hate and anger were both characterized by the similar incidence of "tight muscles" and identical incidence of "tight stomach," "agitation," and "heart palpations" (in opposition to love or jealousy, for which no palpations were reported).

Similar results obtained when Fitness and Fletcher (1993, Study 2) asked the participants to base their descriptions not on actual incidents from their marital lives but on "hypothetical accounts of the most typical love, hate, anger, or jealousy incidents that they could imagine occurring in a marital relationship" (pp. 943–944). Indeed, hate and anger were sufficiently close to be repeatedly confused on the follow-up Study 3. This time Fitness and Fletcher asked the participants to read a series of descriptions of marital interactions and impute one of eight possible emotions (hate, anger, jealousy, worry, love, happiness, relief, and pride) to the story protagonists. The participants were randomly assigned to four "information" conditions. In Condition 1, they received only a very basic description of the emotion-triggering event; Conditions 2 and 3 supplemented this basic description with the information about the characters' evaluations (the appraisal condition) or emotion-prototypical symptoms, urges, and behaviors (the prototype condition), respectively (the information was derived from the participants' accounts in Study 1); Condition 4 brought all of that information together.

For our purposes, the most interesting finding of Study 3 concerns the asymmetry in the participants' tendency to confuse hate and anger when one or the other was the target emotion. When hate was the target emotion, the participants appeared to be as likely to see it as a case of anger as one of hate in both the prototype and the appraisal conditions. Even when, as in the all-information condition, the participants evinced a statistically significant tendency (at the 54% rate) to identify hate accurately, fully 32% thought that anger was the most fitting choice. But the participants hardly ever made the reverse error of characterizing anger as hate in either of the above-mentioned conditions when anger was the target emotion. And anger was never misidentified as hate in the all-information condition. As Fitness and Fletcher (1993) pointed out, this is just the pattern of findings one would expect if the lay concept of hate represented a variation of the more generic anger script.

Contrary to accounts of hatred that emphasize intensity (e.g., Reber & Reber, 2002), there was no difference between anger and hate with respect to intensity (see also Fitness, 2000). And though significantly more hate than anger episodes were reported in the longer-duration categories of days and weeks, 37 % of the participants reported that their hate episodes lasted for only a few seconds or minutes, suggesting that what people ordinarily describe as hate may be experienced both as an episodic emotion and as an episodic disposition. In sum, neither duration nor intensity appears to be criterial to the lay meaning of hate. From the standpoint of lay psychology, hate stands for something other than a stronger, longer-lasting anger. What does it stand for, then? The answer seems fairly consistent across the few available studies.

Going back to Davitz's (1969) study, notwithstanding the many similarities between hate and anger, hate was ascribed some unique features of its own. Most notably, hate involved "a sense of being trapped, closed up, boxed, fenced in, tied down, inhibited" (also characteristic of depression and frustration), a feeling that "it all seems bottled up inside of me" (also characteristic of depression), and a perception of "the world . . .[as] no good, hostile, unfair" (Davitz, 1969, p. 35). Also, unlike anger, hate was described as "more an 'inner' than an 'outer' feeling." Similarly, in Fitness and Fletcher's (1993) report, hate was more likely to be characterized by "a sense" of weakness, inefficacy, and insurmountable obstacles (but it was *not* accompanied by attributions any more global or personalized than those associated with anger). A similar pattern emerges from Fitness's (2000) later study that examined anger in the workplace. In light of her work on marital emotions, Fitness hypothesized that (a) hate involves anger and that (b) insofar as hate involves a self-perception of powerlessness, hate is more likely when the transgressor is a superior than when he or she is a subordinate or a coworker.

Both hypotheses were corroborated by the participants' reports. As expected, there was a significant gap between the proportions of subordinates (45%) and superiors (71%) who confronted the objects of their anger. The majority of those angered by their superiors reported that they failed to defy their apparently insulting treatment "because they feared the consequences of expressing their feelings to a more powerful offender" (Fitness, 2000, p. 155). There were also negative correlations between hate intensity and perceived self-power. That is, perceiving oneself as having little relative power in an interpersonal conflict was associated with the self-attribution of hate. The results of this investigation led Fitness to construct the following hate-dominated "anger script" which is typical of a lower-power worker: The lower-power workers "are likely to become angry over unjust treatment by higher power workers . . . They experience moderate to high levels of hate for offenders, especially if the offenses involved humiliation, and their immediate reactions involve withdrawal" (p. 159). Like Fitness (2000), McKellar (1950) noted that power asymmetry and, consequently, the "unexpressed hostile emotion" (p. 109) felt by the lower-power person toward the higher-power abuser are central features of a prototypic "hate episode":

> In eleven of the cases studied, the other individual had higher status than the subject. Apart from the possibilities of envy and jealousy it was evident that these relations were such as to render any really satisfying expression of experienced anger inexpedient, and to diminish the possibilities of successful defense of oneself, one's status and values. (p. 109)

McKellar (1950) observed the same apparent lack of "successful defense" in many of the remaining cases. In these cases, however, anger remained unexpressed not by virtue of the opponent's superior status but rather because of his or her "dominant personality" (p. 109). He interprets this finding as follows:

Apart from the effect of such a relation on the self-esteem and security of the subject, it is reasonable to suppose that the experience of being powerless to make effective retaliation, to express anger and defend oneself against a more powerful individual, favours the development of lasting hostility rather than mere momentary anger. (p. 109)

An alternative interpretation, one that seems more in line with the work of Davitz (1969), Fitness and Fletcher (1993), and Russell and Fehr (1994), is, of course, that "the experience of being powerless to make effective retaliation . . . against a more powerful individual" represents both an important part of the lay meaning of hate as well as one aspect of its eliciting conditions.

One could say, then, that when people are asked to report hate, they are essentially reporting anger, albeit a particularly helpless, ineffectual, inhibited, "too risky to stick my neck out" kind of anger. This supposition is consistent with the fact that humiliation (or something like it) appears to be the most commonly acknowledged antecedent within the hate script.

For example, the psychoanalytically oriented clinician Fred Pine (1995), whose primary interest lies in a type of jealous revenge-oriented hate that he sees as common among women, traces the origins of this response to a child's experience of being an impotent spectator or an object of her mother's wrath. According to Pine, the defining feature of such an experience is feeling "reduced and objectified and the helplessness to affect it" (p. 106). One interesting aspect of Pine's analysis is its intertwining of clinical case studies with examples derived from some distinguished literary works, such as Euripides's "Medea" or Balzac's "Cousin Bette." He argues that being diminished and remaining helpless to defy one's all-too-powerful opponent is the pattern that lies at the root of both literary and clinically based instances of revenge-driven hate:

> it is of interest that the features of being treated like an object and reduced in one's personhood, as well as a perceived or real helplessness to affect this characterize the position of these women [the hate-prone literary heroines] in male-dominated society, just as those features characterize the position of the female patients as children. (Pine, 1995, p. 106)

The theme of hate as the result of being helplessly "reduced in one's personhood" is also prominent in the work of McKellar (1950). McKellar identified two factors that appeared to be "favourable to the development of hostile attitudes" (p. 109), including hate. The first factor concerned the association between hate and "unexpressed hostility." The second factor concerned the nature of the negative experiences that trigger such hostile responses. Personal humiliation was the single largest category of such experiences. "Physical pain" and "threat to values" were tied for the second place, and "physical pain to another person" (p. 109) came in last. Humiliation and physical pain were the two largest categories for the female and male subgroups, respectively. Moreover, if we consider that the physical pain was usually experienced in connection with being dominated and bullied by a stronger or more aggressive individual, it is likely that such a pain occurred in the context of a humiliating interaction; thus, McKellar's method of classification may have actually underestimated the prevalence of humiliation as the trigger of hate.

The studies of Fitness and Fletcher (1993) give credence to this summary. Their participants' reports revealed that, in contrast to anger, hate-eliciting events were evaluated as more unpredictable, effortful, and less amenable to personal control (hate experiences were associated with greater helplessness and a more negative self-view). Anger incidents were generally elicited by being treated "unfairly," whereas hate incidents were said to follow from being "most often elicited by the perception that the subject had been badly treated, unsupported, or humiliated by the partner" (Fitness & Fletcher, 1993, p. 945). Fitness's (2000) study of anger in the workplace also hypothesized that "humiliating anger-eliciting events will elicit more intense hate than non-humiliating events" (p. 150). The hypothesis has been largely confirmed.

Before drawing out the full implications of these studies, we put them in the context of three conceptual viewpoints, neither of which appears to be specifically about hate.

Essay 1 of Nietzsche's (1969) *On the Genealogy of Morals* represents an account of the "slave revolt" and the ensuing transfiguration of values that Nietzsche saw as the birth of modern morality. The two main protagonists in Nietzsche's dynamic of ressentiment are "the priests" and "the nobles." The priests are portrayed as feeling diminished by the nobles' superiority in commanding the respect and admiration of the people. For our purposes, the most interesting aspect of Nietzsche's account is that the construct of ressentiment (usually interpreted as an impotent grudge-laden resentment; see, e.g., Hampton, 1988) appears to capture some of the lay meaning of hate, and it intimates that this type of reaction may be appropriately ascribed to both individuals and groups.

The second pertinent viewpoint belongs to Sabini and Silver (1998). As part of their more general inquiry into the intersection of the affective and the moral, these authors presented an argument that there may not be a need for a unique psychology of emotion, at least for a subset of emotions they call "the passions" (e.g., anger, envy, fear). Whereas judgments, sensations, and desires are certainly among constituents of the mind, there is not necessarily a fourth entity called "emotions" that is different from the first three. Rather, they claim, "emotion" is a sort of fictional posit that we invoke in two types of situations: (a) the situations when we "do things that we know we shouldn't because we are overwhelmed by desire" (in respect to anger, the *indulged defiance* condition) and (b) the situations in which "we . . . find ourselves devoting cognitive and other resources to preparations to act even though we are quite certain we will not act and we would prefer not to act" (p. 136; in respect to anger, the *inhibited defiance* condition).

For our purposes, the most interesting aspect of Sabini and Silver's (1998) proposal lies in the second condition, which they illustrate with a case of "anger" directed at one's superior. Sabini and Silver asked readers to imagine an untenured professor who is nettled by the self-righteous demeanor of a senior colleague and is contemplating a cutting remark meant to put "the old fool" in his place. It is fortunate that the untenured professor has the presence of mind to realize that directing public insults at his academic betters will have a crippling effect on his budding career; consequently, he decides against lashing out and resigns himself to impotent silence. Suppose further, Sabini and Silver said, that the junior professor is so good at managing his interior life that the mere realization of the imprudence of the "You fatuous old fool"–style diatribe causes him to call off the corresponding desire. However, Sabini and Silver maintained that few people could ever aspire to regulating their desires with such virtuosity. And if the beleaguered assistant professor is like most people, the chances are that there will be a period in his interior life when he will find himself persisting in his desire (and his bodily preparations) to attack the senior colleague, while maintaining the firm awareness that because of his inferior position, no such attack will and should ever take place. It is in this tale of inhibited defiance that Sabini and Silver glimpsed one of the two sets of conditions in which people are likely to diagnose themselves as "feeling angry."

Remarkably, it is this very situation—an inferiority-grounded inhibition of one's desire to attack—that Roseman (1984) viewed as particularly interesting in its failure to accommodate one cardinal feature of a prototypic anger scheme—the perception of one's strength vis-à-vis the perceived transgressor:

> With regard to the emotions directed at another person, it is not difficult to see that one might get angry at someone who caused negative events if one were in a position of strength vis-à-vis that person, but not if one were in a position of weakness. The hypothesized behavioral components of anger (attack) and dislike (distancing) make sense in light of these perceptions. Dislike may be understood as a negative emotional response that, due to weakness, must not be anger. (According to Izard, 1977, p. 331, anger is accompanied by a feeling of power) . . . As with frustration, people who feel anger when seeming to be weak may be powerless to control the negative event but not weak enough to be endangered by feeling or expressing anger. The common observation that people "displace" anger onto targets weaker than themselves is consistent with this view. (pp. 27–28)

Roseman (1984) saw the issue of power as separate from that of legitimacy, which he viewed as another important constituent of a full-fledged anger response. For Roseman, what makes "dislike" so similar and yet so unlike "anger" is that the person who dislikes finds him- or herself (a) legitimated in the urge to retaliate and yet (b) self-inhibited in his or her desire for retaliation because of the asymmetry in power.

It appears, then, that Nietzsche (1969), Roseman (1984), and Sabini and Silver (1998) all, in their own ways, remarked the conceptual significance of this inhibited defiance phenomenon. And as the data suggest, it is precisely this apparent departure from the everyday anger script that forms the tidied-up summary formulation for the lay meaning of *hate*.

Apparently, in agreement with Roseman (1984), the lay conception of anger has embedded in it the notion of a certain power to express, implement, or indulge one's legitimate defiance of the transgressor, with those instances of legitimate defiance that lack such power (but fit the anger model in other respects) being relegated to a conceptual niche of their own.

In this sense, the findings that tie humiliation (physical pain or threat to values) with unexpressed hostility may be explicated as a two-part dynamic: First, humiliation, physical abuse, and the like are the sort of things that people of superior status (strength, dominance, rank, wealth) are far more likely to do to those below them than vice versa. Second, precisely on account of their inferior status or power, the recipients of this abuse (or perceived abuse) are likely to inhibit what they think to be a legitimate urge to defy the higher-status person, while experiencing the physical and mental preparations that otherwise fit the lay script of anger. Thus, the less powerful person is both more likely to be abused and less likely to find it expedient to defy the abuser, making such a person more prone to encounter the maltreatment scenarios that match the lay prototype of hate. In this view, hate is primarily a bottom-up phenomenon, a poor man's anger, and as such it is likely to be shrouded in secrecy. This formulation of the lay meaning of hate prompts at least two reflections.

First, this analysis suggests that the academic community and the lay public may differ in the way they parse the affective realm or name the resulting affective categories (see also Nabi, 2002). Thus, the type of knowledge structure that would be prompted in the mind of an ordinary study participant by the word *hate* seems to be the very same one that a researcher steeped in the conceptual analysis of Sabini and Silver (1998) and Roseman (1984) would code as prototypic "anger" or "dislike," respectively. Conversely, if our introductory overview is any guide, a lay reference to hate would be likely to prompt in the mind of an emotion theorist a very different idea than the layperson had sought to communicate.

Second, it remains an open question to what extent the very existence of the lay concept of hate is a culturally specific phenomenon and to what extent the application of that concept (with its emphasis on avoidance rather than attack) may affect individuals' actual emotional experiences and behaviors. As far as the issue of cultural specificity is concerned (see

Wierzbicka, 1986, 1992, 1999), it is an intriguing possibility that hate, as understood here, is an exclusive property of only those cultures that link the prototypic impulse toward defiance with an ability and, indeed, a mandate to stand up for oneself, irrespective of the transgressor's social rank. A cultural context that lacks this association and places little emphasis on the weakness–power dimension might not have a precise rendition for the anger–hate distinction at all. However, members of such cultures may be able to "re-experience" their past emotional episodes in terms of our concepts anger and hate, once properly acculturated to our point of view (Russell, 2003).

Stipulation

As the name implies, a *stipulative claim* stipulates or constructs a content, rather than aiming to capture the content already associated with the expression—for example, "for the purpose of our discussion 'existent' means 'perceivable'" (Audi, 1995, p. 186). As Audi pointed out, any explicit delineation of a new technical term (e.g., "bloompy" for "a retired Swiss banker") is necessarily stipulative, but his own example shows that everyday terms may be co-opted for stipulative use as well (see also Russell, 1991, on the role of prescriptive analysis). Unlike self-descriptions or (categorical) meta-descriptions, pure stipulations are self-validating. No such statement can ever be shown to be wrong in the sense of having external evidence available against it; this is the sense of "wrong" that should be reserved for meta-descriptive or self-descriptive claims. The worst thing that can be said about such a statement is that it is bizarre (moreover, it is not very useful). But barring some obviously bizarre uses (e.g., "for the purpose of this discussion, *hate* means a small, furry animal that lives in the attic"), a number of perfectly sensible stipulations can coexist side by side in specifying different sets of events falling within the liberally drawn boundaries of notions such as hate, love, or happiness.

In this view, the claim that hate is "generalized anger" is neither more right or wrong nor directly contradictory to the claim that hate is "a blend of anger and fear" or "a disgust for another person" or "a form of inverse attachment" or "an agitation-free, abiding wish for the destruction of a person or a collective of persons." However, when encountered in the context of a scientific inquiry, the stipulative claim concerning hate does incur the additional obligation of constructing a theoretically interesting category that may guide further research into some (but not necessarily all or only) phenomena that are usually understood with reference to hate. Stipulative claims seem to be a part of what Russell and colleagues called the *prescriptive analysis* (e.g., Fehr & Russell, 1991; Russell, 1991), the analysis aimed at delimiting and investigating a class of events in reference to some of which a particular emotion term may be used.

In our view, the evidentiary standard relevant to the research-guiding component of a stipulative claim is twofold: useful demarcated domain and useful relations to other conceptions (Cook & Campbell, 1979). Convergent evidence would indicate that the stipulated conception identifies a domain of behavior or experience that is sufficiently homogenous to support theoretical advances in understanding the causes and consequences of the stipulated conception (this harkens back to the notion of exposing nature at its joints). Discriminant evidence indicates that the stipulated conception can be distinguished theoretically and empirically from related conceptions. For example, constructing hate as a strong aversion to anything or anyone would be poor on the grounds of convergent validity: The way one is averse to drinking fish oil is not the same way one is averse to visiting a dentist or sitting through a documentary on the future of agrarian science. The phenomena in question are just too nonhomogenous to be subsumed under a single construct. However, constructing hate as fear seems to slight discriminant validity: If hate is fear, how is it different from fear, and why study it under the name *hate*? (This is, of course, not to say that fear cannot be a good explanation of certain paradigmatic cases of hate behavior, from genocide to hate crimes).

It seems that with some modest refinements, the Shand-inspired conception of hate as a syndrome of inverse caring could do especially well on the grounds of construct validity by positing a form of antagonistic response that is fairly homogenous and clearly distinct from what is typically meant by anger, fear, or resentment. In a nutshell, it would stipulate that hate and love are not single emotions or blends of emotions but dispositions to experience many different emotions, depending on the fortunes of those loved and hated. Both caring–attachment ("love") and inverse caring–attachment ("hate") represent syndromes of episodic dispositions that go with motivational orientations tracking and reacting to the fortunes of significant others (individuals or groups who occupy a special place in our lives, positively or negatively). In the absence of tracking (which may range from mild to obsessive), inverse caring would probably correspond closer to what we call *dislike* or *negative identification* (McCauley, 2001) and involve emoting inversely to the news of another's fortunes or misfortunes as such news comes to one's attention without seeking it out.

Though puzzling in their own right, one reason that cases of inverse caring should be of great interest to psychologists is that they may help us to shed light on caring proper or vice versa. Like Sternberg's (2003) triadic model of hate, explicitly motivated by his triadic analysis of love, our stipulation encourages the possibility that there is a general capacity that allows for the tracking of and emotional engagement with the fortunes of others, the capacity whose impairment could undercut love and hate alike.

In our view, love and hate, as stipulated above, are likely to be characterized by the following key features:

1. Both hate and love are likely to be associated with a perception or attribution of a negative or positive essence. Briefly, the idea of essence is the hidden something that makes a living thing what it is (e.g., Atran, 1990; Gil-White, 2001; Keil, 1989). Essence is a more primitive idea than genetics and is better represented as *nature* or *spirit* than as a biological concept.
2. The negative or positive evaluation of the target of hate or love is likely to be linked with a moral judgment. The evaluation may be the product of such a judgment or, as in the case of hate, rooted in envious admiration; the moral judgment may emerge as a rationalization for the pre-existing pattern of (direct or inverse) caring.
3. Loves and hates may vary in the extent to which they exclude any possibility of compassion or ill wishing, respectively. The implication is that patriotism, nationalism, and ethnic group identification are particularly extreme expressions of group love, as genocide may be the ultimate expression of group hate (Chirot & McCauley, in press).
4. People may be expected to differ in how vehemently they endorse or identify (Frankfurt, 1971) with their hates. At one extreme, there is a *faint-hearted hater*, someone who is shocked and ashamed to discover that he or she hates whomever he or she hates and who wishes that things were otherwise. At another pole, there is the *wholehearted hater*, someone who endorses his or her hate completely, appropriates it with pride and even fondness, and makes every effort to nurture it to its fullest capacity. In the latter case, hate becomes "sanctified" (Blum, 1995) or fully integrated into one's value system. The same principle applies to love.

An empirical inquiry into the construct of hatred as inverse caring might proceed by asking people to identify relationships in their lives that include a tendency to track and react inversely to another's fortunes. One could then form and test a set of hypotheses regarding possible correlates, consequences, and causal antecedents that characterize such relationships. Do people essentialize the people or groups they are inversely attached to or care about? Do they see the objects of such caring as morally bad? Do they feel good or bad about having such tendencies? Would they ever (and under what circumstances) relent?

An empirical analysis may also reveal that some or all of the above-mentioned elements of hate do not reliably correlate with one another. For example, it is possible to be saddened by another's good outcomes without taking pleasure in his or her bad outcomes; it is possible to do either one without attributing essence or passing a moral judgment.

Explanation of Ostensively Defined Cases

The fourth possible interpretation of a statement such as "Hate is a self-destructive impulse turned outwards" is that it represents a causal explanation—that is, an attempt to specify a mental mechanism most directly responsible for certain paradigmatic instances of "hate-related" behavior. The general idea is that insofar as such paradigmatic instances indicate the immediate effects of hate, working backward to their (relatively proximate) causes should give us a glimpse of hate itself. As noted earlier, the approach to defining hate through paradigmatic instances is common in political science. One context within which hate is commonly discussed and thought to be especially problematic is that of ethnic conflict. In this context, "Hate is a self-destructive impulse turned outwards" would represent an explanatory claim concerning the psychological underpinnings of ethnic conflict; as such, it could be tested empirically by asking if those engaged in ethnopolitical violence are, indeed, driven by a (sublimated) self-destructive impulse.

As we hinted earlier, one potential problem with the ostensive approach to defining hate is that the psychological underpinnings of the relevant paradigmatic cases may be shown to be very different from one's initial intuitions about what hate is or is not. For example, many so-called hate crimes seem to be committed out of some combination of boredom and a desire to show off before one's group (Baumeister, 1997). Indeed, in analyzing Boston police hate crime files, McDevitt, Levin, and Bennett (2002) concluded that the majority (66%) of the perpetrators were motivated by a desire to escape boredom and get some quick thrills and bragging rights, with targets being selected because they were perceived as "somehow different" (p. 307). Of the remaining 34%, 25% seemed motivated by an anxiety-laden desire to protect their neighborhood and families from what the perpetrators perceived as the onslaught of dangerous outsiders, with the criminal behavior being seen as a form of self-defense instrumental to "convincing" the victims to relocate elsewhere as well as forestalling future "intrusions." The Boston police files sample did, indeed, contain a form of motivation that fits well with the classic Aristotelian (1954) notion of hate (see also Elster, 1999; Beck, 1999), namely acting out of a deeply ingrained belief that the "others" are inherently evil or inferior and ought to be eliminated as such. However, this intensely other-focused motivation or affective orientation accounted for less than 1% of the entire sample; it was held by a single person.

Conceding the validity of these observations makes for some tough choices. It seems that either society must allow that most "hate crimes" (assisted as the selection of the victim may be by categorical negative judgments) are neither directly motivated by nor involve hate as their dominant affect, or its current understanding of hate must be expanded.

To give another example, Gaylin (2003, p. 14) proposed that "true hate" is a form of mental disorder ("Hatred is a severe psychological disorder"), and he cited terrorist violence as one of the paradigmatic cases in which such true hate may be found in abundance. In fact, Gaylin appeared to believe that anything short of portraying the terrorists as psychologically disturbed is morally irresponsible—"When we assume that at times we feel like a terrorist, we grant the terrorists a normalcy that trivializes a condition that threatens the civilized world" (p. 22). We fully agree that terrorism is evil and presents a tremendous threat. However, some of the most systematic research into the psychology of terrorism, including the detailed German studies of the Baader-Meinhof Gang, have found psychiatric disorder no more common for terrorists than for the general population that the terrorists emerge from (Konrad, 1998). Again, it seems that something has to give. Gaylin and those who favor his psychoanalytic approach should either surrender the notion that terrorism is a paradigm case of hate or be prepared to revise the concept of hate itself.

The very idea that the conceptual boundaries of hate or any other item of folk psychology can be redrawn on the basis of results of an empirical inquiry may seem foreign to some. However, this type of situation is fairly common in advanced natural science (Griffiths, 1997; Putnam, 1975). For example, some of the earliest definitions of *gold* were, no doubt, ostensive in quality. These definitions could then be unpacked into a prototypical characterization of gold as "that hard, malleable, yellow, shiny stuff we call gold." From the standpoint of an early chemist, the lay meaning of gold merely delimited the domain of inquiry; the scientific meaning of gold was to be sought by investigating the chemical structure manifest in the paradigmatic instances picked out by the commonsense concept gold. The discovery that, chemically speaking, gold is an element with atomic number 79 inaugurated a criterial shift such that it was no longer the lay but the scientific meaning that determined the extension of the concept gold, with genuine gold being clearly distinguishable from "fool's gold" and other substances. Thus, the lay meaning was bent to the results of the scientific discovery.

Consider also the concept of *hysteria*. The phenomenon itself seems real enough and was described by Hippocrates around 460 B.C., accompanied by a theory that the hysterical symptoms are due to wanderings of the uterus and, thus, are restricted to women (Hothersall, 1990, p. 13). Indeed, the term hysteria comes from *hysteron*, the Greek word for uterus. So deeply embedded the uterine theory had become within the concept of hysteria that Freud's 1886 paper "On Male Hysteria" was summarily dismissed by some observers as not being about hysteria at all (Hothersall, 1990, p. 240). Yet neither Freud nor future students of psychoanalysis found it problematic that one may dislodge a certain historically influential account of why paradigm cases of hysteria arise while retaining much of the concept's phenomenological content, thus opening themselves to the possibility of revising the meaning of the concept in the direction of whatever psychic mechanisms could best explain these cases. Similarly, our present folk-theoretical commitment to viewing courage as the opposite of cowardice may simply have to give should we discover that fear, in fact, is the motivation behind many garden-variety courageous acts (think of a female patient who drags herself to a feared and painful medical procedure for the fear that otherwise her life or health may be seriously at risk). There are reasons to believe that the same revisionist logic may be usefully applied to (re)construct the meanings of such folk notions as self-deception (Mele, 1997) and humility (Royzman, Cassidy, & Baron, 2003).

With this in mind, consider Gil-White's (2001) recent argument for a biphasic process whereby cultural differences are first moralized (if you don't act or think like me, you are not just "different," you are bad) and then essentialized (the badness is in your blood and in the blood of all those in your ethnic group) to yield ethnic unrest (see also Hirschfeld, 1995, 1996; see Gelman, 2003, for a broad overview of psychological essentialism). With this in mind, one could argue that, should "hate" be defined as "whatever is going on" in, say, the paradigmatic cases of ethnic conflict, and should "moralization–essentialization" prove to be a good filling for the "whatever" part, the conceptual boundaries of hate may need to be revised accordingly.

Note, however, that what makes this type of criterial shift possible in the case of concepts such as gold or water is not only the overwhelming consensus on what the paradigm instances of these categories are like but also the fact that the domains of inquiry delimited by such instances just happened to match the underlying natural kinds—H_2O in the case of water, a chemical element with atomic number 79 in the case of gold. It is not clear that nominating, say, *ethnic conflict* as a paradigm instance of hate meets either condition. The term ethnic conflict, as currently used, may not pick out a homogenous enough category of natural phenomenon, but there is also no guarantee that it represents the one and only incontestable paradigm case of hate the way that potable, wet, transparent stuff called "water" represents the one and only paradigm case of water. The meaning of hate unearthed in this way may fail to fit other equally compelling paradigm cases identified via other ostensive definitions (e.g., hate as seen in the case of terrorist violence vs. the "admiring hate" of the Sallieri–Mozart type of relationship). Of course, some of these cases, such as the Nazis' genocidal campaign against the Jews, will remain especially central to a cultural consciousness of what hate looks like. It seems that, whenever possible, such core cases should be given preference over their more peripheral counterparts. Still, one may never reach a point when one can say that hate is "really" moralization–essentialization (or something else) with the same tone of confidence with which one can state that gold is "really" an element with atomic number 79 or water is "really" H_2O. Nevertheless, psychologists can recruit all of the above paradigm cases to explore, under the name of hate, the causes of a variety of problems nominally linked to hate from ethnic cleansing to international terrorism, though there is no guarantee that the uncovered antecedents of all or any of these problems will match either the dominant lay meaning of hate (see the previous section) or any of the expert definitions offered in the opening pages of this chapter.

Platonic Insight

It would seem that the four types of claims presented thus far should be able to fit comfortably any conceivable conceptualization of hate, whether offered in a verbal dispute or as a part of a theoretical review. However, it became increasingly clear to us that our taxonomy contained a serious oversight. In arguing that people who commit acts of mass violence cannot be understood in terms of everyday psychology, Gaylin (2003) made a distinction between true hate and the more pedestrian phenomenon that goes by that name in everyday use: "We are capable of transient extremes of rage that we call hatred, but the true haters live daily with their hatred . . . When we confront the true hater, he frightens us" (pp. 4–5). More specifically, Gaylin goes on to state that true hate is a form of mental illness, characterized by displacement and paranoid ideation. What type of claim is this?

First, Gaylin (2003) does not appear to be venturing anything like a (falsifiable) causal hypothesis concerning the motivational underpinnings of a certain type of nominally hate-associated behavior. Rather, he begins by stating what hate is and then goes on to aver a link between that and mass violence. Second, his use of the qualifier "true" in the early pages of the book signals that he does not intend his conception of hate to be taken as a mere stipulative construction (as in "for the purpose of this discussion, I posit *hate* to be . . ."), but as a statement of some deeper truth. The most obvious interpretation would be that Gaylin's intent is to offer a categorical meta-description—that is, to capture the conventional (English-language) meaning of hate. After all, when one says to a foreigner that the "true" or "right" meaning of a word is slightly different from the meaning she appears to be imputing to it, one should be understood as doing nothing more than instructing her about the (historically derived) linguistic conventions governing the use of that word at a given time and place. But this is clearly not what Gaylin was after; he acknowledged that the conventional lay meaning of hate is extreme anger or rage, but he went on to affirm that true hating is different from what we conventionally understand it to be.

In the annals of Western history, there is one major model of word meaning within which such an argument would make perfect sense. We are speaking, of course, of Plato's theory of the Forms. The Platonic Forms or Ideas are eternal, metaphysical essences that permeate and condition the world of sensory experience. Though we may have no direct access to them at the moment, our souls ostensibly knew them as part of their precarnate existence, and it is this implicit memory that is guiding our eventual extension of some common name (*love, piety, justice, good*) to a set of seemingly diverse phenomena. In this view, all things called by the same name must share an essence that is an expression of the corresponding Platonic Idea; thus, all the variegated instances of love, be it the love of God or the love of one's neighbor, the love of a mother for her child or the love of a boy for a girl, the love of a philatelist for his stamps or the love of a patriot for her country, must share a core defining feature, which is but a spatio-temporal expression of the Platonic Idea of Love, the capturing of which will give us one and only one true conception of love.

Within the Platonic system, it makes sense that many people think love to be "X" while declaring that "real love" is something else entirely, with the external fact guaranteeing the truth of one's pronouncement being the objectively extent *Idea* of Love. In his discussion of love, Shand (1920) seemed to be following this very path when he averred that it was poets (primarily the classic British poets of the past 4 centuries), not philosophers, who had a true "insight" into the "nature of love" (p. 54). That is, Shand apparently believed that, irrespective of its conventional meaning, love carries some objective essence, true for all times and places, that some persons (those blessed with the powers of Platonic insight) may fathom better than others. Considering that Shand considered love and hate as structurally equivalent opposites, he must have held a similar view of hate. We call this type of apparently essentialist claims "Platonic" not because we believe that either Gaylin or Shand knowingly subscribed to Plato's theory of the Forms, but because this theory represents the only major intellectual system within which such claims can be rendered fully intelligible. (In one of the long editorial notes to his father's magnum opus [J. Mill, 1878], J. S. Mill complained that "as half the conceptual world are Platonists without knowing it, hence it also is that in the writings of so many psychologists we read of the conception or the concept of so and so; as if there was a concept of a thing . . . other than the ideas in individual minds" [p. 237]. Mill apparently believed that the less conscious we are of our [bad] metaphysics, the more likely we are to be trapped by it.) Granted that neither Gaylin nor Shand were conscious Platonists, how are we to explain their apparent Platonic leanings?

One answer may be that the situation is due to a sort of cultural inertia, that is, a tendency toward the continued acceptance of some cultural idea or practice while no longer giving any credence to the background belief system (i.e., Plato's metaphysics) that originally gave it meaning (see MacIntyre, 1981). An alternative account comes from a recent work of Gelman, Hollander, Star, and Heyman (2000; see also Gelman & Heyman, 1999), which suggests that people are poised to essentialize category names that are lexicalized as common nouns. One could speculate, then, that insofar as the name of the superordinate category such as *emotion* is itself a common noun, all instances of emotion are taken to share a single, objectively discoverable essence, with the result that its subordinate types (love, hate) are understood to be essence holding as well. Assuming that this tendency is linguistically pervasive, it could produce a pattern of thinking about emotion and other folk concepts that fits well with the Platonic worldview.

Whichever explanation proves to be correct, we believe that Platonic musings about one "true," "real," or "essential" nature of hate are scientifically unhelpful and ought to be set aside to make room for the more promising meta-descriptive, explanatory, and stipulative approaches. As recovering Platonists ourselves, we are conscious of the difficulty, but we submit that the resulting gains in clarity and mutual understanding will be well worth the effort.

CONCLUSION

In sum, a statement such as "Hate is a self-destructive impulse turned outwards" lends itself to at least four distinct interpretations. It could be (a) a statement of a categorical meta-opinion, one specifying the predominant meaning of hate within a given linguistic community (e.g., the sense of hate as "personalized anger" among some emotion theorists or the sense of hate as "inhibited defiance" among English-speaking laypersons); (b) a stipulation of a putatively useful theoretical construct (e.g., hate as a syndrome of inverse caring); (c) an explanation of the cause or causes of some nominally hate-related behaviors (e.g., the moralization–essentialization hypothesis); or (d) a statement laying an implicit claim to some form of Platonic insight intent on capturing the objective essence of hate.

There is no reason to expect that any single formulation of hate should be able to satisfy the demands posed by all of these interpretations. Hate as understood by the majority of ordinary English speakers need not be the same phenomenon that motivates "hate crimes" or stirs the fires of ethnic conflict, which, in turn, need not be analogous to the hate that may be posited as a theoretically interesting construct by those with an interest in investigating certain forms of antagonistic motivation.

Thus, the question "What is hate?" must remain largely unintelligible unless the questioner is willing to specify which of the above interpretations he or she has in mind. In the absence of such a specification, it is very hard to interpret either the question or the putative answers. It is this lack of specificity that makes it so difficult to evaluate and compare the various formulations of hate cited in the opening pages of this chapter. We can see now that the disparities among these formulations can be characterized in at least two ways. First, there are substantive differences—is hate a syndrome or an emotional blend? What kind of a syndrome or a blend? Second, there are differences in the nature of the claim being made—is the formulation being offered a stipulation, a meta-description, a causal hypothesis, a Platonic insight, or some combination of these? It will be helpful if future students of hate can be more direct about which type of claim they are making.

Sternberg and Grigorenko (2001) noted recently that many a dispute within psychology may revolve around "false oppositions" that arise when investigators study what is essentially the same construct from divergent methodological and theoretical viewpoints, each believing that his or her approach is the uniquely correct one. Our analysis suggests that false oppositions may also arise when investigators study what are effectively different constructs—constructs specified in accordance with different types of claims—that, nevertheless, operate under the same name.

Although we have distinguished four different ways of thinking about hate, there should be no implication that these are mutually exclusive. Our point is simply that they need not converge in all (perhaps, many) possible cases. A scholar can concede that the way that most people give meaning to, say, *humility* is also the best bet for a stipulated definition that will support evidence of convergent and discriminant validity, which, in turn, offers the best explanation for the relevant behavioral data to be explained with reference to humility. Indeed, our own experience with hate has been a kind of trajectory of interpretations, in which we began with a personal understanding of what hate means, projected this to a hypothesis about what most people mean by hate, hoped that the meta-opinion of hate would provide an explanation of genocide and other forms of intergroup violence, stipulated hate as inverse caring, and recognized belatedly in ourselves a tendency to see meta-opinion, explanation, and stipulation as shadows of a Platonic notion of what hate "really" is.

Our analysis leaves us uncertain about the much-cited link between hate and intergroup violence such as genocide, ethnic riots, or hate crimes. If hate is defined ostensively through paradigm cases of armed conflict and killing, then the notion that hate is responsible for mass violence is a tautology. Conversely, if hate is to be spelled out in terms of its lay meaning, as a form of inhibited defiance, or in terms of a stipulated meaning, for example, as a syndrome of inverse caring, then the empirical evidence for the link between hate and intergroup violence remains to be seen. That is, the very status of hate as a progenitor of evil rests on a prior conceptual decision about which phenomenon one is willing to probe under the heading of hate and which one will opt to see as being "not about hate at all."

Most generally, the four ways of thinking about hate may be helpful in thinking about many other psychological notions that are rooted in lay experience and everyday language. Disgust, shame, humility, and pride; frustration and aggression; value and virtue; the Big Five personality traits—all grow out of lay meanings. We expect that many such items of folk psychology, and the empirical literatures surrounding them, can benefit from the analysis undertaken in this chapter in the service of explicating hate.

REFERENCES

Aristotle. (1954). *The rhetoric and the poetics of Aristotle* (W. R. Roberts, Trans.). New York: Modern Library. (Original work written ca. 340 B.C.)

Atran, S. (1990). *Cognitive foundations of natural history.* Cambridge, England: Cambridge University Press.

Audi, R. (1995). *The Cambridge dictionary of philosophy.* Cambridge, England: Cambridge University Press.

Averill, J. (1982). *Anger and aggression: An essay on emotion.* New York: Springer Verlag.

Averill, J. (1991). Emotions as episodic dispositions, cognitive schemas and transitory social roles: Steps towards an integrated theory of emotion. In R. Hogan (Ed.), *Perspectives in personality: Vol. 3A. Self and emotion* (pp. 139–167). London: Jessica Kingsley.

Baumeister, R. F. (1997). *Evil: Inside human violence and cruelty.* New York: Freeman.

Baumeister, R. F., Stillwell, A., & Wotman, S. R. (1990). Victim and perpetrator accounts of interpersonal conflict: Autobiographical narratives about anger. *Journal of Personality and Social Psychology, 59,* 994–1005.

Beck, A. T. (1999). *Prisoners of hate: The cognitive basis of anger, hostility, and violence.* New York: HarperCollins.

Ben-Ze'ev, A. (2000). *The subtlety of emotions.* Cambridge, MA: MIT Press.

Blum, H. P. (1995). Sanctified aggression, hate, and the alteration of standards of values. In S. Akhtar, S. Kramer, & H. Parens (Eds.), *The birth of hatred: Developmental, clinical and technical aspects of intense aggression* (pp. 17–37). Northvale, NJ: Jason Aronson.

Chirot, D., & McCauley, C. (in press). *Genocide.* Princeton, NJ: Princeton University Press.

Cook, T. D., & Campbell, D. T. (1979). *Quasi-experimentation: Design and analysis issues for field settings.* New York: Rand McNally.

Darwin, C. (1998). *The expression of the emotions in man and animals.* New York: Oxford University Press. (Original work published 1872)

Davitz, J. (1969). *The language of emotion.* San Diego, CA: Academic Press.

Descartes, R. (1989). *On the passions of the soul* (S. Voss., Trans.). Indianapolis, IN: Hackett. (Original work published 1694)

Dozier, R. W., Jr. (2002). *Why we hate: Understanding, curbing, and eliminating hate from ourselves and our world.* Chicago: Contemporary Books.

Ekman, P. (1992). An argument for basic emotions. *Cognition & Emotion, 6,* 169–200.

Elster, J. (1999). *Strong feelings: Emotion, addiction, and human behavior.* Cambridge, MA: MIT Press.

Fehr, B., & Russell, J. A. (1991). The concept of love viewed from a prototype perspective. *Journal of Personality and Social Psychology, 60,* 425–438.

Fitness, J. (2000). Anger in the workplace: An emotion script approach to anger episodes between workers and their superiors, co-workers and subordinates. *Journal of Organizational Behavior, 21*, 147–162.

Fitness, J., & Fletcher, G. J. O. (1993). Love, hate, anger, and jealousy in close relationships: A prototype and cognitive appraisal analysis. *Journal of Personality and Social Psychology, 65*, 942–958.

Frankfurt, H. G. (1971). Freedom of the will and the concept of a person. *Journal of Philosophy, 68*, 5–20.

Fredrickson, B. L., & Branigan, C. (2001). Positive emotions. In T. J. Mayne & G. A. Bonanno (Eds.), *Emotions: Current issues and directions* (pp. 123–151). New York: Guilford Press.

Frijda, N. (1986). *The emotions.* Cambridge, England: Cambridge University Press.

Gaylin, W. (2003). *Hatred: The psychological descent into violence.* New York: Public Affairs.

Gelman, S. A. (2003). *The essential child: Origins of essentialism in everyday thought.* London: Oxford University Press.

Gelman, S. A., & Heyman, G. D. (1999). Carrot-eaters and creature-believers: The effects of lexicalization on children's inferences about social categories. *Psychological Science, 10*, 489–493.

Gelman, S. A., Hollander, M., Star, J., & Heyman, G. D. (2000). The role of language in the construction of kinds. In D. Medin (Ed.), *The psychology of learning and motivation: Advances in research and theory* (Vol. 39, pp. 201–263). San Diego, CA: Academic Press.

Gil-White, F. (2001). Are ethnic groups biological "species" to the human brain? *Current Anthropology, 42*, 515–554.

Griffiths, P. E. (1997). *What emotions really are: The problem of psychological categories.* Chicago: University of Chicago Press.

Hall, G. S. (1898). A study of anger. *The American Journal of Psychology, 10*, 516–591.

Hampton, J. (1988). Forgiveness, resentment and hate. In J. G. Murphy & J. Hampton (Eds.), *Forgiveness and mercy* (pp. 35–87). New York: Cambridge University Press.

Herek, G., Gillis, J. R., & Cogan, J. C. (1999). Psychological sequelae of hate-crime victimization among lesbian, gay, and bisexual adults. *Journal of Consulting and Clinical Psychology, 67*, 945–951.

Hirschfeld, L. A. (1995). Do children have a theory of race? *Cognition, 54*, 209–252.

Hirschfeld, L. A. (1996). *Race in the making: Cognition, culture, and the child's construction of human kinds.* Cambridge, MA: MIT Press.

Hothersall, D. (1990). *History of psychology* (2nd ed.). New York: McGraw-Hill.

Hume, D. (1980). *A treatise of human nature.* Oxford, England: Oxford University Press. (Original work published 1739–1740)

Kaufman, S. J. (2001). *Modern hatreds: The symbolic politics of ethnic war.* Ithaca, NY: Cornell University Press.

Keil, F. C. (1989). *Concepts, kinds, and human development*. Cambridge, MA: MIT Press.

Kolnai, A. (1998). The standard modes of aversion: Fear, disgust and hatred. *Mind, 107*, 581–595.

Konrad, K. (1998). Ideology and rebellion: Terrorism in West Germany. In W. Reich (Ed.), *Origins of terrorism: Psychologies, ideologies, theologies, states of mind* (pp. 43–58). Washington, DC: Woodrow Wilson Center.

Kressel, N. J. (2002). *Mass hate: The global rise of genocide and terror*. Cambridge, MA: Westview Press.

Levin, J., & McDevitt, J. (1993). *Hate crimes: The rising tide of bigotry and bloodshed*. New York: Plenum Press.

MacIntyre, A. (1981). *After virtue*. Notre Dame, IN: University of Notre Dame Press.

McCauley, C. (2001). The psychology of group identification and the power of ethnic nationalism. In D. Chirot & M. Seligman (Eds.), *Ethnopolitical warfare: Causes, consequences, and possible solutions* (pp. 343–362). Washington, DC: American Psychological Association.

McCauley, C. (2002). Psychological issues in understanding terrorism and the response to terrorism. In C. Stout (Ed.), *The psychology of terrorism: Volume 3. Theoretical understandings and perspectives* (pp. 3–30). Westport, CT: Praeger Publishers.

McDevitt, J., Levin, J., & Bennett, S. (2002). Hate crime offenders: An extended typology. *Journal of Social Issues, 58*, 303–317.

McKellar, P. (1950). Provocation to anger and development of attitudes of hostility. *British Journal of Psychology, 40*, 104–114.

Mele, A. R. (1997). Real self-deception. *Behavioral and Brain Sciences, 20*, 91–136.

Mill, J. (1878). *Analysis of the phenomena of the human mind* (Vol. 1, 2nd ed.). London: Longmans, Green, Reader, and Dyer.

Nabi, R. (2002). The theoretical versus the lay meaning of disgust: Implications for emotion research. *Cognition & Emotion, 16*, 695–703.

Nietzsche, F. (1969). *On the genealogy of morals*. New York: Vintage Books.

Oatley, K., & Johnson-Laird, P. N. (1987). Towards a cognitive theory of emotions. *Cognition & Emotion, 1*, 29–50.

Pine, F. (1995). On the origin and evolution of a species of hate: A clinical–literary excursion. In S. Akhtar, S. Kramer, & H. Parens (Eds.), *The birth of hatred: Developmental, clinical and technical aspects of intense aggression* (pp. 105–132). Northvale, NJ: Jason Aronson.

Power, M. J., & Dalgleish, T. (1997). *Cognition and emotion: From order to disorder*. Hove, East Sussex, England: Psychology Press.

Putnam, H. (1975). The meaning of "meaning." In H. Putnam, *Philosophical papers: Vol. 2. Mind, language, and reality* (pp. 215–271). Cambridge, England: Cambridge University Press.

Rachman, S. J. (1978). *Fear and courage*. San Francisco: W. H. Freeman.

Reber, A. S., & Reber, E. (2002). *The Penguin dictionary of psychology* (3rd ed.). New York: Penguin Books.

Roseman, I. (1984). Cognitive determinants of emotion: A structural theory. In P. Shaver (Ed.), *Review of personality and social psychology: Emotions, relationships and health* (Vol. 5, pp. 11–36). Beverly Hills, CA: Sage.

Royzman, E., Cassidy, K. W., & Baron, J. (2003). "I know, you know": Epistemic egocentrism in children and adults. *Review of General Psychology, 7,* 38–65.

Rozin, P., Lowery, L., Imada, S., & Haidt, J. (1999). The CAD triad hypothesis: A mapping between three moral emotions (contempt, anger, disgust) and three moral codes (community, autonomy, divinity). *Journal of Personality and Social Psychology, 76,* 574–586.

Russell, J. A. (1991). Natural language concepts of emotion. In R. Hogan (Ed.), *Perspectives in personality: Vol. 3A. Self and emotion* (pp. 119–137). London: Jessica Kingsley.

Russell, J. A. (2003). Core affect and the psychological construction of emotion. *Psychological Review, 110,* 145–172.

Russell, J. A., & Fehr, B. (1994). Fuzzy concepts in a fuzzy hierarchy: Varieties of anger. *Journal of Personality and Social Psychology, 67,* 186–205.

Ryle, G. (1949). *The concept of mind.* London: Harper & Row.

Sabini, J., & Silver, M. (1998). *Emotion, character, and responsibility.* New York: Oxford University Press.

Scherer, K. R. (1997). The role of culture in emotion-antecedent appraisal. *Journal of Personality and Social Psychology, 73,* 902–922.

Shand, A. F. (1920). *The foundations of character* (2nd ed.). London: Macmillan.

Solomon, R. (1977). *The passions.* New York: Anchor Books.

Spinoza, B. (1985). Ethics. In E. Curley (Ed.), *The collected works of Spinoza* (Vol. 1, pp. 408–617). Princeton, NJ: Princeton University Press. (Original work published 1677)

Sternberg, R. (2003). A duplex theory of hate and its development and its application to terrorism, massacres, and genocide. *Review of General Psychology, 7,* 299–328.

Sternberg, R. J., & Grigorenko, E. L. (2001). Unified psychology. *American Psychologist, 56,* 1069–1079.

Walton, D. N. (1986). *Courage: A philosophical investigation.* Berkeley: University of California Press.

Wierzbicka, A. (1986). Emotions: Universal or culture-specific? *American Anthropologist, 88,* 584–594.

Wierzbicka, A. (1992). Defining emotion concepts. *Cognitive Science, 16,* 539–581.

Wierzbicka, A. (1999). *Emotions across languages and cultures.* New York: Cambridge University Press.

Wittgenstein, L. (1953). *Philosophical investigations.* New York: Macmillan.

2

UNDERSTANDING AND COMBATING HATE

ROBERT J. STERNBERG

The horrific events of September 11, 2001, and the terrorism that has followed in its wake have made it even more important now than in the past to understand the nature of hate. Yet psychologists have had relatively little to say about the nature of hate and its origins compared, say, with what they have had to say about memory, person perception, or even prejudice. Given the overwhelming displays of hate currently being displayed in the world, psychologists have a responsibility to seek an understanding of hate, its causes, and its consequences and how to combat it and achieve a culture of peace (Brenes & Du Nann Winter, 2001; Brenes & Wessells, 2001).

The dictionary definition of *hate* is "1. to have strong dislike or ill will for; loathe; despise. 2. to dislike or wish to avoid; shrink from" (Neufeldt & Guralnik, 1997, p. 617). Although this definition serves as a starting point for an understanding of hate, it is not sufficiently detailed.

SOME EARLIER THEORIES OF HATE

Allport (1954) viewed hatred as an emotion of extreme dislike or aggressive impulses toward a person or group of persons. Fromm (1973/1992) distinguished between two forms of hate: rational and character-conditioned hate. *Rational hate* has a rational basis (e.g., someone swindled you out of fame and fortune), but the much more dangerous kind, character-conditioned hate, does not. With *character-conditioned hate*, targeted groups are chosen to be objects of hate and then aggression. According to Fromm, hatred may arise irrationally because of long-standing, deep-seated prejudices of one group against another or rationally because an out-group is viewed as taking away economic or other resources from the in-group (Olzak & Nagel, 1986).

A number of emotions related to hate can lead to similar outcomes. For example, humiliation can lead to a cycle of hate and violence (Lindner, 2002).

THE DUPLEX THEORY OF HATE

My duplex theory of hate applies to both individuals and groups (Sternberg, 2003). Indeed, evidence suggests that the basic processing system that applies to the formation and processing of impressions about groups and about individuals is the same (Hamilton & Sherman, 1996). The basic thesis to be presented in this chapter makes five fundamental claims:

1. *Hate is very closely related psychologically to love.* The triangular and story elements of the theory of hate, as described later in this chapter, have their analogues in a theory of love (Sternberg, 1998b, 1998c).
2. *Hate is neither the opposite of love nor the absence of love.* Rather, the relationship between love and hate is structurally complex.
3. *Hate, like love, has its origins in stories that characterize the target of the emotion.* The stories of hate often co-occur with each other.
4. *Hate, like love, can be characterized by a triangular structure generated by these stories.* The core elements of the structure are negation of intimacy, passion, and commitment.
5. *Hate is a major precursor of many terrorist acts, massacres, and genocides.* Although such acts are multiply caused, often hate is one major root or root system underlying them.

THE TRIANGULAR THEORY OF THE STRUCTURE OF HATE

Three Components of Hate

According to the proposed theory, hate potentially comprises three components: negation of intimacy, passion, and commitment.

Negation of Intimacy (Distancing) in Hate: Repulsion and Disgust

The first potential component of hate is the negation of intimacy. Whereas intimacy involves the seeking of closeness, the negation of intimacy involves the seeking of distance. Often distance is sought from a target individual because that individual arouses repulsion and disgust in the person who experiences hate. This repulsion and disgust may arise from the person's characteristics or actions or from propaganda depicting certain kinds of characteristics and acts. The propaganda typically depicts the individual as subhuman or inhuman or otherwise incapable of receiving, giving, or sustaining feelings of closeness, warmth, caring, communication, compassion, and respect (Leyens et al., 2000). As with the positive intimacy component, feelings of distancing tend to be somewhat slow to develop and somewhat slow to fade.

Passion in Hate: Anger–Fear

A second potential component of hate is passion, which expresses itself as intense anger or fear in response to a threat. Anger often leads one to approach, or fear to avoid, the object of hate. Galdston (1987) suggested that what is referred to here as the *passion component* of "hatred allows for the super-imposition of a psychosomatic process upon the sensorimotor reflex of fight or flight in response to the stimuli of perceived danger" (p. 371).

Decision–Commitment in Hate: Devaluation–Diminution Through Contempt

The third potential component of hate is decision–commitment, which is characterized by cognitions of devaluation and diminution through contempt for the targeted group. The hater is likely to feel contempt toward the target individual or group, viewing the target as barely human or even as subhuman. The goal of those who foment hate is to change the thought processes of the preferred population so that its members will conceive of the targeted group in a devalued way. Often these changes are accomplished through some kind of instructional or otherwise "educational" program, whether in school or outside of school. In other terms, this kind of program could be viewed as constituting brainwashing.

Taxonomy of Types of Hate

The three components of hate generate, in various combinations, seven different types of hate. They are probably not exhaustive and, because they represent limiting cases, are not mutually exclusive. Particular instances may straddle categories.

1. *Cool hate: Disgust (negation of intimacy alone)*. Cool hate is characterized by feelings of disgust toward the targeted group.

The hater wishes to have nothing to do with the targeted group. Members of the targeted group may be viewed as subhuman, perhaps as vermin of some kind or as garbage. Visceral prejudice may be expressed as cool hate.

2. *Hot hate: Anger–fear (passion alone).* Hot hate is characterized by extreme feelings of anger or fear toward a threat, and the reaction may be to attack or to run away (fight or flight). Sudden flare-ups of hate, such as road rage, are examples of hot hate.

3. *Cold hate: Devaluation–diminution (decision–commitment alone).* Cold hate is characterized by thoughts of unworthiness directed toward the target group. There is something wrong with the members of this group. Indoctrination often portrays the group as evil, as in Ronald Reagan's conjuring up of the "Evil Empire" in referring to the former Soviet Union.

4. *Boiling hate: Revulsion (disgust of negation of intimacy + anger–fear of passion).* Boiling hate is characterized by feelings of revulsion toward the targeted group. The group may be viewed as subhuman or inhuman and as a threat, and something must be done to reduce or eliminate the threat. The targeted group may change from time to time.

5. *Simmering hate: Loathing (disgust of negation of intimacy + devaluation–diminution of decision–commitment).* Simmering hate is characterized by feelings of loathing toward the hated target. The targeted individual or individuals may be viewed as disgusting and as likely always to remain this way. There is no particular passion, just a simmering of hate. Ruthless, calculated assassinations often take this form.

6. *Seething hate: Revilement (anger–fear of passion + devaluation–diminution of decision–commitment).* Seething hate is characterized by feelings of revilement toward the targeted individual or individuals. Such individuals are a threat and always have been. Planned mob violence, often preceded by fiery oratory, sometimes takes on the characteristics of seething hate.

7. *Burning hate: Need for annihilation (disgust of negation of intimacy + anger–fear of passion + devaluation–diminution of decision–commitment).* Burning hate is characterized by all three components of hate. The haters may feel a need to annihilate their enemy, as postulated by Kernberg (1993) for extreme forms of hate.

These types of hate are not related to each other on some kind of encompassing, unidimensional scale. Rather, they are viewed as different but overlapping in kind. The categories are nominal, not ordinal. Moreover, they represent a first-pass attempt to characterize kinds of hate. Research over time may, of course, yield a superior taxonomy.

How can people who hate live with themselves? They may very well establish separate identities for themselves for different roles they enact (Suleiman, 2002). That is, the person who is a hater at a violent rally may go home and become a loving husband or wife. The roles are bifurcated from each other, so that the hater may see him- or herself as a loving and caring person in the roles in which loving and caring seem relevant. Or he or she may engage in moral disengagement by generating excuses for hating or inflicting suffering on others while maintaining a clear conscience (Grussendorf, McAlister, Sandström, Udd, & Morrison, 2002).

Relations of the Components of Hate to Acts of Terror, Massacres, and Genocides

The triangular theory holds that hate is related to massacres and genocides through the number of components of hate experienced:

- *Danger level 0: No hate-based danger*—None of the components of hate is present.
- *Danger level 1: Mild hate-based danger*—One of the components of hate is present.
- *Danger level 2: Moderate hate-based danger*—Two of the components of hate are present.
- *Danger level 3: Severe hate-based danger*—Three of the components of hate are present.

There is another aspect, however, to hate, namely the stories that give rise to different triangles of hate.

A STORY-BASED THEORY OF THE DEVELOPMENT OF HATE

Contents of the Stories Underlying the Development of Hate

Hate propaganda, which proposes story themes, typically accomplishes one or more of three functions. A first function is the negation of intimacy toward the targeted entity (e.g., leader, country, ethnic group). A second function is the generation of passion. And a third function is to generate commitment to false beliefs through the implantation of false presuppositions, the encouragement of people to suspend or distort their critical thinking processes, and the encouragement of people to reach targeted (often false) conclusions based on the pseudologic of false presuppositions and flawed critical thinking.

Stories of hate tend to have a simpler structure than do stories of love. Stories of love have a wide variety of kinds of roles. Stories of hate tend to have two fairly stable roles: perpetrator (who is to be hated) and victim (who is to be the hater). As pointed out by Baumeister (1996), people who do evil things tend to see themselves as victims of those they persecute!

The stories of hate are fomented largely by socialization through propaganda. To a large extent, then, hate is learned (Blum, 1996). The propaganda can emanate from parents, age mates, media of various kinds, teachers, and other sources of information in society. Often, a hated group will be depicted in terms of multiple stories. The list of stories below is neither exhaustive nor uniquely differentiated. Rather, it is intended to be representative of the kinds of stories that are used to foment negation of intimacy, passion, and cognitive commitment to hate.

Why do people create stories about hate? Sometimes the stories may be the result of their attempts to find self-esteem by devaluing others. Freud (1918/1957) proposed what he referred to as the "narcissism of minor differences" (p. 199; see also Gabbard, 1993). Freud believed that people need to find and to exaggerate differences between themselves and those they love to maintain themselves as autonomous individuals. The concept may be extended, perhaps, to include not only loved ones but also all others. To find meaning and autonomy, people may tend to exaggerate differences. And when people's self-esteem is threatened, their tendency to seek to restore it by exaggerating minor differences may be increased. The differences they find may be of many kinds, and at least some of these kinds may correspond to the stories noted next, whereby people take the role of the "good" victim and the hated object takes the role of the "bad" perpetrator. This idea does not emanate only from psychoanalytic thinking. Post (1999), a political psychologist, has suggested that enemies are to be cherished and cultivated, because if people lose them, they also risk losing their self-definition.

Often, people do not create stories, but rather cynical leaders create the stories for them. Often whole governments conspire to create cultures of hate, death, and violence (Lira, 2001). As Post (1999) suggested, "hate-mongering demagogues, serving as malignant group therapists to their wounded nations, can provide sense-making explanations for their beleaguered followers, exporting the source of their difficulties to an external target, justifying hatred and mass violence" (p. 337). These sense-making explanations are what are called *stories* in this chapter.

Keen (1986) and, to a lesser extent, Rhodes (1993) suggested a number of the plots of stories of hate. The following are some of these stories, as well as some others not mentioned by Keen or Rhodes. The list is by no means complete; probably, many more stories of hate could be generated. Moreover, multiple stories can be operative simultaneously or consecutively. The hated object can be understood in terms of whether the hated enemy is

- *a stranger*—The hated object is not like us, but different in a strange way.
- *impure or contaminated*—The hated object is impure and thus needs to be cleansed, whether ethnically or otherwise.
- *a controller*—The hated individual or group is attempting to control others and, perhaps, the world.
- *a faceless foe*—Members of the hated group are all more or less alike—that is, faceless.
- *an enemy of God*—The hated individual/group is an enemy of God and likely in league with Satan.
- *morally bankrupt*—The hated individual or group has no moral scruples.
- *a purveyor of death*—The hated individual or group is a cause of death to people like us.
- *a barbarian*—The hated individual or group is barbaric, a throwback to the Dark Ages (at best).
- *greedy*—The hated individual or group is preoccupied with money, wealth, and symbols of luxury.
- *a criminal*—The hated individual or group is no better than a criminal and, indeed, should be viewed as criminal.
- *a torturer*—The hated individual or group tortures us.
- *a murderer*—The hated individual or group has murdered or will murder people like us.
- *a seducer*—The hated individual or group, despite being loathsome, is seeking to seduce our women.
- *an animal pest*—The hated individual or group is like vermin.
- *a power monger*—The hated individual or group is preoccupied with the accumulation of massive power and total domination.
- *a subtle infiltrator*—There are hated individuals or groups among us, and we do not know who they are.
- *a comic character*—The hated individual or group is clownlike.
- *a thwarter or destroyer of destiny*—The hated individual or group has destroyed or is destroying the destiny that is intended for members of our group.

At the same time that members of the hated group are portrayed through negative stories, members of the preferred group are portrayed positively.

Structure of the Stories of Hate

Because stories of hate tend to be simple, some people might prefer to view them simply as negative stereotypes or as negative images of the enemy. Why use the story concept at all? I use it because, I argue, each is associated with an anticipated set of events and, in particular, with an anticipated beginning, middle, and end. The threat represents a dynamic story, not just a static image or stereotype. It is not the image, per se, that evokes hate, but rather the anticipated events that will follow from the story. Although the particular roles in the story outline are different, the anticipated sets of events that lead to hate are probably not so different. The chain of anticipated events covers roughly five steps. Not all steps need to occur in order for hate to come into being. Indeed, even one step may start the process.

1. *The target is revealed to be anathema.* At some point, often long in the past (and probably, more often than not, in the imagined past), the target reveals itself to be worthy of hatred. Perhaps members of the group killed God, or slaughtered members of what is now the in-group, or plotted the destruction of the in-group, or revealed themselves to be dirty or greedy or whatever. Although the events giving rise to the group's being labeled as anathema may have occurred long ago, they can remain in a metaphorical sort of Jungian collective unconscious.

2. *The target plans actions contrary to the interests of the in-group.* One may not become aware of this problem until after Step 4. But at some point, one becomes aware that for some time, often a long time, the target has been planning actions contrary to the best (and often, any good) interests of the in-group (see discussions of ethnopolitical warfare in Chirot & Seligman, 2001). Whatever the problem is, it is no longer historical in nature; it is current. Because members of the in-group often do not realize they have been "plotted against" until what they perceive to be rather late in the plotting process, they may feel a sense of desperation and urgency.

3. *The target makes its presence felt.* The story often first becomes perceptible when the target appears significantly on the scene. The target may come from outside, either legally (through legal immigration) or illegally (through illegal immigration, invasion, or imposition by outside powers). But the target also may come from inside. Perhaps it has been there a long time. Indeed, people often feel that they missed Step 1 and that only now are they realizing that the threat that has been there for some time. Now the target is becoming powerful and hence is becoming a force to be reckoned with before it is too late.

4. *The target translates plans into action.* Members of the in-group believe they are becoming aware that the period of plotting is over for the target. The target is actively translating thought into action and thus has become a true threat, not just a hypothetical one. Sometimes the action is now perceived to be

already quite far along before individuals realize what is going on; other times, the action is perceived to be just starting up. The exact type of action depends on the content of the story.

5. *The target is achieving some success in its goals.* Unsuccessful targets may be viewed as pathetic, such as members of very small groups that have dreams of taking over the world. But once the target is not only acting but also achieving some success in its actions, feelings of hatred and perhaps the desire to act on these feelings become a force to be reckoned with.

In sum, the images, in themselves, are the contents that fill in the story schema. In a sense, the precise story is less important than how many of the above steps the target group has, in the minds of the in-group, managed to enact. The more steps the target group enacts, the more of a threat they become and the "hotter" the hate is likely to be (i.e., the higher the number of components that are likely to be operative).

The following techniques seem to be common in the use of stories to incite hatred and instigate massacres and genocides:

- intensive, extensive propaganda,
- infusion of hatred and its resultants as an integral and necessary part of societal mores,
- emphasis on indoctrination of youngsters in school and through extracurricular groups,
- importance of obeying orders,
- diffusion of responsibility,
- calls to and rewards for action,
- threats and punishment for noncompliance,
- public examples of compliance and noncompliance,
- system of informers to weed out fifth columnists, and
- creation of an authoritarian cult of a leader.

ARE THERE ANY CURES?

There is no magic bullet cure for hate. There are several possible steps, however. Indeed, Staub (1999, 2000) devised a program for intervening in cases of mass killings and violence (see also Veale & Donà, 2002). At the very least, one can start by modifying negative stereotypes, which can be done with some success (Blair & Banaji, 1996; Mackie, Allison, Worth, & Asuncion, 1992). In general, people need to

- understand the triangular nature of hate and its escalation with successive triangular components so that one can recognize its often subtle presence;

- understand how hate is fomented through stories, often by way of propaganda;
- understand how hate can lead to massacres and genocide through the translation of feeling triangles into action triangles;
- combat feelings of impotence with constructive rather than destructive responses, and act against hate and its consequences rather than stand by as passive observers, as the world so often has done;
- realize that passive observation and often attempts at reason enacted in the hope that hate-based massacres and genocides will go away are perceived as weaknesses and tend to encourage rather than to discourage violence; and
- combat hate with wisdom.

There is no complete cure for hate. Cognitive comprehension of a destructive psychological process does not insulate people from experiencing it. But given the destruction hate has caused over time and geography, there is a need to understand it, its consequences, and ways to at least try to combat it through understanding and especially through action. Indeed, there are few areas of psychology for which it equally can be said that action speaks louder than words.

Many of the ways of combating hate are the same that one would use in resolving conflict situations and achieving peace (Christie, Wagner, & Du Nann Winter, 2001), including creation of win–win situations, building trust between groups, sharing information, each side asking questions of the other, generating multiple alternative options, and seeking understanding of groups to which one does not belong (Boardman, 2002; Isenhart & Spangle, 2000). Sometimes when a group communicates to the other the story of what its members have experienced, they can come to an understanding of each other that is not possible when people stay silent and fail to communicate (Albeck, Adwan, & Bar-On, 2002). When wrongs have been committed, no solution may be possible unless both sides are willing to forgive (Azar & Mullet, 2002). Building tolerance and creating a culture of peace and a society in which people share equally in rights and in participation in the society can go a long way toward resolving problems of violence and hate (Christie & Dawes, 2001; Miall, Ramsbotham, & Woodhouse, 1999; Montiel & Wessells, 2001). The question is whether people have sufficient good will to achieve this goal.

Combating hate requires, first and foremost, taking responsibility for it, its perpetrators, and its consequences. Linn (2001) has pointed out that after World War II, roughly 200 Nazi scientists were protected by the United States from extradition orders to stand trial in Nuremberg. She discussed multiple other instances in which intellectuals failed to come to grips with the crimes of perpetrators of massacres and genocides. People cannot fight hate if they find it tolerable or even acceptable.

Ultimately, the best way to combat hate may be through wisdom (Sternberg, 1998a). Intelligent people may hate; wise people do not. People like Mohandas Gandhi, Martin Luther King, Mother Theresa, and Nelson Mandela had the same human passions as any of us, but in their wisdom, they moved beyond hate to embrace love and peace.

The balance theory of wisdom (Sternberg, 1998a, 2001) defines *wisdom* as the application of intelligence, creativity, and experience toward a common good by balancing one's own interests with others' interests and institutional interests over the long and short terms. By definition, wise people do not hate others because they care about the individual's (or group's) well-being as well as their own or that of their group. They seek solutions that embrace the legitimate interests of others as well as of themselves. Someone who cares about another's interests and well-being cannot hate that person, in part because he or she cannot dehumanize that other.

Schools typically teach children knowledge and to think intelligently. But they rarely teach for wisdom. Indeed, in many schools across the globe, they teach hate for one group or another. Ultimately, if society wishes to combat hate, its schools and institutions need to teach students to think wisely. They then will realize that hate is not the solution to any legitimate life problem. Indeed, it foments rather than solves problems. But to teach for wisdom requires wisdom, and so far, the possession of that wisdom is a challenge that many fail to meet, not because we cannot meet it, but rather, because we choose not to. It is to be hoped that, in the future, people will make the better choice—for wisdom rather than for foolishness and the hate that can arise from it.

REFERENCES

Albeck, J. H., Adwan, S., & Bar-On, D. (2002). Dialogue groups: TRT's guidelines for working through intractable conflicts by personal storytelling. *Peace and Conflict: Journal of Peace Psychology, 8,* 301–322.

Allport, G. W. (1954). *The nature of prejudice.* Reading, MA: Addison-Wesley.

Azar, F., & Mullet, E. (2002). Willingness to forgive: A study of Muslim and Christian Lebanese. *Peace and Conflict: Journal of Peace Psychology, 8,* 17–30.

Baumeister, R. F. (1996). *Evil: Inside human violence and cruelty.* New York: Freeman.

Blair, I. V., & Banaji, M. R. (1996). Automatic and controlled processes in stereotype priming. *Journal of Personality and Social Psychology, 70,* 1142–1163.

Blum, H. P. (1996). Hatred in a delinquent adolescent. In L. Rangell & R. Moses-Hrushovski (Eds.), *Psychoanalysis at the political border* (pp. 35–48). Madison, CT: International Universities Press.

Boardman, S. K. (2002). Resolving conflict: Theory and practice. *Peace and Conflict: Journal of Peace Psychology, 8*, 157–160.

Brenes, A., & Du Nann Winter, D. (2001). Earthly dimensions of peace: The Earth charter. *Peace and Conflict: Journal of Peace Psychology, 7*, 157–171.

Brenes, A., & Wessells, M. (2001). Psychological contributions to building cultures of peace. *Peace and Conflict: Journal of Peace Psychology, 7*, 99–107.

Chirot, D., & Seligman, M. E. P. (Eds.). (2001). *Ethnopolitical warfare: Causes, consequences, and possible solutions.* Washington, DC: American Psychological Association.

Christie, D. J., & Dawes, A. (2001). Tolerance and solidarity. *Peace and Conflict: Journal of Peace Psychology, 7*, 131–142.

Christie, D. J., Wagner, R. V., & Du Nann Winter, D. (Eds.). (2001). *Peace, conflict, and violence: Peace psychology for the 21st century.* Upper Saddle River, NJ: Prentice-Hall.

Freud, S. (1957). The taboo of virginity (Contributions to the psychology of love III.) In J. Strachey (Ed. & Trans.), *The standard edition of the complete psychological works of Sigmund Freud* (Vol. 11, pp. 192–208). London: Hogarth Press. (Original work published 1918)

Fromm, E. (1992). *Anatomy of human destructiveness.* New York: Holt. (Original work published 1973)

Gabbard, G. O. (1993). On hate in love relationships: The narcissism of minor differences revisited. *Psychoanalytic Quarterly, 62*, 229–238.

Galdston, R. (1987). The longest pleasure: A psychoanalytic study of hatred. *International Journal of Psycho-Analysis, 68*, 371–378.

Grussendorf, J., McAlister, A., Sandström, P., Udd, L., & Morrison, T. C. (2002). Resisting moral disengagement in support of war: Use of the "Peace test" scale among student groups in 21 nations. *Peace and Conflict: Journal of Peace Psychology, 8*, 73–83.

Hamilton, D. L., & Sherman, S. J. (1996). Perceiving persons and groups. *Psychological Review, 103*, 336–355.

Isenhart, M., & Spangle, M. (2000). *Collaborative approaches for resolving conflict.* Thousand Oaks, CA: Sage.

Keen, S. (1986). *Faces of the enemy: Reflections of the hostile imagination.* New York: Harper & Row.

Kernberg, O. F. (1993). The psychopathology of hatred. In R. A. Glick & S. P. Roose (Eds.), *Rage, power, and aggression* (pp. 61–79). New Haven, CT: Yale University Press.

Leyens, J.-P., Paladino, P. M., Rodriguez-Torres, R., Vaes, J., Demoulin, S., Rodriguez-Perez, A., & Gant, R. (2000). The emotional side of prejudice: The attribution of secondary emotions to ingroups and outgroups. *Personality and Social Psychology Review, 4*, 186–197.

Lindner, E. G. (2002). Healing the cycles of humiliation: How to attend to the emotional aspects of "unsolvable" conflicts and the use of "humiliation entrepreneurship." *Peace and Conflict: Journal of Peace Psychology, 8*, 125–138.

Linn, R. (2001). Conscience at war: On the relationship between moral psychology and moral resistance. *Peace and Conflict: Journal of Peace Psychology, 7,* 337–355.

Lira, E. (2001). Violence, fear, and impunity: Reflections on subjective and political obstacles for peace. *Peace and Conflict: Journal of Peace Psychology, 7,* 109–118.

Mackie, D. M., Allison, S. T., Worth, L. T., & Asuncion, A. G. (1992). The generalization of outcome-biased counter-stereotypic inferences. *Journal of Experimental Social Psychology, 28,* 43–64.

Miall, H., Ramsbotham, O., & Woodhouse, T. (1999). *Contemporary conflict resolution.* Cambridge, MA: Polity Press.

Montiel, C. J., & Wessells, M. (2001). Democratization, psychology, and the construction of cultures of peace. *Peace and Conflict: Journal of Peace Psychology, 7,* 119–129.

Neufeldt, V., & Guralnik, D. B. (1997). *Webster's new world college dictionary* (3rd ed.). New York: Macmillan.

Olzak, S., & Nagel, J. (1986). *Competitive ethnic relations.* Orlando, FL: Academic Press.

Post, J. M. (1999). The psychopolitics of hatred: Commentary on Ervin Staub's article. *Peace and Conflict: Journal of Peace Psychology, 5,* 337–344.

Rhodes, A. (1993). *Propaganda the art of persuasion: World War II: an allied and axis visual record, 1933–1945.* Broomal, PA: Chelsea House Publishers.

Staub, E. (1999). The origins and prevention of genocide, mass killing, and other collective violence. *Peace and Conflict: Journal of Peace Psychology, 5,* 303–336.

Staub, E. (2000). Genocide and mass killing: Origins, prevention, healing, and reconciliation. *Political Psychology, 21,* 367–382.

Sternberg, R. J. (1998a). A balance theory of wisdom. *Review of General Psychology, 2,* 347–365.

Sternberg, R. J. (1998b). *Cupid's arrow: The course of love through time.* New York: Cambridge University Press.

Sternberg, R. J. (1998c). *Love is a story.* New York: Oxford University Press.

Sternberg, R. J. (2001). Why schools should teach for wisdom: The balance theory of wisdom in educational settings. *Educational Psychologist, 36,* 227–245.

Sternberg, R. J. (2003). A duplex theory of hate and its development and its application to terrorism, massacres, and genocides. *Review of General Psychology, 7,* 299–328.

Suleiman, R. (2002). Minority self-categorization: The case of the Palestinians in Israel. *Peace and Conflict: Journal of Peace Psychology, 8,* 31–46.

Veale, A., & Donà, G. (2002). Psychosocial interventions and children's rights: Beyond clinical discourse. *Peace and Conflict: Journal of Peace Psychology, 8,* 47–61.

3

THE ORIGINS AND EVOLUTION OF HATE, WITH NOTES ON PREVENTION

ERVIN STAUB

Prejudice, hostility against groups and their members, and hate are everyday realities. They are expressed in words and actions: White supremacist groups attacking members of minority groups, attacks by Palestinians against Jews, the killing by a Jewish settler of worshiping Palestinians, the killings of doctors who perform abortions, genocide in Rwanda and mass killing in Bosnia, and the 9/11 attacks on the United States.

Not all acts of violence arise from hate. Violence can be instrumental, people aiming to accomplish some goal while harming others as means to their ends. It can be defensive, or it can be hostile-angry (when a person who is frustrated or attacked feels anger and hostility and strikes out). Hate is an intense negative view of, accompanied by intense feelings against, the objects of hate. A hater sees the object of his or her hate as profoundly bad, immoral, dangerous, or all of these. The intense devaluation and the associated feelings make it satisfying to have the hated other suffer, experience loss, and be harmed. A violent act is hateful when it is based on intense, persistent negative views of the other, which give rise to the desire to harm, make suffer, and even destroy the other.

Hate may arise out of seeing someone as a threat to the self or to one's group or to important values or as standing in the way of something important (the creation of a way of life, of a kind of world advocated by an ideology). The objects of hate can be individuals, although in this chapter the focus is on groups and their members as the objects. Hate may evolve out of already existing prejudice or devaluation of people. It is promoted or intensified by actions that harm the people who are devaluated or come to be hated. Hate is based on perception of the other but also has a great deal to do with the self, with one's past history, and with its effects on one's thoughts, feelings, beliefs and personality, and especially identity, often a threatened identity. Conditions of adversity in the lives of individuals and groups may give rise to and often intensify hate.

In summary, hate is built out of a complex of cognitions and emotions. The cognitive components are likely to include devaluation or a negative view of some other and the perception of threat from that other. The emotional components are likely to include dislike, fear, anger, and hostility. Another likely element of hate is a sense of rightness or justice about acting against the object of one's hate.

US AND THEM: THE DEVALUATION OF GROUPS OF PEOPLE

Hate is rooted in and develops from the human tendency to differentiate between *us* and *them* and the many ways that people come to devalue *them* (Brewer, 1978; Staub, 1989; Tajfel, 1978, 1982; Tajfel, Flamant, Billig, & Bundy, 1971). The line between *us* and *them* can be and has been drawn on many bases, and it can be arbitrarily and, given the human potential to create such a differentiation, easily created. Frequent bases of such differentiation have been race, religion, ethnicity, nationality, social class, and political beliefs. But there can be many others, for example, rooting for one sports team versus another (Buford, 1992) or going to one school versus another. Religions, which proclaim love but at the same time almost always identify other religions as false and as the wrong way to worship God, have been both a frequent basis of differentiating *us* and *them* and a source of hate for those of other faiths.

A common form of devaluation is to see the "other," or *them* as unintelligent, lazy, and unappealing. A stronger form is also to see the other as morally deficient and bad, which can be accompanied by the belief that the other has gained wealth, power, or influence dishonestly, manipulatively, and at one's own expense. This has been a persistent form of the devaluation of Jews (Staub, 1989). For this or for different reasons, the other can be seen as violating, by their actions or their very being, important moral norms. People strongly opposed to abortion may hate those advocating and, especially, those performing abortions and may view them as violating central, essential moral norms. Another important form of the negative view of the other is a person or group seeing the hated person or group as a danger to his or her life, loved ones' lives, or the lives of members of his or her group. Hitler and the Nazi propaganda propagated the view of Jews as posing a threat to Germans individually (exploiting them, seducing German girls and women) and collectively (aiming to destroy Germany).

How does a group of people, or a whole society, develop devaluation of another group of people, often a subgroup of society? One way is that, for various historical reasons, one group becomes poorer and less privileged, with fewer rights in society, and this is justified by their devaluation. Differences in societal status, the discrimination that usually follows, and devaluation mutually support each other. Another source of devaluation may be a group's differentness in habits, customs, beliefs, and values and perhaps, even more, in physical characteristics. This has been one source of racism against Black people by Whites. Sometimes the differentness is at least in part imposed, such as forcing Jews at various times and places in Europe to wear certain clothes or distinguishing marks (like a yellow star, as early as the 5th century), which then becomes a further source of devaluation (Girard, 1980), or prohibiting slaves in the United States to learn to read and write and then devaluing them because of their ignorance.

Given already existing devaluation, possibly due to differentness, a group of people can be subjugated and exploited, which may then be justified by their further devaluation. This was probably an important source of racism in America (Staub, 1996). Devaluation may also be a response to difficult conditions of life, which frustrate basic human needs (discussed later in this chapter). People may scapegoat some group as responsible for life problems or elevate their own group by diminishing some other group to make themselves feel better in the face of life problems (Staub, 1989, 1996; Tajfel, 1978).

Devaluation is not the same as hate, but it is an essential ground out of which hate can grow. Certain types of devaluation are less likely and others more likely to give rise to or be associated with hate. Seeing members of a group as less intelligent, less able, or lazy is a devaluation, but not one that is likely to give rise to hate. Members of a group who are seen as exploitative or morally deficient but who are at the same time in a relatively good economic (or social) position in a society are especially likely to become the objects of genocidal violence that is driven by hate. This was the case with the Jews in Germany, the Armenians in Turkey (Staub, 1989), and the Tutsis in Rwanda (Des Forges, 1999; Mamdani, 2002; Staub, 1999a).

Once it has developed, devaluation (as well as antagonism and even hate) can be transmitted by a culture through written and pictorial material, through everyday conversations and the examples of people's behavior, or through guidance and instruction by parents. Social conditions such as difficult life conditions, which can give rise to devaluation, as I have noted, tend to intensify already existing devaluation and move it toward hate. Both experiences that affect whole groups and personal experiences by individuals, such as past victimization, can create or increase the inclination to accept devaluation and develop hate.

To overcome devaluation requires corrective experiences. Information that humanizes the other, positive descriptions and images of devalued people, and positive behavior toward them by respected public figures are of great value. In addition, however, personal experiences of significant contact, ideally contact in which people work together for shared goals, is important to overcome devaluation (Aronson, Stephan, Sikes, Blaney, & Snapp, 1978; Pettigrew & Tropp, 2000). Structural conditions, such as the absence of discrimination and increased equality between groups, are also important.

IDEOLOGY AS A SOURCE OF HATE

Hate on the group level is often promoted by an *ideology*, or system of beliefs about desirable or ideal social arrangements that offer the promise of a better life for a nation or for all humanity. Such ideologies tend to specify the desirable structure of society or the desirable relationship between groups. The ideology may elevate the group, advocating social arrangements in which the group that holds the ideology has superiority over others in general or over particular others (nationalistic as well as racist ideologies), or advocating that the group be purified by eliminating others from its midst who contaminate it.

Or the ideology may advocate a "better world," social arrangements that would presumably be better for all, such as communism. These ideologies become a basis of hate and are destructive because they specify certain groups of people that stand in the way of the ideology's fulfillment: capitalists and imperialists standing in the way of communism, Armenians standing in the way of creating a new Turkey that would redeem the losses and humiliations that Turkey suffered in the 19th and early 20th century, and so on.

Ideals like communism can have variations, like total social equality propagated by the Khmer Rouge in Cambodia, who then proceeded to destroy everyone who they believed could not live in or contribute to the creation of a totally equal society. Included among such people were intellectuals, who had presumably learned too much to have the proper humility. A person could be identified as an intellectual simply by wearing glasses; presumably, such a person had ruined his or her eyes by reading too much. Members of minority groups were also killed (Staub, 1989).

At times seemingly genuinely positive visions become destructive because they identify enemies who must be "dealt with." Even if it does not start that way, the way of dealing with the other often becomes destroying the other. At times the vision that the ideology offers is the world without the particular, hated other. This was the case with the ideology of "Hutu Power" in Rwanda and its associated Hutu 10 commandments. The better world for the Hutu was a world without Tutsis (Des Forges, 1999).

Hate groups in the United States are also guided by ideologies that affirm the biological supremacy of White people, seen as God's chosen people. The enemies these ideologies focus on are Black people, who are seen as biologically inferior, as "mud people," there to serve White people but claiming for themselves rights they should not have given their biological nature, and Jews, who are seen as the children of Satan who try to subvert and take over the rightful place of White people (Ezekiel, 1995, 2002).

HISTORY, VULNERABILITY, AND THE FRUSTRATION OF BASIC HUMAN NEEDS

Past group (or individual) trauma and the resulting mistrust and generally negative view of people create a vulnerability to threat, such as difficult life conditions and group conflict. In the absence of healing or redeeming experiences, past trauma, especially victimization, can lead to perceiving hostility from others, fearing and devaluing others, and can create the potential for hate. Painful, difficult experiences intensely frustrate basic human needs—this is at the core of a sensitivity to or inclination for hate. Scapegoating, prejudice, and the creation of destructive ideologies can be destructive attempts to satisfy basic needs.

Early theorists, especially Maslow (1968, 1971), described theories of universal human needs. Others developed somewhat different theories about human beings possessing "basic" psychological needs (Burton, 1990; Kelman, 1990; Pearlman & Saakvitne, 1995; Staub, 1989, 1996, 1999b, 2003). In my conception, these universal needs include the need for security, the need for a positive identity, the need for feelings of effectiveness and control over important events, the need for positive connection to other human beings, and the need for autonomy. In addition, people have a profound (basic) need to understand the world, to have a view of how it operates and of their place in it. When these needs are reasonably satisfied, another important need emerges: the need to go beyond concern with one's own self, the need for transcendence. However, at times, what looks like transcendence can be an escape from the self, rather than going beyond the self, in the form of giving oneself over to groups and movements however destructive they are. I have called this *pseudotranscendence* (Staub, 2003, in press).

When needs are not fulfilled constructively, they continue to press for satisfaction. People then often attempt to fulfill them, at least minimally, in destructive ways. Need satisfaction is destructive when it is harmful to the self, when fulfilling one need makes it difficult to fulfill another need (e.g., a focus on control by controlling other people can interfere with positive connections to people), or when it is harmful to other people (e.g., when someone fulfills the need for effectiveness by aggression against others; Staub, 1989, 1999b, 2003, in press).

The potential for hate can be generated in children who are neglected or badly treated, which frustrates their basic needs. They may develop hostility toward people in general. Some of them, when they grow older, may join ideological movements or terrorist groups (McCauley & Segal, 1989) or White supremacist or "hate groups" (Ezekiel, 1995, 2002). These groups may help them fulfill basic needs for connection, identity, and comprehension of reality and, as they take action against others, the need for effectiveness. In addition, to the extent their past experience has led them to feel hostility toward people, the views and purposes of such groups, their hostility to some devalued other or enemy, fits the orientation that such persons have developed.

In his exploration of White supremacist groups in the United States, Ezekiel (1995, 2002) interviewed youths belonging to such a group in Detroit. Many of them had experienced severe losses in childhood, often the loss of a father early in life who left the family and disappeared. They had no redeeming social contact with other caring adults, either relatives or others outside the family. Although Ezekiel reported less on this, they apparently had no deep peer friendships, which can also be a source of resilience and healing (Staub, in press). A number of these youths had shown early interest in the Ku Klux Klan, writing to the Klan as early as in junior high school to receive literature about the Klan. Nonetheless, Ezekiel found them racist but not hating. However, their already existing racist inclination had been further developed by the leaders of the group. In Ezekiel's view, their main motivation for membership was what I would call the fulfillment of basic human needs—for connection, identity, security, and worldview.

Children who have been badly treated may grow into adults whose hostility and potential for hate can manifest itself in varied ways, depending on other aspects of their personality and other shaping influences. People who are expressively violent and who harm others not to gain some advantage for themselves but rather to enhance their self-image or their image in the eyes of others (Toch, 1969/1993) often were abused as children (Gilligan, 1996; Widom, 1989a, 1989b). In addition to their orientation to the self, their orientation to others and disconnection from and feelings of hostility to others are likely to be sources of their frequent violence.

Harsh treatment contributes to boys' aggression. Aggressive boys tend to see other people as hostile to them and strike out in what they see as self-defense (Dodge, 1980, 1993; Dodge, Bates, & Pettit, 1990). Seeing the world as hostile may lead to fear and withdrawal. In aggressive people, however, in addition to fear and the perception of hostility, there seems also to be hostility toward others. Such hostility can be channeled toward vulnerable or already devalued individuals or groups and intensified into hate.

An important issue is the extent to which parents who treat children with love and affection and provide positive guidance but at the same time greatly devalue and express hate toward some out-group will generate hate in the children. The child rearing of such parents enhances their influence over their children. At the same time, their loving practices are in contradiction to the hate they model and teach. Nonetheless, given the power of *us–them* differentiation, such parents can be effective agents in creating devaluation and probably hate as well. On one hand, even when a whole group devalues another, because of the love that children experience and because loving parents may be less hostile to people, such parents may inculcate less negativity to the "other." On the other hand, loving, nurturant parenting is not likely, by itself, to develop inclusive caring in children or caring for people outside the group, especially for people who are devalued by the group. To develop inclusive caring, which inoculates against hate, requires additional practices (Colby & Damon, 1992; Staub, 2002, 2003, in press).

In addition to individuals, whole groups—that is, collections of individuals—can be deeply victimized or traumatized in other ways. Individuals and groups who have been greatly traumatized, who have had extremely painful experiences that were or felt life threatening over which the person or group did not have the capacity to exercise control, to defend against and cope with, may have an increased potential for hate. This is especially true of trauma that is created by victimization, that is, by harmful actions against the self or important others. Victimization makes people feel diminished, to see other people as untrustworthy and hostile and the world as dangerous (Staub, 1998; Staub & Pearlman, 2001). Perceived fear and hostility toward others create a strong potential for devaluation and hate. When whole groups have been victimized, as in individuals, their diminished self, vulnerability, and view of the world as dangerous create a potential for "defensive violence," that is, violence that is seen as defensive but is actually unnecessary. In the process the group can become a perpetrator.

Becker (1975) proposed a particular form of the potential for threat to create violence. He suggested that human beings cannot tolerate or accept their death. Power over the life of others gives them a sense of invulnerability. In Becker's view, this was one reason for human sacrifice in many cultures. Following this line of thinking, social psychologists who have developed terror management theory found that when people are reminded of death, their negative reaction to the other intensifies (Greenberg et al., 1990). I would hypothesize, however, that this is more likely with people who have been significantly victimized, so that suffering and the possibility of death are closer to them. Such people, in the face of threat, may be more easily guided to hate those who threaten them.

Of course, people who have been victimized will not necessarily become hostile or hateful or inappropriately violent in their self-defense. Some of them may even become what I have called "altruists born of suffering" (Staub, 2003, in press). Such people try to protect others from suffering. For this to happen, they require healing experiences. An important form of this is a loving connection to people. In children who come from difficult backgrounds, resilience, or the ability to function effectively, is promoted by connections to caring adults, whether a parent, relative, schoolteacher, or counselor. Even deep connections to peers are likely to have such a positive effect (Staub, in press). For people who have suffered, such connections can provide hope because they show the possibility of a different world from what they have experienced, the possibility of love and caring.

Self-awareness may be another important antidote to the inclination toward hate that may result from painful experiences. Freud has proposed that the need to deny negative, problematic parts of oneself leads to their projection into other people. Seeing the other as the possessor of the unacknowledged negative, unacceptable characteristics in turn leads to hostility toward the other. The disapproval by adults of various characteristics can lead children to deny the existence of these characteristics in themselves and both to project them onto others and judge them harshly in others. Helping children, and adults, to gain self-awareness and to process their own experience can diminish this tendency.

ROLE OF SOCIAL CONDITIONS AND GROUP CONFLICT IN GENERATING HATE

Difficult life conditions in a society, such as intense economic problems, great political turmoil, and even rapid culture change, tend to frustrate people's basic needs. In response, people often scapegoat some group, blame them for life problems, and develop destructive ideologies. These responses fulfill basic needs, but destructively (Staub, 1989, 2003). Scapegoating and ideology both offer an understanding of reality, create connections among people who scapegoat together or join an ideological movement, offer the possibility of effective action against the scapegoat or ideological enemy, or encourage other actions to fulfill the ideology (Staub, 1996, 2003). Individuals also tend to shift from an individual identity, because seeing themselves as separate persons who stand on their own has become burdensome, to a group identity as members of an ethnic, religious, or racial group or of some ideological movement. Such a shift is, of course, relative, as normally people see themselves to some extent as both individuals and group members. But the relative weight of identity shifts.

Conflict between groups can be another starting point for hate. When the conflict becomes intractable, resistant to resolution, and violent, it comes to intensely frustrate basic needs. Groups tend to justify their own conduct, their violence, and blame the other (Bar-Tal, 2002). The ability to consider the other's needs and points of view, usually limited in groups, further declines. Harm doing may be mutual, but what people see is the harm done to their own group, which gives rise to deep pain and rage (Staub & Bar-Tal, 2003). Out of pain, hurt, anger, and out of the justification of one's group's actions as right and moral and the other's actions as wrong and immoral, hate can and often does arise.

THE EVOLUTION OF HATE

Intense violence—even individual violence, but especially violence by groups—develops step by step (Staub, 1989). Hate also develops progressively. When a person harms another to a small degree (e.g., a husband hitting a wife; Beck, 2000) or members of a group harm members of another group to a small extent (discriminating against them in education or exploiting them in work), unless there are countervailing forces, an evolution of hate is likely to start.

As people harm others, they change and become capable of harming their victims more. Unless witnesses or bystanders powerfully communicate that such behavior is unacceptable, or unless bystanders or victims create painful consequences for the actors, people justify what they have done by seeing their actions as a rightful response to the victim's actions or character (Lerner, 1980; Staub, 1989). The perpetrators devalue the victims more and more. In the end, in their eyes the usual moral and human considerations cease to apply to the victims (Opotow, 1990; Staub, 1989, 1990). As hate intensifies, it can lead to a fanatic commitment to "deal with" the hated person or group. Killing is a way of dealing with them to which haters all too often resort. In the end there may be a reversal of morality, whereby killing the members of a hated group becomes the right thing to do.

The evolution expands on the origins out of which hate develops, such as devaluation and ideology; it shapes them and enlarges them. It limits empathy, because perpetrators (and bystanders) distance themselves from victims, perpetrators to be able to engage in their violent acts and bystanders to diminish their own empathic suffering. The evolution removes obstacles and develops building blocks or rudimentary tendencies into hate. This is an evolution not only in feelings, thoughts, and actions but also in social norms, which undergo changes in the kind of conduct toward the hated other that becomes acceptable and normal, and in institutions, which are created or develop into promoting and enacting hate.

Hate is a complex emotion, and the building of hate is a complex matter. For example, Christians have claimed love as their motivation to convert others, such as Jews or colonized peoples, and the intention to save the souls of those to be converted. This already involves a devaluation of the beliefs of others as false faiths and most likely of the people themselves. In the course of these conversions, much cruelty was inflicted, especially when people resisted and wanted to hold on to their beliefs. Resistance certainly increased devaluation, as well as created discrimination and persecution, all elements in the evolution to hate.

Dynamics in Groups: Ideological Movements and Terrorist Groups

Hate can be an individual matter; a person may hate someone because of his or her experiences with this other person or because of experiences that made the hater vulnerable to feeling hate, or a combination of the two. Often, however, hate is shared; members of a terrorist cell or an ethnic, religious, political, or some other group together develop a shared view, attitude, and feeling toward some other. When there has been prior devaluation of some group in a culture, it may develop into hate when individuals join with like-minded others who hold this devaluation especially strongly. In ideological movements, it may be those with the most negative views of the devalued other or ideological enemy who come to have leadership roles. This was the case, for example, among the Nazi stormtroopers or paramilitary of the 1930s in Germany whose leaders were more anti-Semitic than the rank-and-file members (Merkl, 1980).

The dynamics in the group can further develop devaluation and negative images and through this, as well as through contagion and other processes, intensify hate. For example, members of terrorist groups have been described as acting on behalf of both cause and comrades (McCauley & Segal, 1989). They are committed to the cause, but they also are committed to and want to be loyal to their fellow group members, which intensifies their commitment to the ideology and their hate for the identified enemy. Moreover, members of the group striving for leadership take initiatives that move the group further in the direction they have already started.

In mobs, there can be a speedy loss of the boundaries of the self, a giving of oneself over to the group, with a speedy spread of feelings in the crowd, a contagion of emotions. Negative feelings toward an object of group hostility can easily intensify and move a crowd of people to action (Staub & Rosenthal, 1994).

Leaders Generating Hate

Leaders often fuel hatred, sometimes because of their own beliefs, sometimes as a political tool, and sometimes because of a combination of the two. Ezekiel (2002) described White supremacist leaders as very interested in power and highly cynical about people, including their own followers. I have suggested, however, that leaders are also often affected by the conditions that affect their group or potential and actual followers, including difficult life conditions, past victimization and the resulting woundedness, and a history of devaluation of another group (Staub, 1989, 1999a). Whatever the leaders' motivation, the inclinations of leaders and followers join. In the course of the evolution of devaluation, discrimination, violence, and hate, followers come to identify with the leaders and with the ideology they propagate.

Once it develops, hate does not remain under the leaders' control. It is deeply rooted in perceptions and beliefs, is intensely felt, and grows into people's identity. It cannot be changed overnight; it is extremely difficult to change at all. When groups like Jews and Palestinians that have lived in antagonism, hostility, and mutual violence begin to move toward peace, hate often flares up. Leaders can move many people, but they cannot easily change those who already hate by changing their political course.

Haters may feel desperate about the potential disconfirmation of their beliefs, identity, and ideological vision or about the objects of their hate getting away without punishment and continuing to endanger them. But another problem is that leaders often change their political course half-heartedly. For example, while engaging in negotiations with Israelis following the Oslo accords, Palestinian leaders continued to use hate speech about Israelis in talking to their own people. Palestinian textbooks continued to present highly negative images of Jews. Israeli leaders, while taking actions to move toward peace, continued to build settlements and exercise at times harsh control over Palestinians, expressing disregard for the rights of Palestinians and encouraging devaluation.

However, even when leaders make genuine efforts toward peace between groups that have developed intense hostility or hate, certain processes are required to change feelings and thoughts. Hate does not change simply because external circumstances have changed. Processes that change the orientation toward the other include healing, reconciliation, deep contact, working for shared goals in joint projects, understanding the roots of the violence and hostility, and creating a history of the past that is acceptable to both parties and humanizes the other (Staub & Bar-Tal, 2003; Staub & Pearlman, 2001, 2004).

HATE, TERRORISM,
THE ATTACKS ON THE UNITED STATES,
AND THE RESPONSE

Although minorities in the United States have experienced devaluation, discrimination, and even hate, for many the experience of September 11, 2001, was shocking because of the degree of violence against Americans, the fact that it occurred on their own soil, and the hate that fueled it. The attacks deeply frustrated basic needs for security, for positive identity (who are we, the most powerful nation in the world, if this is possible?), for comprehension of reality, and others.

One possible reaction would have been increased empathy with others who have suffered from genocide, mass killing, or other violence against them. But it is not surprising that this has not happened. This would be an element, a psychological underpinning, for altruism born of suffering. And as I have suggested, that requires prior healing. Instead, people in the United States turned to their leaders, who moved them to fulfill their basic needs— to reestablish security, a positive identity, and so on—by striking out. To what extent was this guided by the need for security? To what extent was it guided by the need to reestablish a positive identity, feelings of effectiveness and control, and a comprehension of reality by destructive means—destructive in the sense that a violent response was supported by the people even if not directed at those who caused the harm? In a *New York Times* poll before the attack on Afghanistan, over 60% of the respondents supported an attack, even if they were not sure who was responsible for the attack on us. There may have been a need for revenge also, which carries elements of hate and given its intensity can lead to an attack on the wrong target.

An important course of action would have been to try to understand, much more deeply than was the case, the possible reasons for anger and hate against the United States. Some of the reasons for anger seem legitimate; the U.S. boycott of Iraq did great harm to ordinary people in Iraq, and aspects of U.S. economic policies and support for autocratic regimes have negatively affected people. Other reasons may be less legitimate; for example, the spread of U.S. culture into traditional societies, some of which are also repressive, and the resulting psychological and social upheaval that create antagonism (Staub, 2004). Considering the roots of hate against the United States would have been one way to address the psychological impact of the 9/11 attacks and may have enabled the people and the leaders of the United States to be more reflective about the response to them.

CONCLUSION

I have discussed a variety of influences that contribute to hate. In general terms, they include culture and what it transmits to people, social conditions such as difficult life conditions and the processes they generate, group relations such as conflict, especially intractable conflict, and the personal experience of individuals and the orientation it creates to human beings in general, to the self, and to members of particular groups. This chapter discusses specific forms of many of these influences.

I have also noted some processes that help prevent hate. They include love and affection that children (and adults) experience and the constructive fulfillment of basic human needs; humanizing the other and the experience of positive connections to people who belong to different groups, which help develop inclusive caring; self-awareness both as an individual and as a group member, which among other benefits enables people to see the impact of their actions on others; and healing from past victimization and reconciliation between groups and individuals who have harmed each other. Helping young people who come from difficult backgrounds or who have had painful experiences to fulfill basic needs for security, identity, effectiveness, connection, and worldview through positive means, joining constructive rather than destructive groups, is of great importance. So is the behavior of witnesses or bystanders who respond to and attempt to stop or counteract devaluation and harmful actions against people. Constructive ways of responding to difficult conditions in society are also of great value, such as the creation of positive visions for the future that do not identify enemies and bring all people together to work for a better future (see also Staub, 1989, 1999a, 1999b, 2003, in press; Staub & Pearlman, 2004).

REFERENCES

Aronson, E., Stephan, C., Sikes, J., Blaney, N., & Snapp, M. (1978). *The jigsaw classroom*. Beverly Hills, CA: Sage.

Bar-Tal, D. (2002). Collective memory of physical violence: Its contribution to the culture of violence. In G. Salomon & B. Nevo (Eds.), *Peace education: The concept, principles and practice around the world* (pp. 27–36). Mahwah, NJ: Erlbaum.

Beck, A. T. (2000). *Prisoners of hate*. New York: HarperCollins.

Becker, E. (1975). *Escape from evil*. New York: Free Press.

Brewer, M. B. (1978). Ingroup bias in the minimal intergroup situation: A cognitive–motivational analysis. *Psychological Bulletin, 86*, 307–324.

Buford, R. (1992). *Among the thugs: The experience, and the seduction, of crowd violence*. New York: Norton.

Burton, J. W. (1990). *Conflict: Human needs theory*. New York: St. Martin's Press.

Colby, A., & Damon, W. (1992). *Some do care*. New York: Free Press.

Des Forges, A. (1999). *Leave none to tell the story: Genocide in Rwanda*. New York: Human Rights Watch.

Dodge, K. A. (1980). Social cognition and children's aggressive behavior. *Child Development, 51*, 162–170.

Dodge, K. A. (1993). Social cognitive mechanisms in the development of conduct disorder and depression. *Annual Review of Psychology, 44*, 559–584.

Dodge, K. A., Bates, J. E., & Pettit, G. S. (1990, December 21). Mechanisms in the cycle of violence. *Science, 250*, 1678–1683

Ezekiel, R. S. (1995). *The racist mind*. New York: Penguin Books.

Ezekiel, R. S. (2002). The ethnographer looks at Neo-Nazi and Klan groups: *The Racist Mind* revisited. *American Behavioral Scientist, 46*(1), 51–57.

Gilligan, J. (1996). *Violence: Our deadly epidemic and its causes.* New York: Putnam.

Girard, P. (1980). Historical foundations of anti-semitism. In J. Dimsdale (Ed.), *Survivors, victims and perpetrators: Essays on the Nazi Holocaust* (pp. 55–73). New York: Hemisphere Publication Services.

Greenberg, J., Pyszczynski, T., Solomon, S., Rosenblatt, A., Veeded, M., & Kirkland, S. (1990). Evidence for terror management theory: II. The effects of mortality salience on reactions to those who threaten or bolster the cultural world view. *Journal of Personality and Social Psychology, 58,* 308–318.

Kelman, H. C. (1990). Applying a human needs perspective to the practice of conflict resolution: The Israeli–Palestinian case. In J. Burton (Ed.), *Conflict: Human needs theory* (pp. 283–297). New York: St. Martin's Press.

Lerner, M. (1980). *The belief in a just world: A fundamental delusion.* New York: Plenum Press.

Mamdani, M. (2002). *When victims become killers.* Princeton, NJ: Princeton University Press.

Maslow, A. H. (1968). *Toward a psychology of being* (2nd ed.). New York: Van Nostrand.

Maslow, A. H. (1971). *The farther reaches of human nature.* New York: Viking Press.

McCauley, C. R., & Segal, M. D. (1989). Terrorist individuals and terrorist groups: The normal psychology of extreme behavior. In J. Groebel & J. F. Goldstein (Eds.), *Terrorism* (pp. 40–64). Sevilla, Spain: Publicaciones de la Universidad de Sevilla.

Merkl, P. H. (1980). *The making of a stormtrooper.* Princeton, NJ: Princeton University Press.

Opotow, S. (1990). Moral exclusion and injustice: An introduction. *Journal of Social Issues, 46*(1), 1–20.

Pearlman, L. A., & Saakvitne, K. W. (1995). *Trauma and the therapist: Countertransference and vicarious traumatization in psychotherapy with incest survivors.* New York: Norton.

Pettigrew, T. F., & Tropp, L. R. (2000). Does intergroup contact reduce prejudice? Recent meta-analytic findings. In S. Oskamp (Ed.), *Reducing prejudice and discrimination: Social psychological perspectives* (pp. 93–114). Mahwah, NJ: Erlbaum.

Staub, E. (1989). *The roots of evil: The origins of genocide and other group violence.* New York: Cambridge University Press.

Staub, E. (1990). Moral exclusion, personal goal theory and extreme destructiveness. *Journal of Social Issues, 46*(1), 47–65.

Staub, E. (1996). The cultural–societal roots of violence: The examples of genocidal violence and of contemporary youth violence in the United States. *American Psychologist, 51,* 17–132.

Staub, E. (1998). Breaking the cycle of violence: Healing and reconciliation. In J. Harvey (Ed.), *Perspectives on loss: A sourcebook* (pp. 231–241). Washington, DC: Taylor & Francis.

Staub, E. (1999a). The origins and prevention of genocide, mass killing and other collective violence. *Peace and Conflict: Journal of Peace Psychology, 5,* 303–337.

Staub, E. (1999b). The roots of evil: Personality, social conditions, culture and basic human needs. *Personality and Social Psychology Review, 3,* 179–192.

Staub, E. (2002). From healing past wounds to the development of inclusive caring: Contents and processes of peace education. In G. Solomon & B. Nevo (Eds.), *Peace education: The concepts, principles, and practices around the world* (pp. 73–89). Mahwah, NJ: Erlbaum.

Staub, E. (2003). *The psychology of good and evil: Why children, adults and groups help and harm others.* New York: Cambridge University Press.

Staub, E. (2004.) Understanding and responding to group violence: Genocide, mass killing, and terrorism. In A. J. Marsella & F. M. Moghaddam (Eds.), *Understanding terrorism: Psychosocial roots, consequences, and interventions* (pp. 151–169). Washington, DC: American Psychological Association.

Staub, E. (in press). The roots of goodness: The fulfillment of basic human needs and the development of caring, helping and nonaggression, inclusive caring, moral courage, active bystandership, and altruism born of suffering. In C. Edwards & G. Carlo (Eds.), *Nebraska Symposium on Motivation. Moral motivation across the life span.* Lincoln: University of Nebraska Press.

Staub, E., & Bar-Tal, D. (2003). Genocide, mass killing and intractable conflict: Roots, evolution, prevention and reconciliation. In D. Sears, L. Huddy, & R. Jarvis (Eds.), *Oxford handbook of political psychology* (pp. 710–751). New York: Oxford University Press.

Staub, E., & Pearlman, L. A. (2001). Healing, reconciliation and forgiving after genocide and other collective violence. In S. J. Helmick & R. L. Petersen (Eds.), *Forgiveness and reconciliation: Religion, public policy and conflict transformation* (pp. 205–229). Radnor, PA: Templeton Foundation Press.

Staub, E., & Pearlman, L. A. (2004). *Advancing healing and reconciliation.* Unpublished manuscript, University of Massachusetts at Amherst.

Staub, E., & Rosenthal, L. (1994). Mob violence: Social–cultural influences, group processes and participants. In L. Eron & J. Gentry (Eds.), *Reason to hope: A psychosocial perspective on violence and youth* (pp. 281–313). Washington, DC: American Psychological Association.

Tajfel, H. (1978). Social categorization, social identity and social comparison. In H. Tajfel (Ed.), *Differentiation between social groups* (pp. 61–76). London: Academic Press.

Tajfel, H. (1982). Social psychology of intergroup relations. *Annual Review of Psychology, 33,* 1–39.

Tajfel, H., Flamant, C., Billig, M. Y., & Bundy, R. P. (1971). Societal categorization and intergroup behavior. *European Journal of Social Psychology, 1,* 149–177.

Toch, H. (1993). *Violent men: An inquiry into the psychology of violence*. Washington, DC: American Psychological Association. (Original work published 1969)

Widom, C. S. (1989a, December 9). The cycle of violence. *Science, 224,* 160–166.

Widom, C. S. (1989b). Does violence beget violence? A critical examination of the literature. *Psychological Bulletin, 106,* 3–28.

4

A COGNITIVE PERSPECTIVE ON HATE AND VIOLENCE

AARON T. BECK AND JAMES PRETZER

Whether one considers intimate violence between family members, the carnage of the World Wars, the wholesale slaughter of genocides around the world, or the tragic actions of terrorists, the damage that humans can do to each other presents a serious threat to all of us. Theorists from Freud to the present have faced the challenge of developing an understanding of hate and violence. In recent decades, cognitive–behavioral[1] formulations have proven useful in understanding many aspects of psychopathology and in improving treatment efficacy. Recently, a cognitive perspective on hate and violence has been advanced (Beck, 1999, 2002) in the hope that it can contribute to our understanding of this serious topic and lead to effective interventions.

---

[1]A number of different cognitive and cognitive–behavioral approaches to therapy have been developed in recent years. Although these various approaches have much in common, there are important conceptual and technical differences among them. To minimize confusion, we refer to the specific approach developed by Aaron T. Beck and his colleagues as *cognitive therapy,* whereas the term *cognitive–behavioral* will be used to refer to the full range of cognitive and cognitive–behavioral approaches.

Role of Cognition in Emotion and Behavior

The cognitive approach developed initially out of observations made in the course of psychotherapy. One seminal insight was the observation that the content of individuals' thoughts influences their emotional and behavioral response. Thoughts of failure, rejection, and loss lead to feelings of sadness and a tendency to give up. Thoughts of gain, achievement, and approval by others lead to feelings of pleasure and a tendency to keep trying or to try harder. Thoughts of danger or threat lead to anxiety and a tendency to avoid. Thoughts of being wronged or mistreated produce anger and an impulse to retaliate. The relevant thoughts are fleeting, involuntary, and often not recognized by the patient until the therapist teaches him or her to watch for these *automatic thoughts*. However, these thoughts often trigger strong emotional reactions and have an important impact on behavior.

A second important insight was the observation that the automatic thoughts that play a role in problems frequently are out of proportion to the situation that elicits them. For example, an anger-prone individual may blow a minor slight out of proportion, react intensely, and want to punish the offender severely. Two factors are seen as contributing to patients' exaggerated interpretations of mundane events. First, humans are subject to a variety of thinking errors, *cognitive distortions*, which can have a significant impact on the individual's interpretation of events (see Table 4.1). Anger-prone individuals often interpret impersonal events egocentrically ("Why does this have to happen to *me*?"), exaggerate the frequency of noxious events ("He *always* does that!"), and exaggerate the severity of noxious events ("She *never* shows me *any* respect!"). Second, people interpret experiences on the basis of beliefs and assumptions they have acquired from previous experience. These include unconditional core beliefs such as "I don't count," conditional beliefs such as "If you don't have respect, you don't have anything," and interpersonal strategies such as "You have to *make* people respect you." These beliefs and assumptions lie dormant until a relevant situation arises and then automatically become active and shape the individual's responses when a relevant situation is encountered. Dysfunctional beliefs can influence which aspects of the situation people focus on, how they interpret those experiences, and how they respond to them.

Clinical observation shows that, left to themselves, patients typically accept their exaggerations and misinterpretations at face value. When this is the case, their emotional and behavioral reactions are in proportion to these dysfunctional automatic thoughts. However, when patients learn to focus attention on their automatic thoughts, to look critically at them, and to intentionally replace dysfunctional thoughts with more realistic thoughts, this proves useful as one part of helping them overcome their problems. For example, when an easily provoked mother was able to recognize her thought "They're bad, they must be punished" and replace it with "They're just

TABLE 4.1
Common Cognitive Distortions

Type of distortion	Definition	Example
Dichotomous thinking	Viewing experiences in terms of two mutually exclusive categories with no shades of gray in between	Believing that one is *either* a success *or* a failure and that anything short of a perfect performance is a total failure
Overgeneralization	Perceiving a particular event as being characteristic of life in general rather than as being one event among many	Concluding that an inconsiderate response from one's spouse shows that he or she doesn't care, despite having showed consideration on other occasions
Selective abstraction	Focusing on one aspect of a complex situation to the exclusion of other relevant aspects of the situation	Focusing on the one negative comment in a performance evaluation received at work and overlooking the positive comments contained in the evaluation
Disqualifying the positive	Discounting positive experiences that would conflict with the individual's negative views	Rejecting positive feedback from friends and colleagues on the grounds that "They're only saying that to be nice" rather than considering whether the feedback could be valid
Mind reading	Assuming that one knows what others are thinking or how others are reacting despite having little or no evidence	Thinking, "I just know he thought I was an idiot!" despite the other person's having given no apparent indications of his reactions
Fortune telling	Reacting as though expectations about future events are established facts rather than recognizing them as fears, hopes, or predictions	Thinking, "He's leaving me, I just know it!" and acting as though this is definitely true
Catastrophizing	Treating actual or anticipated negative events as intolerable catastrophes rather than seeing them in perspective	Thinking, "Oh my God, what if I faint?" without considering that although fainting may be unpleasant or embarrassing, it is not terribly dangerous
Maximization or minimization	Treating some aspects of the situation, personal characteristics, or experiences as trivial and others as very important independent of their actual significance	Thinking, "Sure, I'm good at my job, but so what? My parents don't respect me"
Emotional reasoning	Assuming that one's emotional reactions necessarily reflect the true situation	Concluding that because one feels hopeless, the situation must really be hopeless

continues

TABLE 4.1 *(Continued)*

Type of distortion	Definition	Example
"Should" statements	The use of "should" and "have to" statements that are not actually true to provide motivation or control over one's behavior	Thinking, "I shouldn't feel aggravated; she's my mother, I have to listen to her"
Labeling	Attaching a global label to oneself rather than referring to specific events or actions	Thinking, "I'm a failure!" rather than "Boy, I blew that one!"
Personalization	Assuming that one is the cause of a particular external event when, in fact, other factors are responsible	Thinking, "She wasn't very friendly today; she must be mad at me" without considering that factors other than one's own behavior may affect the other individual's mood

behaving like normal kids," she found that her anger was less intense and subsided more quickly.

The cognitive model that emerged from observations of patients in psychotherapy and research into the role of cognition in emotion and behavior was not simply "thoughts cause feelings and behavior." Rather, thoughts are seen as an important part of a cycle through which thoughts influence feelings and behavior and through which feelings and actions influence thoughts as well (see Figure 4.1).

Thus, when the easily provoked mother discussed above was faced with childish misbehavior, she tended to respond with critical, punitive thoughts

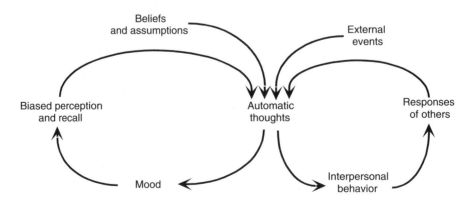

Figure 4.1. Cognitive–interpersonal cycle.

(e.g., "He should know better"; "I can't let him get away with this"), and these thoughts quickly elicited irritation or annoyance. However, the cycle does not stop at that point. Although thoughts influence mood, mood also biases cognition in mood-congruent ways. As a result, once the mother in this example was irritated or annoyed, she tended to selectively recall her son's previous transgressions, to be vigilant for additional misbehavior, and to have more extreme cognitions in response to continued misbehavior (e.g., "He *always* does this!" "If I've told him once, I've told him a *thousand* times!" "He *never* shows *any* respect!"). These cognitions, of course, elicited a more intense emotional reaction that further biased cognition and set the stage for even more extreme automatic thoughts.

The model depicted in Figure 4.1 has an interpersonal component as well. Thoughts such as "He's old enough to know better" and "People will think I can't control my child" are likely to elicit attempts to control the child's misbehavior. If the mother's initial attempts at controlling her child's behavior are effective, then her cognitions are likely to gradually change (perhaps to "He's finally being good"), and her mood is likely to improve. However, if the mother's initial attempts at controlling her child's behavior are ineffective, the misbehavior is likely to continue, and she is likely to have more extreme thoughts about her inability to control her child's behavior (perhaps, "What kind of a mother am I if I can't control a 5-year-old? I have to *make* him obey!"). This will result in more intense attempts to control the child's behavior, and if these attempts are unsuccessful, the conflict is likely to become more and more intense.

Role of Cognition in Hate and Violence

The model described thus far may account for the role that cognition plays in mundane reactions. However, an understanding of the cognitive–interpersonal cycle that results in a mother becoming quite angry with her child does not provide an understanding of hate and violence. After all, everyone feels angry from time to time, but this momentary experience of anger does not usually lead to either hate or violence. Most people who become angry handle the situation without punching their antagonist or shooting up their workplace.

Figure 4.2 summarizes the sequence of events leading to an episode of spouse abuse. If a man interprets his wife's comments in a way that leaves him feeling belittled, hurt, or mistreated, this is distressing in itself. However, if he sees her behavior as unjustified and inexcusable, then he is likely to see himself as the victim of mistreatment, to feel angry, and to experience the impulse to retaliate and punish his wife. The greater the extent to which additional cognitions legitimize a violent response, the greater the likelihood of violence (see Beck, 1999, pp. 128–132 and pp. 247–268, for a more detailed discussion).

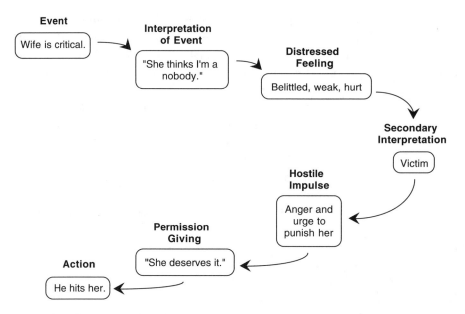

Figure 4.2. Sequence of events in an episode of marital violence.

The cognitive view of "hot" violence (i.e., violence that is associated with anger and does not involve prolonged planning and preparation) is based on the idea that the violently hostile individual often has strong negative biases toward the victim. The greater the degree of bias and distortion, the stronger the affect and the greater the likelihood of violence. In almost all forms of hot violence, the perpetrator or perpetrators believe that they have a legitimate grievance and that, therefore, violence is justified. When individuals or groups perceive themselves as having been wronged, damaged, coerced, or corrupted by another individual or group, the response is an impulse to retaliate, seek revenge, rebel, or destroy the source of the corruption. In addition, beliefs and perceptions that decrease inhibitions against violence or that provide justifications for violence increase the likelihood that anger will progress to overt violence. Beliefs such as "Don't get mad, get even" or "It's them or us" or "God is on our side" can increase the perception that violence is necessary and justified.

When the adversary is demonized (viewed as different, alien, subhuman, and evil), this intensifies the sense that violence is justified and reduces inhibitions about violence and killing. Under the force of a momentary surge of anger, thinking becomes more polarized and inhibitions regarding violence decrease, at the same time that the impulse toward violence increases. Often, the results are disastrous. "In the heat of the moment" individuals and groups may commit acts of violence that they would not normally commit and that they regret deeply once their anger subsides.

Many of the same factors play a role in "cold" violence (i.e., violence that is the end result of planning and preparation). In this case, the perception (realistic or not) is that one is persistently wronged, damaged, coerced, or corrupted. The response is to feel persistent hatred and to have a continuing desire to retaliate, seek revenge, rebel, or destroy the source of the corruption. The thinking of terrorists, perpetrators of planned genocide, and others who commit acts of cold violence against persons whom they do not know personally show a number of cognitive distortions. These include *overgeneralization*—the transgressions of specific members of the enemy group may be seen as characterizing all members of the group—and *dichotomous thinking*—*we* are good, *they* are bad. In addition, perpetrators show *tunnel vision*—a single-minded focus on their image of the enemy to the exclusion of information and experiences that might contradict their polarized view.

The dichotomous thinking in combination with the demonized view of the enemy enhances the individual or group's self-image (i.e., If I fight that which is evil, corrupt, and depraved, then I see myself as good, righteous, and just). This enhancement of self-image provides an incentive for dichotomous thinking and demonization of the enemy. The greater the extent to which an individual or group has legitimate grounds for feeling victimized, the fewer distortions are needed to produce a persistent sense of having been wronged and a persistent impulse to retaliate. The greater the extent to which one's family and culture endorse beliefs that justify violence and views that dehumanize others, the easier it is for persistent hate to culminate in violence. Selective association with a group or subculture that promulgates views that support hate and violence can greatly reinforce the individual's own views. However, there need not be legitimate grounds for hate and violence. Individual experiences, cognitive distortions, and idiosyncratic beliefs can lead to hate and violence if the conditions are right.

Applying the Cognitive Model to Groups, Cultures, and Nations

The cognitive approach to understanding violence perpetrated by groups is based on the premise that people are people whether they are operating individually or in groups. Table 4.2 shows the parallels that Beck (1999) saw in the thinking of individuals who abuse spouses or children, individuals who react violently under provocation, individuals who persecute members of other groups, and members of aggressive nations. The nature of the perceptions and cognitions that lead to violence are the same whether the person is involved in beating a spouse or in a collective assault on members of another tribe or nation. Thus, if a substantial portion of a group, culture, or nation shares a view that they (or those they care about) have been wronged by an identifiable adversary and believe that a violent response is called for, group-on-group violence is a possible outcome.

TABLE 4.2
Commonalities Observed in Hate and Aggression
Across a Variety of Contexts

Factor	Spouse or child abuser	Reactive offender	Persecutors	Aggressive nations
Image of self	Blameless victim	Victim	Victim	Victim
Image of victim	Victimizer	Victimizer	Victimizers	Victimizers
Orientation	Egocentric	Egocentric	Group egoism	Group egoism
Attitude toward violence	Permissive	Permissive	Permissive	Permissive
Thinking	Dualistic	Dualistic	Dualistic	Dualistic

However, in considering hatred, persecution, and violence on a societal level, it is important to use a broad frame of reference and a level of analysis that is appropriate to the questions being addressed. For example, an analysis of the relationship between economic conditions and hate crimes in the United States shows that the lynchings of Blacks in the South increased each time economic hardship increased during the years between 1882 and 1930. However, since 1930, economic fluctuations have not been associated with increases in lynchings. Analysis of the role of racist political elites and organizations shows that they actively fomented resentment towards Blacks and instigated anti-Black violence. As societal attitudes toward prejudice and anti-Black violence changed over time, these changes stripped racist groups of much of their power to instigate violence (Green, Glaser, & Rich, 1998). Cultural attitudes such as the belief that one's group has a history of being victimized by a particular group, that one must right current or past wrongs, that the other group is different in a way that makes them less human, or that violence is the appropriate way to address grievances form the substrate for group violence.

In addition to automatic thoughts and individual factors such as cognitive distortions and beliefs that legitimize violence, group interactions can play an important role in hate and violence. Group conformity can reinforce the sense of having been wronged, the demonization of the individual or group seen as responsible for this, and the conviction that violence is justified. Group interactions that reinforce these views can lead to a much more extreme response than would be the case if each individual reached these conclusions separately.

If influential group members endorse extreme views or if the communication media are used to spread extreme views, the group as a whole is moved toward hate and violence. Examples illustrating the impact that within-group communications can have include Hitler's speeches, the role of radio stations in the Rwandan genocide, and the impact of White supremacist Web sites. If group members who are seen as legitimate leaders advocate hate and violence, they can mobilize the rest of the group and legitimize violence.

Once a sufficient portion of a group adopts extreme views, those individuals who do not endorse those views may voluntarily leave or may be excluded from the group. As a result, the group ideology may become more extreme over time. In addition, influential group members who do not directly commit violence may do a great deal to organize, encourage, and reward the violent acts of others. A good general can contribute greatly to the effectiveness of a fighting force without firing a gun himself.

HOW CAN HATE BE ASSESSED?

Assessing Hate in Individuals

In clinical practice, cognitive therapists find that it often is necessary to rely on self-reports because many of the factors of interest, such as automatic thoughts and dysfunctional beliefs, are not directly observable and because it is often impractical for the therapist to do extensive in vivo observation and data collection. We recognize that self-reports are an imperfect source of data because they are open to a wide range of potential biases and distortions. However, they are often the most practical source of information regarding an individual's day-to-day experiences. Self-report information can be quite useful in clinical practice when the therapist can take an active role in helping the individual gain access to cognitions that normally operate outside of awareness and in testing the validity of the self-reports. Table 4.3 summarizes suggestions for increasing the validity of self-reports adapted from Freeman, Pretzer, Fleming, and Simon (1990).

Unfortunately, there are problems with relying on simple self-report measures in research. Use of this methodology assumes that individuals can reliably report their automatic thoughts and rate the strength of their dysfunctional beliefs or schemas.[2] However, cognitive therapists report that many individuals require considerable help before they are able to reliably report their automatic thoughts. According to cognitive theory, dysfunctional schemas often operate outside of awareness, and in clinical practice it often takes significant time and effort to identify clients' dysfunctional beliefs. Clear evidence that self-report measures actually assess the cognitions they purport to measure, not more superficial attitudes, is needed before they are

---

[2]*Schemas* are unconditional core beliefs that serve as a basis for screening, categorizing, and interpreting experiences (e.g., "I'm no good," "Others can't be trusted," "Effort does not pay off"). Schemas often operate outside of the individual's awareness and often are not clearly verbalized.

TABLE 4.3
Guidelines for Increasing the Validity of Self-Reports

Guideline	Description
1. Motivate the client to be open and forthright.	Make sure that it is clear that providing full, honest, detailed reports is in the client's interest by • providing a clear rationale for seeking the information, • demonstrating the relevance of the information being requested to the client's goals, and • demonstrating the value of clear, specific information by explicitly making use of the information in therapy.
2. Minimize the delay between event and report.	Minimizing this delay will result in more detailed information and will reduce the amount of distortion due to imperfect recall. For events occurring outside of the therapist's office, use an in vivo interview or self-monitoring techniques when possible.
3. Provide retrieval cues.	Review the setting and the events leading up to the event of interest either verbally or by using imagery in order to improve recall.
4. Avoid possible biases.	Begin with open-ended questions that ask the client to describe his or her experience without suggesting possible answers or requiring inference. Focus on "What happened?" not on "Why?" or "What did it mean?" Do not ask clients to infer experiences they cannot remember. Wait until after the entire experience has been described to test your hypotheses or ask for specific details.
5. Encourage and reinforce attention to thoughts and feelings.	Clients who initially have difficulty monitoring their own cognitive processes are more likely to gradually develop increased skill if they are reinforced for accomplishments than if they are criticized for failures. Some clients may need explicit training in differentiating between thoughts and emotions, in attending to cognitions, or in reporting observations rather than inferences.
6. Encourage and reinforce acknowledgment of limitations in recall.	If the therapist accepts only long, detailed reports, this increases the risk of the client's inventing data in order to satisfy the therapist. It is important for the therapist to appreciate the information the client can provide and to encourage the client to acknowledge his or her limits in recalling details, because incomplete but accurate information is much more useful than detailed reports fabricated in order to please the therapist.
7. Watch for indications of invalidity.	Be alert for inconsistencies within the client's report, between the verbal report and nonverbal cues, and between the report and data obtained previously. If apparent inconsistencies are observed, explore them collaboratively with the client without being accusatory or judgmental.

continues

TABLE 4.3 *(Continued)*

Guideline	Description
8. Watch for factors that may interfere.	Be alert for indications of beliefs, assumptions, expectancies, and misunderstandings that may interfere with the client's providing accurate self-reports. Common problems include • the fear that the therapist will be unable to accept the truth and will become angry, shocked, disgusted, or rejecting if the client reports his or her experiences accurately • the belief that the client must do a perfect job of observing and reporting the experiences and that he or she is a failure if the reports are not perfect from the beginning • the fear that the information revealed in therapy may be used against the client or may give the therapist power over him or her • the belief that it is dangerous to closely examine experiences involving strong or "crazy" feelings for fear that the feelings will be intolerable or will "get out of control."

Note. From *Clinical Applications of Cognitive Therapy* (p. 35–36), by A. Freeman, J. L. Pretzer, B. Fleming, and K. M. Simon, 1990, New York: Plenum Press. Copyright 1990 by Plenum Press. Adapted with permission.

relied upon in research. Alternative methods for assessing relevant cognitions are available and should be used more widely. These include Thought Sampling or Experience Sampling methodology (Hurlburt, Leach, & Saltman, 1984), laboratory tasks that provide a more direct method for assessing schemas (e.g., McNally, Riemann, & Kim, 1990), and content analysis of responses to schema-relevant stimuli (e.g., Eckhardt, Barbour, & Davison, 1998).

In assessing beliefs related to hate and violence, it is important to remember that the beliefs may be dormant until they are activated by a relevant stimulus. It may be important to "prime" aggressive beliefs through the use of relevant stimuli to assess them reliably (see Eckhardt et al., 1998).

Assessing Hate in Groups, Cultures, and Nations

To date, cognitively oriented investigators have focused primarily on individuals, couples, and families and have not yet developed specific methods for assessing hate in larger social groupings. The theoretical model discussed in this chapter emphasizes the content of individuals' cognitions, the presence of cognitive distortions, within-group communications that reinforce hate-compatible thoughts and beliefs, and within-group interactions that result in suppression of information incompatible with hatred and the exclusion of group members who hold views that are incompatible with hate. Established research methods used in social psychology, sociology, anthropology, and related fields should provide useful strategies for assessing these variables.

HOW CAN HATE BE COMBATED?

Combating Hate in Psychotherapy

Psychotherapy provides one option for combating hate on the individual level, at least on the occasions when the individual recognizes that hate and violence are a problem and is motivated to change. Exhibit 4.1 summarizes the general principles of cognitive therapy. The idea of "collaborative empiricism" is central to the practice of cognitive therapy. In the course of therapy, the cognitive therapist works with his or her client to collect detailed information regarding the specific thoughts, feelings, and actions that occur in problem situations. These observations provide a basis for developing an individualized understanding of the client that facilitates strategic intervention. Collaborative empiricism continues to play an important role as the focus of therapy shifts from assessment to intervention. Many of the specific techniques used to modify dysfunctional thoughts, beliefs, and strategies emphasize first-hand observation and "behavioral experiments" to test the validity of dysfunctional automatic thoughts or dysfunctional beliefs and to develop more adaptive alternatives. Rather than relying on the therapist's expertise, theoretical deductions, or logic, cognitive therapy assumes that empirical observation is the most reliable means for developing valid conceptualizations and effective interventions.

Persons unfamiliar with cognitive therapy sometimes assume that cognitive therapists focus solely on modifying the individual's cognitions and ignore behavioral interventions. It is important to know that a broad range of behavioral interventions and emotion-focused interventions are also a

EXHIBIT 4.1
General Principles of Cognitive Therapy

Therapist and client work collaboratively toward clear goals.
The therapist takes an active, directive role.
Interventions are based on an individualized conceptualization.
The focus is on specific problem situations and on specific thoughts, feelings, and actions.
Therapist and client focus on modifying thoughts, coping with emotions, and changing behavior as needed.
The client continues the work of therapy between sessions.
Interventions later in therapy focus on identifying and modifying predisposing factors, including schemas and core beliefs.
At the close of treatment, therapist and client work explicitly on relapse prevention.

---

part of cognitive therapy. Table 4.4 summarizes a number of interventions that can be used in cognitive therapy with problems of anger, hate, and violence.

TABLE 4.4
Possible Interventions With Anger, Hate, and Violence

Goal	Possible interventions
To reduce the intensity of anger in response to provocation	If the client tends to suppress or deny anger until he or she reaches a "breaking point," help the client recognize the value of dealing with anger before reaching the breaking point and develop adaptive ways of handling anger. If dysfunctional cognitions amplify anger, identify and modify dysfunctional thoughts using "standard" cognitive therapy techniques. Increase understanding of the other person's point of view and feelings. Increase understanding of any valid justifications of the other person's behavior. If it is desirable for the client to be able to respond more calmly in the face of provocation, use Anger Management Training or Stress-Inoculation Training (imaginal exposure combined with applied relaxation).
To eliminate maladaptive or inappropriate expression of anger (including violence)	Identify cognitions that justify inappropriate expression of anger, and challenge them. Frame problematic expressions of anger as inappropriate and unjustified. Identify more adaptive alternatives, address cognitions that maintain dysfunctional behavior or block adaptive alternatives, use role-play or imagery to practice the alternatives, implement the alternatives in situations that are of low to moderate intensity first and then in more intense situations. Help the client learn to implement alternative responses before the anger becomes too intense. Consider simultaneously working to reduce the intensity of anger in order to facilitate more adaptive responses. Persistently focus attention on the actual consequences of the maladaptive or inappropriate behavior. Identify alternatives that produce better results. If dysfunctional interaction patterns trigger or perpetuate the problem, consider whether marital, family, or conjoint intervention is needed.
To increase appropriate assertion	Identify cognitions that block assertion, and modify them. Teach assertion skills if necessary. Use role-play or imagery to practice assertion in real-life situations that are of low to moderate intensity first and then in more intense situations.
To decrease the client's tendency to "hold a grudge"	Watch for cognitions that encourage prolonged anger and address them. Address cognitions that intensify anger, and address any tendency to suppress anger. Identify adaptive alternatives (e.g., communication, assertion, relaxation, exercise, "cooling off"), and put them into practice.

Unfortunately, psychotherapy has serious limitations as a means of preventing individual or group violence. It is most appropriate when an individual recognizes his or her own hate and violence as a problem and is motivated to change, but many perpetrators of violence do not seek help and do not wish to change. Furthermore, even if more perpetrators of violence were willing to seek treatment, individual or group psychotherapy is too expensive and requires too many resources to be broadly applicable. Methods are needed for intervening on a societal level to decrease hate and violence.

Combating Hate in Groups, Cultures, and Nations

Strategies applicable with larger groups include reframing individuals' perceptions of the presumed adversary, reducing their emotional investment in their previously established positions and ideology, encouraging more pragmatic goals, and increasing attention to information incompatible with the demonized image of the opponent. Unfortunately, interventions useful in dealing with conflict among individuals or small groups generally are not adequate in volatile political environments. It is difficult to induce leaders to abandon or moderate ideological or self-interested positions. In factional disputes, assertion of superior power and determination is often necessary to move the opponent to a more moderate position where logical argument and positive experiences in interactions with the opponent can then help resolve the conflict. However, because dichotomous thinking is more likely when individuals feel threatened, the assertion of superior power and determination does not necessarily result in opponents shifting to more moderate and reasonable positions.

Michael Duffy, Kate Gillespie, and their colleagues have established the Centre for Trauma and Conflict Resolution in Omagh, Northern Ireland. Their program for moderating the conflict between Republicans and Loyalists (based on Beck, 1999) includes a number of interventions:

- psychoeducational sessions for mediators and community leaders;
- group sessions for former opponents;
- facilitation of meetings where perpetrators of violence and the victims meet and consider each other's perspectives; the program includes acknowledgment of suffering, taking responsibility for violent deeds, ventilation and processing of feelings, and challenging negative appraisals and overgeneralized interpretations of events; and
- training therapists who will use their skills in this challenging area of work.

When intervening with individuals, couples, and small groups, it may be feasible for the practitioner to remain comfortably in his or her office.

However, in order for interventions to be effective with larger groups, there must be some means of disseminating the interventions throughout the larger community. This could include training a corps of individuals who will intervene through the community, making use of the mass media, intervening with influential group members who will then influence other members of the community, organizing mass events that have an influence throughout the community, or organizing ongoing programs that have a persistent effect over time. Programs that incorporate a number of these interventions over time should be more effective than those that rely on a single, short-term intervention.

Group narcissism, in which the interests of the group are pursued to the exclusion of the interests of other groups, plays a central role in many conflicts. A long-term antidote would be the establishment of a humanistic orientation as an alternative to tribalism, nationalism, and militant religiosity. A moral code emanating from this orientation would incorporate considering the other person's perspectives, respecting the rights of others, feeling responsibility for the welfare of others, and balancing one's own needs with the needs of others. Although dissemination of this type of orientation is clearly a long-term project, we would expect that the likelihood of violent conflict within a community or state would decrease as the proportion of the population with a humanistic orientation increases.

Conflict between states or between a state and external militant groups, as exemplified by the recent terrorist attacks against the United States, requires a different level of solution. Although the interventions discussed above are likely to be relevant, it is likely to be necessary for the interventions to be implemented simultaneously with each of the parties in the conflict. We hope that understanding each of the antagonists' perspectives in cognitive terms will assist in finding solutions.

EMPIRICAL SUPPORT FOR THE COGNITIVE MODEL OF HATE AND VIOLENCE

Cognitive therapy's general model of the role of cognition in human functioning and in psychopathology is based on a large body of research accumulated over several decades. A review of this extensive literature is beyond the scope of this chapter. In this section we will present a number of illustrative studies to give an idea of the type of research that supports the cognitive perspective and will refer interested readers to sources for more detailed reviews of the literature. The April 2000 volume of *Cognitive Therapy and Research* is devoted to a special issue on cognitive factors in male intimate violence and provides good coverage of empirical research into this topic.

Evidence Regarding the Cognitive Model of Hate and Violence

One of the central principles on which cognitive therapy is based is the hypothesis that the content of an individual's momentary thoughts influences the emotions that he or she experiences. Wickless and Kirsch (1988) had a large nonclinical sample record their thoughts and emotions whenever they felt angry, anxious, or sad over a 3-day period and conducted structured interviews with participants each day. As predicted, they found that anxiety was associated with thoughts of threat, sadness was associated with thoughts of loss, and anger was associated with thoughts of transgressions committed against the participant. In particular, the theme of being "wronged" was most frequently associated with anger.

Experimental confirmation of the role of cognitive distortions in anger is provided by the work of Eckhardt and his colleagues (1998). Male participants with and without a history of marital violence verbalized their thoughts in response to anger-arousing and non-anger-arousing audiotapes depicting an imaginary interaction with their wives. Responses were coded by trained raters. The results showed that maritally violent men were more likely than nonviolent men to show three types of cognitive distortions hypothesized to contribute to violence: magnification, dichotomous thinking, and arbitrary inference.

After reviewing the available evidence regarding the role of cognition in marital violence, Eckhardt and Dye (2000) concluded that the empirical evidence suggests that maritally violent men do, indeed, think differently than their nonviolent counterparts. Although there is a need for additional research, and although issues related to assessment methodologies and research design complicate interpretation of some studies, the available research provides support for cognitive therapy's hypotheses about the role played by the content of automatic thoughts, attitudes, beliefs, and causal attributions.

Evidence Regarding the Effectiveness of Cognitive Therapy With Hate and Violence

Quite a few studies have investigated the effectiveness of cognitive–behavioral therapies (CBT) with anger problems. R. Beck and Fernandez (1998) conducted a meta-analysis of 50 studies including a total of 1,640 participants. These studies included participants from a wide range of anger- and hostility-related domains such as prison inmates, abusive parents, abusive spouses, juvenile delinquents, adolescents in residential treatment, aggressive children, and college students who reported anger problems. The meta-analysis found that the average CBT recipient was better off than 76% of the untreated participants in terms of anger reduction.

Although there is room for improvement, the empirical support for using cognitive therapy and related approaches to reduce hate and violence in individuals, couples, and families is encouraging. Ideas for use of these approaches on the societal level are of more recent vintage and have not yet been the subject of extensive research. Hopes are high among proponents of this approach, but the challenge is great, and much remains to be learned.

RELATIONSHIPS TO OTHER PERSPECTIVES ON HATE AND VIOLENCE

The evolution of cognitive therapy has been influenced by a wide range of theorists and clinicians. In fact, it can be argued that cognitive therapy is a highly integrative approach (Alford & Beck, 1997; Alford & Norcross, 1991; Beck, 1991). The three primary theoretical influences cited in discussions of the evolution of cognitive therapy have been the phenomenological approach to psychology, psychodynamic depth psychology, and cognitive psychology (Weishaar, 1993). The clinical practice of cognitive therapy has been strongly influenced by client-centered therapy and by contemporary behavioral and cognitive–behavioral approaches to therapy. Among the influences Beck considered to have been most important are phenomenological perspectives dating back to the Greek Stoic philosophers and presented more recently by Alfred Adler, Otto Rank, and Karen Horney; the structural theory and depth psychology of Kant and Freud; the cognitive perspectives of George Kelley, Magda Arnold, and Richard Lazarus; the emphasis on a specific, here-and-now approach to problems taken by Austen Riggs and Albert Ellis; Carl Rogers's client-centered therapy; the idea of preconscious cognition from writers such as Leon Saul; and the work of cognitive–behavioral investigators including Albert Bandura, Marvin Goldfried, Michael Mahoney, Donald Meichenbaum, and G. Terrence Wilson (Weishaar, 1993).

In applying the cognitive perspective to understanding hate and violence, Beck (1999) attempted to incorporate a wide range of perspectives and to integrate the available data. Psychoanalytic theory has been one of the most influential approaches to understanding hate and violence, influencing writers in political science, sociology, history, and criminology. In comparing his cognitive model with psychoanalytic theory, Beck (2002) proposed that the cognitive model is more parsimonious and has stronger empirical support. He argued that his generic cognitive model applies equally well to understanding normal human functioning, psychopathology, and hate and violence.

CONCLUSION

The cognitive perspective on hate and violence is consistent with a large body of empirical research and with the detailed observations made in the course of psychotherapy. It can easily be applied retrospectively to episodes of hate and violence by individuals and groups as long as sufficient information about thoughts and feelings is available. Further studies are necessary to test the predictive value of the model and its relevance to effective interventions. Fortunately, the model can generate testable propositions and is amenable to empirical research.

We look forward to future research that will refine and improve the theoretical model and that will test the effectiveness of interventions and programs designed to reduce hate and violence. A particular focus on the collective self-image of antagonistic groups and their image of the Enemy can provide a basis for understanding the conflict. Further, a composite picture of the contrasting perspectives, attitudes, malevolent attributions, and cognitive distortions can facilitate finding political solutions between warring factions. Recent decades have demonstrated the vast destructive potential of individuals and groups motivated by hate. We hope that the cognitive model can offer a fresh approach to reducing the ubiquitous tendency toward hate and destruction.

REFERENCES

Alford, B. A., & Beck, A. T. (1997). *The integrative power of cognitive therapy*. New York: Guilford Press.

Alford, B. A., & Norcross, J. C. (1991). Cognitive therapy as integrative therapy. *Journal of Psychotherapy Integration, 1*, 175–190.

Beck, A. T. (1991). Cognitive therapy as *the* integrative therapy: Comments on Alford and Norcross. *Journal of Psychotherapy Integration, 1*, 191–198.

Beck, A. T. (1999). *Prisoners of hate: The cognitive basis of anger, hostility, and violence*. New York: HarperCollins.

Beck, A. T. (2002). Prisoners of hate. *Behaviour Research and Therapy, 40*, 209–216.

Beck, R., & Fernandez, E. (1998). Cognitive–behavioral therapy in the treatment of anger: A meta-analysis. *Cognitive Therapy and Research, 22*, 63–74.

Eckhardt, C. I., Barbour, K. A., & Davison, G. C. (1998). Articulated thoughts of maritally violent and nonviolent men during anger arousal. *Journal of Consulting and Clinical Psychology, 66*, 259–269.

Eckhardt, C. I., & Dye, M. L. (2000). The cognitive characteristics of maritally violent men: Theory and evidence. *Cognitive Therapy and Research, 24*, 139–158.

Freeman, A., Pretzer, J. L., Fleming, B., & Simon, K. M. (1990). *Clinical applications of cognitive therapy*. New York: Plenum Press.

Green, E. P., Glaser, J., & Rich, A. (1998). From lynching to gay bashing: The elusive connection between economic conditions and hate crimes. *Journal of Personality and Social Psychology, 75,* 77–92.

Hurlburt, R. T., Leach, B. C., & Saltman, S. (1984). Random sampling of thought and mood. *Cognitive Therapy and Research, 8,* 263–276.

McNally, R. J., Reimann, B. C., & Kim, E. (1990). Selective processing of threat cues in panic disorder. *Behaviour Research and Therapy, 28,* 407–412.

Weishaar, M. E. (1993). *Aaron T. Beck*. Thousand Oaks, CA: Sage.

Wickless, C., & Kirsch, I. (1988). Cognitive correlates of anger, anxiety, and sadness. *Cognitive Therapy and Research, 12,* 367–377.

5

ROOTS OF HATE, VIOLENCE, AND EVIL

ROY F. BAUMEISTER AND DAVID A. BUTZ

Hate is a significant source of violence and trouble in the world. *Hate* is a stable emotional pattern marked by severely negative feelings toward some person or group. Many people come to hate specific other people whom they believe have mistreated them in some way. Other people have long-standing hatred even of people they have never met, simply on the basis of belonging to groups in conflict. This would be bad enough if the emotional states were the end of it, but all too often these feelings result in violent acts. During the 20th century, these feelings sometimes contributed to large-scale mass killings, in Armenia, in Germany, in the Soviet Union, in Cambodia, in Rwanda, in Yugoslavia, in China, and elsewhere (although hate was certainly not the only cause of those horrific acts).

In recent years, social scientists have devoted much empirical attention to understanding why people act and behave aggressively toward others, with comparatively less attention given to understanding why people hate. Although there have been many scholarly advances in the domain of aggression, the domain of hate remains largely enigmatic and lacking a strong empirical foundation. In light of the absence of much empirical work concerning hate, our analysis of hate draws on the extant research in aggression and prejudice, with the intent of applying these relevant findings to the understanding of hate.

Because hate is often linked to violence, our approach to hate starts with the four roots of violent and evil acts proposed by Baumeister (1997). To be sure, not all violence is motivated by hate. But the sources of violence offer a starting point for considering the roots of hate. The four roots proposed in that earlier work are as follows. First, instrumental and pragmatic concerns sometimes prompt people to resort to violence to get their way. Second, some people turn violent when their favorable images of themselves are attacked or threatened. Third, some violence is motivated by idealistic pursuits and goals, such as when people believe that violent means will make the world a better place. And fourth, a small amount of violence is driven by sadism, which is to say that some people get pleasure and satisfaction out of inflicting violence on others.

INSTRUMENTAL AGGRESSION

A great deal of aggression is simply a means to an end. Some people use it to win arguments or get their way in disputes. Others use it to pursue goals that are widely seen as acceptable (even though the violent means are not acceptable): money, sex, power. Aggressive tendencies probably evolved because social life presents endless possibilities for conflict and dispute and because aggression is one way for certain animals to influence others and get what they want.

In that respect, the expected payoff serves as the motivation for people to commit aggressive acts toward others. People who engage in instrumental aggression are motivated by a desire for a reward, which does not entail any wish to harm or a hatred of others. If they could obtain the same goals by not aggressing toward others, instrumental aggressors would be expected to do so (Baumeister, 1997). Thus, it is the desire to reap personal benefits that attracts an instrumental aggressor to a victim, not a desire to inflict harm on that victim. People can commit instrumental acts of aggression without hating the victim and, in some instances (e.g., robberies and murders), without even knowing the identity of their victim.

Then again, if two individuals or two groups repeatedly come into conflict, hate may well develop. Repeated conflicts establish the two parties as chronic enemies. Once an enemy has been identified and the pattern of repeated conflict has given some basis to expect further conflicts in the future, negative feelings could well develop.

One implication of competing for scarce resources is that it naturally creates in-groups and out-groups. For example, people who pose an obstacle to attaining desired resources (i.e., other competitors) constitute an out-group in relationship to another group who is competing for the same resources. Forming groups and differentiating between who belongs in an in-group and an out-group is seemingly natural and universal. In the context of competition for resources, ensuring that an in-group succeeds and gains the desired resources is also natural. Indeed, the finding that people favor in-groups is widely cited in the psychological literature (e.g., Hewstone, Rubin, & Willis, 2002; Tajfel & Billig, 1974).

We said that there is no inherent reason for the aggressor to hate his or her victim if the motive for aggression is instrumental. In that respect, instrumental aggression might not be accompanied by hate. However, instrumental violence may well foster hate in the victim. The person who is unjustly deprived of material or other assets would understandably feel angry, hostile, and resentful toward the aggressor, and over time (especially if there are repeated incidents) these could harden into hate.

The view of instrumentally aggressive victimization as a cause of hate leads to two predictions that could be tested empirically. First, when two people or two groups find themselves in a relationship in which one is generally the aggressor and the other the victim, the ensuing development of hate should be more pronounced in the chronic victim than in the chronic aggressor. That is, if one group regularly uses aggression to exploit another or appropriate its resources, then the exploiting group may not have to hate its victims, but the victim group may come to hate its oppressors.

If victim groups come to hate their oppressors, this pattern might be expected in the attitudes of Blacks toward Whites, insofar as Whites have historically oppressed and exploited Blacks. That is, Blacks may hold more negative attitudes toward Whites than Whites hold toward Blacks. To be sure, little empirical work has investigated the attitudes of victim and oppressor groups toward each other. However, Judd, Park, Ryan, Brauer, and Kraus (1995) examined the perceptions that Whites have of Blacks and the perceptions that Blacks have of Whites. They found that Blacks judged Whites more stereotypically than they judged their own in-group. There was little difference between how Whites rated their in-group and how they rated Blacks. Although Blacks showed patterns of ethnocentrism, this pattern was not found for Whites.

Although negative views of other groups do not necessarily translate into hate toward members of that group, recent work suggests that people belonging to low-status groups may come to hate oppressor groups if they have been treated with prejudice. Participants in a study by Tropp (2003) were told that they would be taking part in an experiment on communication styles among over- and underestimators, a trait they were further told was an important determinant of behavior. All participants were assigned to the underestimator group, and devalued group status was manipulated by telling group members that people belonging to the overestimator group (of which none of the participants was a part) are generally perceived more positively in society. Next, participants were told they would interact with an overestimator who was a confederate to the study. Some participants then heard the confederate make a prejudiced comment (the confederate asked the experimenter to switch partners because he or she preferred not to interact with an underestimator). Other participants just heard the confederate make a neutral comment. Tropp found that participants in the prejudice condition reported feeling more hostile than participants in the neutral condition. In addition, participants in the prejudice condition were less positive about interacting with their partner. The important finding from this study was that being a victim of prejudice led to feelings of hostility toward the perpetrator of prejudice. Thus, members of low-status groups may come to hate dominant group members if they perceive that they were the victims of prejudice.

There is other evidence that corroborates the idea that victim groups may come to hate their oppressors. Branscombe and Wann (1994) demonstrated that when a group identity is threatened, the dominant group that represents a threat to the minority group is then derogated. Further, Branscombe, Schmitt, and Harvey (1999) showed that attributions to prejudice among Blacks lead to both increased hostility toward Whites and to greater minority group identification. Consistent with the idea that Blacks may develop hate toward Whites because Blacks have historically been the victims of prejudice, Monteith and Spicer (2000) examined essays written by White and Black undergraduates about attitudes toward the other group. Whereas the essays written by White participants revealed themes consistent with modern racism (e.g., that Blacks get more than they deserve), the essays for Black participants revealed themes suggesting that their negative attitudes toward Whites are rooted in perceived prejudice and discrimination. Taken together, these findings suggest that people who are the victims of prejudice may foster hate toward the perpetrators of such prejudice.

Hate crime statistics also support the idea that victim groups may come to hate their oppressors. According to U.S. Department of Justice FBI hate crime statistics for 2002, 61.8% of all hate crime offenders were White, whereas 21.8% were Black. In that sense, White people commit over three times as many hate crimes as Blacks. But the preponderance of White hate crimes must be understood in the context of different population sizes. Population projections for 2002 from the U.S. Census Bureau estimate that White people account for 80.6% of the U.S. population and Black people for 12.7%. Thus, Black people commit more hate crimes against Whites relative to their representation in the population. It is likewise almost certain that Black people regard themselves as traditional victims of Whites more than the reverse. Thus, the patterns of hate-based racial violence are consistent with the view that victims develop hate toward their oppressors. On a more individual level, one of the most vivid accounts of committing a hate crime was reported by McCall (1994). He and several Black friends attacked a White bicyclist and beat him until he lost consciousness (after which they inflicted further injuries). McCall noted that he and his friends felt that such attacks were morally justified because Black people had been oppressed by White people in the past.

The second prediction is that hate should be especially common when two parties have a long series of conflicts and some of them are resolved by aggression, even if neither one is invariably the winner. Countries should be more likely to hate their neighbors than far-off, distant ones, even though one might think that similarity and solidarity could make countries align with their neighbors and hate the far-off ones. Over a long period of time (even centuries), each side will sometimes find itself defeated by the other and therefore perceive itself as unjustly deprived of various material assets.

Instrumental aggression may not directly lead to hating others, but it does provide an account of the universality of dividing people into groups. At a basic level, people who are competing for the same resources are natural enemies. Because dividing into groups appears to be an automatic part of human nature, it might also be true that prejudice and disliking of certain groups could be similarly natural and universal.

Having negative expectations about someone (even a total stranger) belonging to an out-group has been demonstrated by social psychologists to be effortless and automatic (e.g., Devine, 1989). According to Devine, the negative stereotype of Black men (for example, as unintelligent or aggressive) may be automatically activated in Whites on coming in contact with a Black man. The fact that intergroup perceptions lead so automatically toward negative attitudes suggests that intergroup conflict can be a basis for hate.

In summary, the concept of instrumental aggression suggests that acts of aggression against an out-group can be motivated by a desire to obtain rewards for the in-group. Hating or disliking an out-group member is not necessarily part of an instrumental aggressor's motivations, though it may be appealing as a way to rationalize one's exploitation, and moreover losers in instrumental conflicts may develop hate toward those they believe have unjustifiably exploited or oppressed them. From an evolutionary perspective, the need to procure resources to sustain life or enhance the quality of life may lead to instrumental aggression if aggressing toward competitors increases the chances that an aggressor will become the victor.

Instrumental aggression also naturally creates groups comprising people who will benefit from the fulfillment of rewards (i.e., the aggressors) and groups comprising people who pose a threat to fulfillment of rewards (i.e., the competitors). The basic and universal nature of division into groups is also a theme common to the domain of prejudice, where encounters with out-group members may lead to automatic attitudes and prejudice responses.

Aggression may also serve as a means for some people to get even with others who pose a threat to or challenge their positive self-views. For people who think very highly of themselves, receiving information that compromises this positive self-view could be damaging to their self-concept if they were to accept it as true. Thus, people may lash out at the perceived source of the negative evaluation, in doing so refuting the evaluation and asserting symbolic dominance over the other person (Baumeister, Smart, & Boden, 1996).

Appraisals of the self that are favorable, along with the desire to receive such favorable self-evaluations, constitute egotism. *Egotism* is defined as a motivational investment in gaining or keeping a favorable global evaluation of the self (Baumeister et al., 1996). Aggression may stem from one's having high self-regard and suffering a blow to one's ego. It is posited that ego threats lead to negative affect, which may become directed outward toward others. The need to boost self-esteem after incurring an ego threat may serve as a potential motivation for prejudice and hate toward out-group members.

The idea that low self-esteem causes violence and aggression has been a long-standing tradition in the psychological literature. For example, in their book on hate crimes, Levin and McDevitt (1993) discussed low self-esteem as a cause of aggression and hate crimes. Toch (1969/1993) suggested that violence may serve as a means to boost people's low self-esteem. In his studies attempting to link men to violence, however, he was unable to demonstrate that low self-esteem led to violence. In fact, Toch presented evidence that casts doubt on this claim and seemingly bolsters the idea that high self-esteem may lead to violence. He referred to violent men as having "exaggerated self-esteem" and as demanding "unwarranted respect" (p. 136). Elsewhere it has been asserted that terrorists (Long, 1990), murderers (Kirschner, 1992), wife beaters (Gondolf, 1985), abusive mothers (Oates & Forrest, 1985), and Black violent criminals (Schoenfeld, 1988) commit crimes as a result of low self-esteem. Indeed, the array of out-groups for which low self-esteem has been linked to aggression and violence is seemingly credible evidence that a link between low self-esteem and aggression should exist.

This link tying low self-esteem to negative outcomes, however, may not be as clear-cut as thought by some. From a Freudian perspective, it was plausible that people who felt bad about themselves might have displaced this negative self-directed affect onto others. Therefore, in terms of theorizing regarding hate, it would seem plausible that those low in self-esteem might be likely to hate others and that low self-esteem would be one cause of hate, both of the self and of others. However, if this were true, there should be data to support either one or both of the following patterns. First, there should be evidence that groups known to have low self-esteem also have higher crime rates. Second, it might be expected that groups with higher crime rates should also have low self-esteem.

The data, however, consistently point toward the opposite conclusions, namely that groups with lower self-esteem are generally less violent (and vice versa). Women have been found to have lower self-esteem than men (e.g., Kling, Hyde, Showers, & Buswell, 1999), but they are not more violent and in fact are far less likely to commit crimes or other acts of violence (except in the domestic sphere; see Wilson & Herrnstein, 1985; see also Archer, 2000). Depressed people are also known to have low self-esteem (e.g., Allgood-Merten, Lewinsohn, & Hops, 1990; G. W. Brown & Harris, 1978; Tennen & Herzberger, 1987), but a link has been found only between depression and family violence. Violence directed toward others does not appear to stem from people suffering from depression.

It might also be expected that members of groups who have higher rates of crime and violence should have lower self-esteem. Thus, examining the self-esteem of groups with higher crime rates may also shed some light on the tentative link between self-esteem and violence. Hare (1993) showed that psychopaths tend to have very positive or narcissistic self-views but also have egos that are susceptible to insults. Crocker and Major (1989) demonstrated that Black people do not have lower self-esteem than do White people. On the contrary, self-esteem among Black people is generally found to be higher than among Whites (e.g., Gray-Little & Hafdahl, 2000; Twenge & Crocker, 2002). Attributing aggression and increased crime rates to having lower self-esteem may therefore be problematic in light of the data that show groups who have largely positive self-appraisals also have higher rates of violence.

The empirical evidence does not seem to fit the idea that low self-esteem directly leads to violence, nor does it suggest that the opposite is necessarily true—that high self-esteem leads to violence. Rather, as Baumeister et al. (1996) proposed, high self-esteem may interact with situational threats to one's ego, which together may lead to violence and aggression. According to the threatened egotism theory, aggression and violence may arise in people who have positive self-views but receive negative appraisals from others. If the recipient of the negative appraisal rejects the evaluation as untrue, the appraisal from the other person may result in negative affect, aggression, and violence directed at the source of the negative evaluation (Baumeister et al., 1996).

Laboratory evidence has confirmed that threatened egotism leads to aggression. Bushman and Baumeister (1998) measured both self-esteem and narcissism. (*Narcissism* involves a highly favorable, even inflated self-view along with a motivation to have this favorable view of self confirmed by others.) Narcissists were no more aggressive than anyone else when praised, but when they were criticized or insulted they became highly aggressive. Self-esteem alone did not predict aggression in either condition. Thus, the most egotistical persons were also the most aggressive, but only when their egotism had come under attack. Moreover, they were aggressive only toward the person who had offended them; they did not displace these aggressive feelings toward innocent third parties.

In fact, people may be so willing to act negatively toward the person who insults their pride that they will also incur costs to themselves to carry out the retaliation, as first shown by B. R. Brown (1968). Participants in Brown's experiment were all young men who were taking part in a game in which they owned a trucking company and could earn real money by driving their trucks down a stretch of road. One person, a confederate in the experiment, owned a portion of the road and could charge the other person, the participant, a toll for using that part of the road. The confederate exercised this opportunity often, causing the participant to lose a great deal of money in tolls. Taxing rules applied to the game, such that the more a person earned in tolls, the more he would have to pay in "road taxes." Thus, charging low tolls was profitable, but high tolls incurred a cost to the person charging the toll in that he lost money through having to pay taxes. The only goal of the game was to earn money, which made it even clearer that charging large tolls to the other person would come at a huge cost to the person charging the large toll.

In this experiment, participants were in one of two conditions: people who did or did not incur ego threats. B. R. Brown (1968) delivered ego threats by telling participants that while they were playing the game they had been observed by an audience who was evaluating them. Some people were told that the audience thought that even though they had lost some money, they had played their part well. Others, those in the condition that led to ego threat, were told that the audience thought the confederate made them "look like a sucker" by charging the high tolls. Of particular interest was what those who had just been humiliated by the audience did next. In the next round, the roles were reversed, and the participant was given control of the toll road. Participants who were insulted charged the other person high tolls, even though this meant they were themselves losing money. In contrast, participants who were not insulted by the audience did not sock the other person with large tolls.

The results of this experiment demonstrate that people who experience insults to their pride might be willing to sacrifice personal gain to engage in revenge. That is, if people experience a blow to their ego, they might then be willing to go beyond revenge that is pragmatic. Pragmatic revenge would entail trying to win back money that was lost. However, as was seen in B. R. Brown's experiment, people who received the unfavorable evaluation did not merely charge the other person a moderate amount so that they could win back money they lost in the first round. Instead, they forfeited the money they could have won and instead went about making sure the other person lost money. Although it would perhaps be premature to speak of "hate" between a participant and confederate in a one-shot laboratory experiment, the willingness to sacrifice one's own money simply to hurt someone else suggests an intensity of irrational, negative feelings that could well be the beginning of a hating relationship if the interactions were to continue in that vein.

It should also be noted that threatened egotism may not lead directly to aggression. Rather, there is an intermediate step that should be considered. That is, threatened egos are likely to result in negative affect, which then should be directly associated with aggression and violence. The direction of this negative affect, whether it is directed inward toward the self or outward toward others, is posited to be decided at the point when the person either accepts or rejects the threat. If a person were to accept an insult from another person as true, he or she might then experience negative self-directed affect, which would likely lead to withdrawal. However, if a person were to reject the insult from the other person, he or she might then experience negative other-directed affect, which would potentially lead to aggression or violence (Baumeister et al., 1996).

There could also be other situational factors that contribute to when people aggress toward others. For example, the stability of one's self-esteem may be a relevant factor to weigh when determining whether high self-esteem will lead to aggression. Kernis, Grannemann, and Barclay (1989) found that people whose self-esteem was high but changed from day to day (i.e., was unstable) were more likely than those whose self-esteem was high but stable to report negative affect toward others. Therefore, it is important to consider both the level of one's self esteem (high or low) and the stability (stable versus unstable) when determining who is likely to commit acts of aggression and violence.

To this point it has been discussed that ego threats may engender negative affect, and this may lead to aggression and violence toward others. The link between threatened egos and hate, however, may be clear if it is considered what people who suffer an ego threat may gain by hating others. One potential answer may be found in the prejudice and stereotyping literature, where it has been suggested that hate directed toward others in the wake of an ego threat may lead people to feel better about themselves. Hate, then, may serve a purpose to the perpetrator—it could make a person feel better about himself or herself when others threaten these positive self-views.

Fein and Spencer (1997) examined the need to bolster self-esteem and its implications for stereotypes. In their first study they used stereotypes of Jewish women (whom they called Jewish American princesses, or JAPs). They manipulated the need to bolster self-esteem by having some participants self-affirm by choosing from several values important to their self-concept and then writing about why this one value was important to their self-concept. Participants in the no-affirmation condition were asked to choose the value that was least important to them and write about why this value might be important to another person. Participants were then told that their job was to act as a manager of an organization and to evaluate a female job candidate's credentials, which were either stereotypically Jewish (i.e., containing references to Jewish organizations) or non-Jewish and accompanied by a photograph of a woman dressed either to look Jewish (e.g., wearing a Star of David) or to look non-Jewish. They found that people who had not self-affirmed evaluated the Jewish target more negatively, compared with the non-Jewish candidate and compared with people who had self-affirmed. Thus, the most negative feelings toward the target (certainly not hate, but at least hostile and prejudicial) came from the combination of lower feelings of self-esteem and evaluating an out-group member.

Fein and Spencer (1997) also conducted a study in which they measured state self-esteem at two time points: after the participants received either bogus positive or negative feedback about their intelligence and after they rated the female job candidate. The bogus intelligence test was important in that it provided a threat to the participant's ego. Fein and Spencer found that participants whose egos were threatened evaluated the Jewish candidate worse than if they thought she was not Jewish and if their egos had not been threatened. Also, participants who evaluated the Jewish candidate and received negative feedback experienced the greatest increase in state self-esteem from the time they received the feedback until after they evaluated the candidate. Fein and Spencer concluded that derogating the out-group member had positive implications for the evaluator. That is, evaluating the out-group member more negatively boosted the evaluator's own self-esteem. Put more bluntly, people's self-esteem was boosted by expressing hostile prejudice.

Receiving blows to one's ego has the potential to result in negative affect, as well as aggression and violence directed at the perceived source of the negative evaluation. This may be particularly true for people who think favorably of themselves, who have high self-esteem, or who are narcissistic. It has also been shown by B. R. Brown's study (1968) that people whose egos are threatened may even incur a cost to themselves to pay back the negative evaluation they have received. Though aggression may come at a price to people, they are willing to pay this price if others have insulted them—that is, if others are deserving of revenge.

Like instrumental aggression, hate has the potential to serve a purpose to the perpetrator. People may not merely commit acts of hate spontaneously but may be motivated by reasons relating to the self. This reason, to bolster self-esteem, may then lead people to derogate out-group members if by doing so they feel better about themselves.

People might also be motivated to commit acts of aggression or hate even if their egos have not been threatened. If people believe that acting aggressively toward others is done for the protection of the greater good or for the pursuit of collective high ideals, this may legitimize acting badly toward others. Though perpetrators of aggression may be committing a fair share of aggressive or violent deeds, if they are motivated by idealism they might come to believe that they are actually doing good.

IDEALISM

Idealism is another root of violence. Although many people associate violence with evil and regard perpetrators of evil as immoral, it is important to recognize that many perpetrators themselves regard their actions as pursuing or upholding positive moral values. In a war, for example, it is not uncommon for both sides to regard themselves as on the side of virtue and goodness and to perceive their enemies as evil.

It may be ironic that the pursuit of positive moral ideals can produce horrific violence and bloodshed, but the pattern is indisputable. If anything, idealistic violence produces greater carnage than any other type. Of all the violent crimes in the 20th century—by all accounts an exceptionally bloody century—the highest body counts were perpetrated in the name of high ideals. These included the utopian (communist) schemes that guided the Chinese Cultural Revolution and the Stalinist purges, both of which claimed over 20 million victims. The atrocious mass killings of Nazi Germany were also perpetrated in pursuit of a utopian dream of creating a society in which all the right people would supposedly live together in peace, harmony, and virtue. The Khmer Rouge in Cambodia killed nearly 2 million people out of a population of around 8 million, and they too sought to install an ideal society.

Such violence is not confined to the 20th century. An important prototype was the French Revolution and its Reign of Terror. The Committee of Public Safety, which presided over the terror, was explicitly devoted to installing a Reign of Virtue in France, but its legacy was memories of the guillotine and the seeming arbitrariness of injustice. It was an attempt to create a better society founded on philosophical thought and on the ideals of liberty, equality, and fraternity. Yet it so discredited democracy that France soon welcomed back monarchy.

Hate is almost certainly a factor in idealistic violence. If God and goodness are on our side, then those who oppose us must have embraced the cause of evil, and therefore it is appropriate (perhaps even obligatory) to hate them. Any individual who lacks sufficient zeal in hating the enemy may be upbraided by colleagues because a lack of hating the devil suggests a deficit in one's love for God and goodness. For example, Conquest (1986) described how during the Ukrainian terror-famine of the 1930s, many low-level cadres took pity on the starving peasant families whose last scraps of food they were confiscating. Yet they reproached each other for showing mercy or even for feeling pity.

Idealistic structures particularly contribute to hate by legitimizing it. Animosity that arises from whatever root may be sustained and increased insofar as the legitimizing values and ideals justify it. People who might normally seek to curb their animosity toward some target may instead cultivate it when collectively held ideals designate it as appropriate.

Once again, research on prejudice provides some converging evidence. By most accounts, overt anti-Black prejudice in the United States declined precipitously in the 1960s, due in part to a cultural campaign that promoted ideals of racial equality and stigmatized prejudice as evil. However, some negative feelings toward Black citizens shifted into a new form. Kinder and Sears (1981) characterized the newly emerging form as symbolic racism, and they noted that it was rooted more in moral objections to the behavior of Black people than in traditional notions of White supremacy and innate racial differences. Thus, whereas early 20th-century racists had simply asserted that Black people were innately, genetically inferior to Whites, the new symbolic racists could assert that Black and White people were born equal but that some animosity toward Black people was justified on moral grounds. Black people were criticized for being excessively violent, for preferring to live off government subsidies and other handouts instead of working for a living, for sexual immorality and promiscuity, for paternal irresponsibility, and for other alleged moral deficiencies.

It is possible that some individuals embraced these "symbolically racist" (in Kinder and Sears's term, 1981) views out of a sincere belief that Black people were more prone than other races to perform immoral behaviors. For others, however, it seems likely that symbolic racism was merely a continuation of racial antagonism and even racial hatred, just on new terms. The new American ideal of racial equality made people uncomfortable in asserting that the races were innately or genetically different, but by citing moral ideals they could feel justified in retaining their antagonistic, hostile feelings. In plainer terms, it may have been simple for some people to shift from "I hate Black people because they are different" to "I hate Black people because they behave badly."

Centuries earlier, the Spanish Inquisition may have offered some people a similar opportunity to sustain and act on their petty personal hatreds by invoking high ideals (Roth, 1964). Jews and Christians had lived near each other relatively peacefully in Spain for some time. Jews were barred from many professions and opportunities, but they performed important socioeconomic functions, such as lending money. (Christians regarded charging interest as sinful, on the grounds that it meant profiting by time, and time belonged to God, but the ban on charging interest had the unintended effect of making it difficult to find anyone from whom one could borrow money.)

A rise in religious enthusiasm led to a royal decree that all Jews must either leave the country or convert to Christianity. The very short time frame made it impractical for most Jews to emigrate, so a great many accepted the

Christian faith, at least in public oaths. This, however, had the unintended side effect that these new Christians found themselves freed from all the traditional barriers and restrictions that had held Jews back in society. Many of them therefore became immensely successful. This excited considerable envy and resentment among their neighbors, who grumbled that the forcible conversions had been intended as a way to promote the true faith (in their eyes) and not to enrich ex-Jews. These individuals cast about for some more acceptable basis for their animosity, finally settling on the complaint that some of the ostensible new Christians had been insincere about their conversion. The Inquisition grew out of this as a means of investigating whether these converts were sincere, genuine Christians or instead harbored Jewish (or other un-Christian) beliefs.

As Roth (1964) and others noted, it is likely that some people denounced others to the Inquisition out of a sincere desire to promote Christian faith and ideals, but others acted out of petty personal animosities. The Inquisition provided a structure of legitimized punishment that some people used as a way of justifying and acting on their personal hatreds.

Perhaps ironically, opposition to prejudice may fuel hate in today's America. This is because current American ideals condemn prejudice and therefore render it appropriate to hold strongly negative views toward anyone who is seen as prejudiced or even as supporting prejudice. Probably the most hated intellectuals in America in recent years are the authors of *The Bell Curve* (Herrnstein & Murray, 1994), a book that purportedly documented a racial difference in intelligence. Many people condemned the book and its authors, even without reading it. It is not our intention to defend the book but simply to indicate that whereas once prejudice was a source of hate, now opposition to prejudice can fuel hate simply because of a shift in the collective ideals of the society.

SADISM

Sadism was the fourth root of evil Baumeister (1997) identified. *Sadism* refers to taking pleasure in inflicting pain and suffering on others. It is probably less common than the other roots but is nonetheless a genuine factor that contributes to some violent acts.

One could extrapolate from sadistic violence to hate insofar as some people may get pleasure from hating. There is, however, little reason to speculate that hating is directly satisfying. (It is theoretically plausible that people can get direct pleasure from inflicting harm on others.) It is generally assumed that most states of negative affect are inherently aversive, and this would presumably extend to hate as well. In that sense, it seems a priori unlikely that people could derive pleasure, joy, or other positive gratifications from hating. It is hard to rule out entirely, though. We raise this as an issue for further research: Do some people garner direct satisfaction or pleasure from the act of hating someone else?

A perhaps more plausible link between sadism and hate is that hate may contribute to sadism. It does seem plausible that people may derive pleasure or satisfaction from inflicting harm on those they hate. For example, soldiers may experience a broad range of emotional reactions to killing an enemy in battle, but the more pleasant emotions would seemingly be more likely to the extent that the soldier hates the enemy.

CONCLUSION

In this chapter, we have sought to provide theoretical bases for understanding hate by looking for converging evidence from related phenomena, specifically aggression and prejudice. First, material, instrumental conflicts produce both aggression and prejudice, and we speculate that these may or may not contribute to hate as well. In particular, chronic victims of aggression and prejudice may come to hate those who they believe have victimized and oppressed them.

Second, threatened egotism gives rise to aggression and may contribute to prejudice as well, and it seems a very promising candidate as a source of hate. That is, people may come to hate those who threaten their self-esteem or otherwise impugn their favorable images of self.

Third, idealism contributes to both aggression and hate. Though idealism is often a positive force, its very positivity lends it power to justify and legitimize a wide range of actions, and it may also be used to legitimize hate, or even to make hating seem obligatory under some circumstances.

A fourth root of aggression, sadism, seemed less promising as a conceptual basis for hating. It also lacked the convergence of findings from the study of prejudice.

These considerations lead to the following conclusions. Hate may be prone to arise among people who feel that their self-esteem has been threatened, and in that case it would be mainly directed at the source of those threats. Hate may arise out of either material or idealistic conflicts. Hate could be intensified if idealism offers justification for hating or if losing a material conflict leads to resentment toward the winners of those conflicts.

REFERENCES

Allgood-Merten, B., Lewinsohn, P. M., & Hops, H. (1990). Sex differences and adolescent depression. *Journal of Abnormal Psychology, 99*, 55–63.

Archer, J. (2000). Sex differences in aggression between heterosexual partners: A meta-analytic review. *Psychological Bulletin, 126*, 651–680.

Baumeister, R. F. (1997). *Evil: Inside human violence and cruelty*. New York: Freeman.

Baumeister, R. F., Smart, L., & Boden, J. M. (1996). Relation of threatened egotism to violence and aggression: The dark side of high self-esteem. *Psychological Review, 103*, 5–33.

Branscombe, N. R., Schmitt, M. T., & Harvey, R. D. (1999). Perceiving pervasive discrimination among African Americans: Implications for group identification and well-being. *Journal of Personality and Social Psychology, 77*, 135–149.

Branscombe, N. R., & Wann, D. L. (1994). Collective self-esteem consequences of outgroup derogation when a valued social identity is on trial. *European Journal of Social Psychology, 24*, 641–657.

Brown, B. R. (1968). The effects of need to maintain face on interpersonal bargaining. *Journal of Experimental Social Psychology, 4*, 107–122.

Brown, G. W., & Harris, T. (1978). *The social origins of depression: A study of psychiatric disorder in women*. London: Tavistock.

Bushman, B. J., & Baumeister, R. F. (1998). Threatened egotism, narcissism, self-esteem, and direct and displaced aggression: Does self-love or self-hate lead to violence? *Journal of Personality and Social Psychology, 75*, 219–229.

Conquest, R. (1986). *The harvest of sorrow: Soviet collectivization and the terror-famine*. New York: Oxford University Press.

Crocker, J., & Major, B. (1989). Social stigma and self-esteem: The self-protective properties of stigma. *Psychological Review, 96*, 608–630.

Devine, P. G. (1989). Stereotypes and prejudice: Their automatic and controlled components. *Journal of Personality and Social Psychology, 56*, 5–18.

Fein, S., & Spencer, S. J. (1997). Prejudice as self-image maintenance: Affirming the self through derogating others. *Journal of Personality and Social Psychology, 73*, 31–44.

Gondolf, E. W. (1985). *Men who batter*. Holmes Beach, FL: Learning Publications.

Gray-Little, B., & Hafdahl, A. R. (2000). Factors influencing racial comparisons of self-esteem: A quantitative review. *Psychological Bulletin, 126*, 26–54.

Hare, R. D. (1993). *Without conscience: The disturbing world of the psychopaths among us*. New York: Simon & Schuster/Pocket.

Herrnstein, R. J., & Murray, C. (1994). *The bell curve: Intelligence and class structure in American life*. New York: Free Press.

Hewstone, M., Rubin, M., & Willis, H. (2002). Intergroup bias. *Annual Review of Psychology, 53*, 575–604.

Judd, C. M., Park, B., Ryan, C. S., Brauer, M., & Kraus, S. (1995). Stereotypes and ethnocentrism: Diverging interethnic perceptions of African American and White American youth. *Journal of Personality and Social Psychology, 69*, 460–481.

Kernis, M. H., Grannemann, B. D., & Barclay, L. C. (1989). Stability and level of self-esteem as predictors of anger arousal and hostility. *Journal of Personality and Social Psychology, 56*, 1013–1022.

Kinder, D. R., & Sears, D. O. (1981). Prejudice and politics: Symbolic racism versus racial threats to the good life. *Journal of Personality and Social Psychology, 40,* 414–431.

Kirschner, D. (1992). Understanding adoptees who kill: Dissociation, patricide, and the psychodynamics of adoption. *International Journal of Offender Therapy and Comparative Criminology, 36,* 323–333.

Kling, K. C., Hyde, J. S., Showers, C. J., & Buswell, B. N. (1999). Gender differences in self-esteem: A meta-analysis. *Psychological Bulletin, 125,* 470–500.

Levin, J., & McDevitt, J. (1993). *Hate crimes: The rising tide of bigotry and bloodshed.* New York: Plenum Press.

Long, D. E. (1990). *The anatomy of terrorism.* New York: Free Press.

McCall, N. (1994). *Makes me wanna holler: A young Black man in America.* New York: Random House.

Monteith, M. J., & Spicer, C. V. (2000). Contents and correlates of Whites' and Blacks' racial attitudes. *Journal of Experimental Social Psychology, 36,* 125–154.

Oates, R. K., & Forrest, D. (1985). Self-esteem and early background of abusive mothers. *Child Abuse and Neglect, 9,* 89–93.

Roth, C. (1964). *The Spanish Inquisition.* New York: Norton.

Schoenfeld, C. G. (1988). Blacks and violent crime: A psychoanalytically oriented analysis. *Journal of Psychiatry and Law, 16,* 269–301.

Tajfel, H., & Billig, M. (1974). Familiarity and categorization in intergroup behavior. *Journal of Experimental Social Psychology, 10,* 159–170.

Tennen, H., & Herzberger, S. (1987). Depression, self-esteem, and the absence of self-protective attributional biases. *Journal of Personality and Social Psychology, 52,* 72–80.

Toch, H. (1993). *Violent men: An inquiry into the psychology of violence.* Washington, DC: American Psychological Association. (Original work published 1969)

Tropp, L. R. (2003). The psychological impact of prejudice: Implications for intergroup contact. *Group Processes and Intergroup Relations, 6,* 131–149.

Twenge, J. M., & Crocker, J. (2002). Race and self-esteem: Meta-analyses comparing Whites, Blacks, Hispanics, Asians, and American Indians and comment on Gray-Little and Hafdahl (2000). *Psychological Bulletin, 128,* 371–408.

United States Census Bureau. (2004, June 14). *Table 3: Population projections of the United States by age, sex, and Hispanic or Latino origin (2001–2003).* Retrieved July 2, 2004, from http://eire.census.gov/popest/data/national/tables/NC-EST2003-03.pdf

United States Department of Justice. (2002). *Hate crime statistics 2002: Uniform crime reports.* Washington, DC: Federal Bureau of Investigation.

Wilson, J. Q., & Herrnstein, R. J. (1985). *Crime and human nature.* New York: Simon & Schuster.

6

THE DIMINUTION OF HATE THROUGH THE PROMOTION OF POSITIVE INDIVIDUAL–CONTEXT RELATIONS

RICHARD M. LERNER, AIDA BILALBEGOVIĆ BALSANO,
RUMELI BANIK, AND SOPHIE NAUDEAU

It is a curious subject of observation and inquiry, whether hatred and love be not the same thing at bottom. Each, in its utmost development, supposes a high degree of intimacy and heart-knowledge; each renders one individual dependent for the food of his affections and spiritual life upon another; each leaves the passionate lover, or the no less passionate hater, forlorn and desolate by the withdrawal of his object. Philosophically considered, therefore, the two passions seem essentially the same, except that one happens to be seen in a celestial radiance, and the other in a dusky and lurid glow.
—Nathaniel Hawthorne, *The Scarlet Letter* (1850/2003, p. 244)

The concept of *hate* can be operationalized as an instance of negative prejudice. As such, hate is a prejudice held by a person toward another individual, group, social object, category, or institution; it has distinct cognitive and emotional components. Hate is marked by intense emotional arousal and high meaningfulness, or conceptual salience, to the person. But so is love.

THE NATURE OF HATE: A DEVELOPMENTAL SYSTEMS PERSPECTIVE

In this chapter, we discuss hate through the lens of negative prejudice. We note that, historically, the scientific study of hate has been split from the

The writing of this chapter was supported in part by grants from the National 4-H Council, the William T. Grant Foundation, and the Jacobs Foundation.

study of love or of other positive feelings toward others (e.g., friendliness, camaraderie, affection). We argue that this conceptual split is associated with problems pertinent to understanding the development of hate and to devising ideas to diminish it. We suggest that the problems associated with a split conception of hate can be transcended and, if this is done, that an integrated understanding of the genesis of hate and of positive feelings may result in ideas to diminish hate as both an individual and social phenomenon. The integrative approach we take is associated with developmental systems theory and emphasizes the promotion of positive and reciprocal relations between individuals and contexts (represented as individual–context relations). The model we put forward points to the promotion of social liberty and of individual thriving as means to ensure the diminution of hate.

THE NATURE OF SPLIT CONCEPTIONS OF HATE

As suggested in the epigraph from Hawthorne's (1850/2003) *The Scarlet Letter*, hate need not be juxtaposed with love, as opposite emotions or as noncommensurate feeling states that have little if any shared psychosocial "territory" or psychic overlap. Yet precisely such a conceptual separation has been the predominant approach to studying hate.

For instance, as illustrated by Freud's (1949, 1920/1961) theory of Eros versus Thanatos, or by Adorno, Frenkel-Brunswik, Levinson, and Sanford's (1950) specification of the defining features of the fascistic, antidemocratic, authoritarian personality, hate and its presumed genesis are ordinarily split off as separate from the positive emotions (love, affection, positive attraction) and their presumed ontogenetic origins. In essence, then, some split approaches to understanding or reducing hate have focused (in the main) on its psychogenic origins (e.g., pathological prejudice, conceptual or behavioral rigidity), to the exclusion of nuanced assessment of the role of interactive contextual variables in moderating interindividual developmental variation (Adorno et al., 1950, is an example of this approach). In turn, other split approaches have assessed proximal through distal sociogenic influences (e.g., parent-rearing patterns through social stereotypes, respectively) and regarded individual characteristics as either derived from the "molding" social context or as noncausal (e.g., McCandless, 1967, is an example of this approach; see also Allport, 1954; Brown, 1965, for reviews).

These Cartesian splits between hate and love are just instances of a common conceptual stance in psychological science and, arguably, especially in developmental science, where splits between nature and nurture, organism and environment, continuity and discontinuity, and stability and instability are common means for framing conceptual debates, theoretical positions, and research agendas (Overton, 1998, 2003; see also Lerner, 2002). Despite the absence of an impressive or even credible record of the diminution of hate and its behavior concomitants associated with split conceptualizations, across the history of psychological science split models have remained the major frames for discussing the nature and development of hate (Allport, 1954; McCandless, 1967). At least in part, this historical focus derives from the fact that the theoretical zeitgeist has not been sympathetic to alternative, more integrative theories until about the last 2 decades, and only within the last decade have such models come to the forefront of developmental science (Cairns, 1998; Overton, 1998, 2003).

We have noted that this integrative orientation to hate and love is legitimated by concepts associated with developmental systems theories, which stress that the basic process of human development involves bidirectional, mutually influential relations between people and the ecology of human development (e.g., Lerner, 1998, 2002). In practice, strategies that promote positive individual–context relations offer ideas for applications to policies and programs that contrast with those that are predicated on split approaches to human development.

However, the historical focus on split ideas is derived from the fact that, after World War II, there was a societal need to make sense of the horrendous events the world had experienced due to the Nazi atrocities and the Holocaust, and social scientists, using the theoretical models available to them (e.g., Adorno et al., 1950; Allport, 1954), performed important services to their disciplines and to civil society by making such previously unimaginable and incomprehensible horrors perpetrated on humanity the focus of sustained scholarly inquiry.

POST-WORLD WAR II ATTEMPTS TO UNDERSTAND THE DEVELOPMENT OF HATE AND ITS BEHAVIORAL CONCOMITANTS

Following World War II, B'nai Brith supported Adorno et al. (1950) in investigating the personality characteristics associated with individuals' embracing the antidemocratic attitudes of fascism. In the most well-known portion of their work, Adorno et al. developed a Fascism (or F) scale to measure "the authoritarian personality." As indexed by this scale, individuals who endorsed antidemocratic attitudes had personalities marked by conformity, hostility, rigidity, intolerance to ambiguity, pathological prejudice, ethnocentrism, and sexual stereotypy (Brown, 1965).

Literally hundreds of studies involving the F scale followed the publication of *The Authoritarian Personality* (Adorno et al., 1950). However, methodological controversies surrounded the measurement characteristics of the instrument (Brown, 1965). In addition, there was an absence of longitudinal data sets directly testing the nature-based psychoanalytic-oriented ideas about the origin of fascistic ideology in individuals (e.g., authoritarianism was seen to arise through arrests of healthy libidinal development that occurred as a consequence of inadequate parenting during the anal stage of development); similarly, there were no longitudinal data provided about the translation of this ideology into behavior (McCandless, 1967). Eventually, there was a drop off in scientific activity associated with the empirical use of the F scale and a diminution of interest in Adorno et al.'s ideas about the origins and nature of the authoritarian personality.

The Contributions of Gordon Allport

Even before the waning of scholarly interest in the work of Adorno et al. (1950) occurred, other major frames emerged for understanding the nature of the unbridled hatred of the "other" that is associated with fascism. Allport's (1954) *The Nature of Prejudice* is the exemplar of scholarship pertinent to hatred that, although at this writing 50 years have past since its publication, still has a great deal of scientific currency. Allport defined prejudice as "an aversive or hostile attitude toward a person who belongs to a group, simply because he belongs to that group, and is therefore presumed to have the objectionable qualities ascribed to the group" (p. 7). In other words, the hostile attitude becomes a reflection of the use of negative emotional arousal coupled with the conceptual salience prototypic of hate. Allport went on to say the following:

> [An] adequate definition of prejudice contains two essential ingredients. There must be an *attitude* of favor or disfavor [toward a person or a thing]; and it must be related to an overgeneralized (and therefore erroneous) *belief*. Prejudice statements sometimes express the attitudinal factor [e.g., I would not want to marry someone who is Catholic.], sometimes the belief factor [e.g., All Muslims are terrorists.]. . . . When we find one, we usually find the other. Without some generalized belief concerning a group as a whole, a hostile attitude could not long be sustained. . . . [In addition,] the belief system has a way of slithering around to justify the more permanent attitude. The process is one of *rationalization*—of the accommodation of beliefs to attitudes. (pp. 13–14)

Allport (1954) distinguished between negative and positive prejudice, explaining that in both instances of prejudice, individuals holding pejorative attitudes made exceptionless generalizations (or, in other words, maintained social stereotypes) about others based on their membership in particular social categories, such as Jews, Muslims, African Americans, women, men, Liberals, Conservatives, beautiful people, physically unattractive individuals, endomorphs, or mesomorphs (e.g., see Lerner, 1976, 2002, for discussions). Once placed into a positive or negative category, the target of prejudice would be believed to possess all of the behavioral, mental, and physical characteristics of all others placed within the same social category.

We believe that the features and functions of negative prejudice specified by Allport serve as an effective operationalization of hate.

Allport (1954) explained further that not only were targets of prejudice believed to be exceptionless possessors of the behaviors associated with their category, but, in turn, the holder of the pejorative attitudes would behave appetitively or aversively to positive or negative targets, respectively. In regard to targets of negative prejudice, Allport noted that there were five ways in which such attitudes were translated into the behaviors of the prejudiced person: antilocution, or use of racial epithets to describe a target person; avoidance of interactions with the target; discrimination, or prevention of interaction with the target; physical attack; and genocide. In other words, there are many ways in which hate may be expressed behaviorally.

The Contributions of Boyd R. McCandless

The distinction between positive and negative prejudice introduced by Allport (1954) was explored further by McCandless (1961, 1967), who sought to explain through a drive-reduction, social learning model of development the association between social category membership and the behavior of individuals placed into these categories. Proposing what may be termed a "social inculcation" hypothesis, McCandless (1961, 1967) and his students (e.g., Staffieri, 1967) argued that targets of both positive prejudice (e.g., men with muscular or "mesomorphic" body builds) and negative prejudice (e.g., men with fat or "endomorphic" body builds) would be rewarded or punished (i.e., stimulation would be afforded that would or would not reduce physical and social drives) for behaviors that were consistent or inconsistent, respectively, with social stereotypes. Through such differential regimens of reward and punishment, behaviors would be socially molded to fit stereotypes and, in effect, to create a self-fulfilling prophecy.

McCandless (1967) went on to note that negative prejudice (hate, by our operationalization) could be distinguished by whether it was normal or pathological in character. For instance, hate toward a racial or religious group could be learned by social experiences within a given culture at a particular time in its history. However, if such social learning was amenable to modification by new socialization experiences or by direct didaction (i.e., if negative prejudice could be unlearned or extinguished), then hateful attitudes reflected only the person's understanding of the lore of his or her culture (McCandless, 1967). Hate would be seen to have served no psychic need in such cases; negative prejudice would not be regarded, then, as an overt "symptom" of an underlying psychopathological problem.

However, when negative prejudice could not be extinguished either by countervailing experiences with target people or through new learning regimens, McCandless (1967) believed that pathological prejudice was present. In such cases, hate could in fact be regarded as indicative of the sort of personality problems associated by Adorno et al. (1950) with the authoritarian personality. McCandless did not offer an explanation of the ontogenetic circumstances that resulted in the development of the pathological prejudice, although, given his social learning, nurture orientation, it is likely that he would not have endorsed the Adorno et al. psychoanalytically oriented formulation.

McCandless (1967) thus placed the study of negative prejudice (hate) within a developmental model attentive to potentially manipulable experiences of individuals and, in so doing, offered a "split," nurture-oriented alternative to the essentially split, nature-oriented ideas presented by Adorno et al. (1950). However, as already noted, neither McCandless nor Adorno et al. had available or had themselves generated longitudinal data pertinent to their models, and thus their ideas either about the failure of normative stage progression or about socialization inculcating a negatively pejorative cultural lore have not been subjected to adequate empirical tests. Nevertheless, although both sets of ideas are also flawed on the basis of their reliance on counterfactual, split conceptions of developmental processes (Overton, 1998, 2003), there are several important contributions of these ideas, ones that usefully inform the developmental systems ideas that succeeded these split conceptions of the development of hate.

PROBLEMATICS OF THE SPLIT CONCEPTIONS OF THE DEVELOPMENT OF HATE AS NEGATIVE PREJUDICE

The work of both Adorno et al. (1950) and of McCandless (1967) represents a commitment to the idea that hate and the negative prejudice that may surround it are developmental phenomena. Although we may not agree with Adorno et al. and McCandless in regard to the characteristics of the process involved in such development, we agree with their commitment to understanding the succession of ontogenetic events that give rise to hate, and thus we support their implicit rejection of an appeal to the innate presence of the source of hate, for example, to a fanciful "hate gene" whose influence is, for instance, estimated through the computation of a heritability coefficient (cf. Schneirla, 1966; see also Garcia Coll, Bearer, & Lerner, 2004, for a discussion).

Both Adorno et al. (1950) and McCandless (1967) pointed to the role of the social context in the development of hate within individuals, even though their respective approaches to both developmental processes and the context of development share the conceptual and empirical problems of other split and reductionist approaches to understanding ontogenetic change (see Lerner, 2002, and Overton, 1998, 2003, for discussions). Nevertheless, Adorno et al. directed scientific attention to personality and behavioral characteristics that are linked universally (i.e., across contextual variations) with, for instance, an anal syndrome—that is, the type of adult character that, when present in men and women, is associated with "rigid-moralistic patterns of behavioral [and] totalitarian-moralistic typologizing" (p. 448). In turn, McCandless highlighted the important role that institutions, such as the family, the school, and the community, play in providing learning environments for the developing person.

However, neither McCandless nor Adorno et al. adequately addressed interindividual differences in the parent–child relations or broader context they described. For instance, McCandless (1961), describing what he characterized as the neopsychoanalytic theory of Adorno et al. (1950), depicted their viewpoints by indicating that "the authoritarian personality is the result of child-rearing practices (most specifically, those connected with toilet training)" (p. 359). In turn, Adorno et al. indicated that the anal syndrome that they identified among the adults they studied "may be considered as an outcome of a certain type of child training" (p. 448). However, by what means would individuals developing within such ecologies not become hateful people (or would adopters of the McCandless or the Adorno et al. theoretical positions maintain the easily falsifiable position that there can be no interindividual variance)? In turn, what would account for the emergence of fascistic characteristics among youths not developing with such contextual circumstances?

In addition, is there no variation between the normal and pathological types of prejudice that McCandless (1967) described? Are there interindividual differences in the time needed to acquire or to extinguish normally prejudiced attitudes? If there are such variations, where do they come from, and does it matter for the person's psychological health and for his or her behaviors toward the targets of prejudice? More fundamental, what developmental processes result in the development of normal and pathological prejudice, and does a person possessing normal but nonextinguished prejudice behave differently toward a target as compared with a person possessing pathological prejudice?

Finally, what interventions, both at an individual and at a contextual level, are possible in regard to pathological prejudice, and what is the attitude of a formally prejudiced person (be he or she formally, normally, or pathologically prejudiced) toward the former target? Under what circumstances might the target person come to be regarded neutrally or as a target of positive prejudice? What contextual changes might help formally prejudiced people maintain the emotions and thoughts associated with positive regard? Critically, what are the developmental bases of the development of either positive or negative prejudice, and, in the case of positive prejudice, how do the thoughts and emotions associated with such positive regard correspond to the thinking and feeling characteristics prototypic of other positive mental orientations to others, such as love, attachment, fondness, caring, compassion, admiration, esteem, and adoration?

Indeed, although negative prejudice seems closely related to hate, both in its genesis and in its common manifestations, it is unclear to what extent positive prejudice is related to love. Furthermore, this asymmetry seems to undergo change as a result of developmental processes. For instance, it may be that in adolescence love might entail an idealized image of the target person, thus indicating a close connection with positive prejudice at this particular developmental stage. However, more mature love may be more nuanced and may entail a less idealized image of the target person. Therefore, at this more advanced developmental level, such love may be distant psychologically from positive prejudice. How can this asymmetry in the relationship of hate and love to negative and positive prejudice, respectively, inform developmentally appropriate interventions aimed at reducing hate and promoting love? Clearly, answers to these questions cannot be found in the extant literature.

TOWARD THE TRANSCENDENCE
OF SPLIT CONCEPTIONS OF HATE

Adorno et al. (1950), McCandless (1967), and Allport (1954) provided ideas that, in different ways, referenced individual and contextual variables as sources of: negative prejudice and, if not of nonstereotype-based positive orientations to other people, then at least of the absence of negative prejudice and, for Allport, the presence of positive prejudice. Interest in these ideas was enhanced by the events of the historical eras within which the ideas were formulated, that is, from the post-World War II period through, within the United States, the civil rights period, to the beginning of the Vietnam War era (1950 through 1976).

In addition, these ideas reflected the theoretical conceptions of human development that were current during this span of history. Overton (1973; Overton & Reese, 1973, 1981) and Reese (1993; Reese & Overton, 1970) explained that these ideas were associated with either mechanistic or organismic metatheories. Overton (1998, 2003) explained that theories associated with either metatheory were inherently reductionistic in character in that they split the individual–context system of human development into either a model predicated on maturationally or genetically predetermined epigenetic changes (e.g., associated with libidinal changes creating the anal stage of psychosexual development, as in Adorno et al., 1950) or a model predicated on environmentally shaped changes (e.g., associated with social learning through drive-reducing experiences, as in McCandless, 1961, 1967).

In other words, these post-World War II developmental models were not devised within a scientific era (which emerged only beginning in the 1970s; Cairns, 1998; Lerner, 2002) that stressed that human development was a relational, not a split, phenomenon; was therefore derived from fusions between the developing individual and his or her changing, multilevel context; and, as a consequence, was a phenomenon that involved bidirectional individual–context relations. Because these relations occur between individuals having unique combinations of genotypes (Gottlieb, 1997, 1998, 2004; Hirsch, 1997, 2004) and unique sets of interpersonal, family, community, institutional, cultural, and historical experiences and events, all people are understood to be systematically individually different across time and place (Elder, 1998; Elder, Modell, & Parke, 1993). It is this set of ideas, ones associated with developmental systems models of human development (e.g., such as developmental contextualism; Ford & Lerner, 1992; Lerner, 2002), that afford conceptual transcendence of split conceptions of hate and, instead, provide a frame for both explanation and application that is predicated on integrative, relational ideas about the development of hate and of emotions of positive mental orientations to others.

DIMINISHING HATE THROUGH THE PROMOTION OF POSITIVE INDIVIDUAL–CONTEXT RELATIONS

The maintenance of hate and of the emotions associated with negative prejudice (e.g., disdain, disgust, abhorrence, enmity, revulsion) may not only exact a toll on the psychological health of a person. When translated into behaviors, along any point of the continuum suggested by Allport (1954), hate exacts a toll on other people. Hate-based behaviors may compromise target people's sense of well-being, and when discrimination, physical attack, and genocide occur, there are both threats to people's physical safety and assaults on democracy and civil society. Examples of such hate-based behaviors have occurred throughout history, most certainly during World War II, but also more recently and around the world, from Cambodia to Guatemala, Bosnia-Herzegovina, Rwanda, Sierra Leone, Liberia, and even in New York City, to name just a few instances. Accordingly, to promote the health of individuals and of the institutions of society that ensure social justice, equity, and liberty, developmental scientists should seek to understand both the genesis of hate and the individual–context relations that promote the development of hate or diminish, if not eliminate, it.

From the perspective of models associated with developmental systems theories (e.g., Lerner, 2004; Lerner, Brentano, Dowling, & Anderson, 2002; Lerner, Dowling, & Anderson, 2003), the key to understanding the trajectory of individual–context relations that results in either positive or negative development is found through focusing on the character of developmental regulation, that is, the relation between the ways in which individuals influence contexts and the ways in which contexts influence individuals. Lerner (2004; Lerner et al., 2003) explained that these relations between individual and context are changing interdependently across time (history) and that this temporal embeddedness means that there always exists across life the potential for change in person–context relations.

Nevertheless, regardless of whether hate is harbored and expressed by an individual or by a society as a whole, there is always a possibility that a change in individual–context relations can lead to either the development or the diminution of hate in both the individual and his or her context. Indeed, a system open for a change for the better is also open for a change for the worse. When developmental regulations are supportive of negative, unhealthy development, they can lead to increased feelings and expressions of hate. Equally, when developmental regulations are supportive of positive development, they are mutually beneficial for all levels of the system; they support the healthy maintenance and perpetuation of the interacting levels (e.g., of both the person and of his or her community).

There are two important concepts associated with this view of the potential to change human life and its ecology: relative plasticity and developmental regulation. *Relative plasticity* pertains to the potential for at least some systematic change in the structure and function of individual–context relations across the life span. *Developmental regulation* pertains to the reciprocal influence of one level of organization within the developmental system on the nature of, and changes in, the structure and function of other levels in the developmental system.

The concepts of relative plasticity and developmental regulation frame a conceptualization of an optimal life span developmental process that may be labeled as "thriving" (Lerner, 2004). Across his or her development, a thriving person is an individual who, within the context of his or her individual set of physical and psychological characteristics and abilities, takes actions that serve his or her own well-being and, at the same time, the well-being of parents, peers, community, and society. A thriving young person is on a life path toward a hopeful future (Damon, Menon, & Bronk, 2003), a path that eventuates in becoming an ideal adult member of a civil society. In other words, thriving people, young and adult alike, show exemplary positive development in the present, and they are generative members of their community, making positive contributions to self, others, and civil society (Lerner, 2004).

The growth among individuals of these contributions to self and society is a matter of relationships between changes in the person and changes in the nature of his or her social world. Thriving people—individuals who make these mutually beneficial contributions to self and to society—are people whose sense of self involves a combined moral and civic commitment to contributing to society in manners reflective of their individual strengths, talents, and interests (Lerner, 2004). Accordingly, thriving individuals are on a life journey that involves productive civic engagement and valued contributions to other people and to the institutions of their communities (Benson, 2003). As well, thriving people are individuals who live in a society valuing and supporting the freedom to take the initiative to make such individual contributions. Lerner (2004) described such a mutually beneficial relationship between person and society as *liberty*.

Promoting Liberty and Thriving as Means to Diminish Hate

In a system marked by liberty, thriving is enabled by a civil society that supports the rights of the individual to develop his or her abilities as best as he or she can and in ways valued by the person thriving. A civil society supporting individual freedom and justice can exist only when the people in that society act to support, protect, and extend the societal institutions affording such liberty for all of its citizens. And when individuals do so because of their belief that such actions constitute the "right thing to do," that these actions define the morally correct path, there is, then, a mutual or reciprocal relationship between individual thriving and civil society that may be represented as the "thriving individual–civil society" relationship. This relationship involves the development in a person's life of a sense of self (a self-definition or an "identity") wherein civic engagement and moral thought and action are synthesized (Lerner, 2004; Lerner et al., 2003). In human life, integrated moral and civic identity may emerge prototypically in adolescence, when the person's self-definition is undergoing significant and singular changes (Lerner, 2002, 2004).

Across development, but especially during the adolescent years, the thriving individual–civil society relationship is actualized by the attainment of several key characteristics of positive development. These characteristics have been summarized as the "Five Cs" of positive youth development—that is, competence, character, confidence, social connections, and compassion (Lerner, 2004). When these characteristics are present simultaneously, they create a person who is developing successfully toward an "ideal" adulthood, one marked by contributions to self, others, and the institutions of civil society (Lerner, 2004; Lerner et al., 2003).

Of course, the content of developmental regulations that support the development of thriving and such characteristics of positive development may vary culturally and temporally. It can also vary interindividually and intraindividually (i.e., developmentally). Not all instances of such variation may reflect adaptive (mutually beneficial) exchanges between individuals and contexts. From a developmental systems perspective, nonadaptive developmental regulations would be predicted to be instable, although there is no extant longitudinal work that affords a priori empirical specification or estimation of the time course of instability for different levels of the system. Nevertheless, whatever the time course for change, developmental systems theory would, for instance, predict that totalitarian (e.g., fascistic) contexts that emphasize benefits to the state rather than to the individual should be less stable than democratic states that ensure social justice and equity. In turn, individual goals that reflect zero-sum game strategies, that stress the manipulation or denigration of other individuals or groups, or that exploit the social and physical ecology should be less developmentally stable than goals that integrate personal meaning and civic contributions.

There are some data sets (e.g., associated with the work of Search Institute in regard to youth–community relations; Benson, 2003) that suggest that the individual variation that may characterize developmental regulation is linked to differences in the presence and quality of assets or resources for positive development. Such assets are the "building blocks" or "social nutrients" for positive youth development (Benson, 2003) and may be marked by such ecological characteristics as the presence of positive, healthy adult–youth relationships and the provision by families or communities of safe environments, boundaries and expectations, skill-building activities, and opportunities for participation in and leadership of the civic life of the community. Low levels of developmental assets are linked to engagement in internalizing and externalizing behaviors (e.g., Benson, Leffert, Scales, & Blyth, 1998; Leffert et al., 1998), many of which reflect actions consistent with behaviors that have been associated with the negative emotions toward others, or even toward oneself, that are prototypic of hate. However, high levels of assets are associated with thriving among youths (Scales, Benson, Leffert, & Blyth, 2000).

Accordingly, both noble and ignoble purposes, behaviors, and emotions—ones reflective of positive regard for self and others or of hate—may develop through variation in developmental regulations within the developmental system. To promote the adaptive developmental regulations that will result in the emergence of stable, noble purposes, behaviors, and emotions, then, developmental scientists must apply their understanding of the nature and character of individual and ecological developmental assets in ways that maximize their mutually supportive alignment for individuals and communities.

For instance, developmental psychologists need to translate knowledge about the thriving individual–civil society relationship into programs that are effective in engaging individuals productively and positively with their communities, and again, because of an interest in building positive life spans, they should focus such efforts especially on children and adolescents. Accordingly, they should strive to promote the "big three" features of effective youth-serving programs: positive and healthy adult–youth relationships; positive skill building; and the opportunity for youth participation and leadership that contribute to oneself, others, and the society as a whole (Lerner, 2004).

In addition, developmental psychologists should support policies that ensure that all individuals will have the opportunity to be civically engaged and to thrive (Lerner, 2003). We suggest that the concept of "family-centered community building for youths" provides a frame for such policy development (Gore, 2003; Gore & Gore, 2002).

Family-Centered Community Building for Youths

How may developmental psychologists build a policy and program context for the development of people who are thriving, who manifest the Five Cs of positive development, and who embrace positive and democratic attitudes, emotions, and behaviors toward others and eschew the mental and behavioral characteristics associated with hate and negative prejudice? In other words, how can people build communities in this nation that integrate healthy, thriving young people and the institutions of civil society in mutually beneficial ways that link citizenship, civic engagement, and moral commitment to foster the development of young people into adults committed to democracy, to social justice, and to making positive contributions to self, family, community, and national and global civil society?

To sustain the individual and societal benefits of mutually beneficial person–context relations (adaptive developmental regulations), families and communities must promote a moral orientation among youths. This orientation supports the idea that good is created through a commitment to build the institutions of civil society, that is, to construct the ecological "space" for individual citizens to promote in their communities institutions of social justice, equity, and democracy. To attain this type of orientation, citizens need to align public policies and community actions (e.g., community-based, youth-serving programs) in support of the development of such an integrated moral and civic identity.

These ideas are instantiated in an approach to community building envisioned by former Vice President Al Gore. Gore (e.g., 2003; Gore & Gore, 2002) believed that this nation can create a developmental system across generations that builds integrated moral and civic identities in its citizens and that such citizens will be able to sustain and to enhance the institutions of civil society. To create this socially just developmental system, Gore indicated that policies should be developed to enhance in communities the capacities of families to provide children with the resources needed for their positive development, for example, with the developmental assets suggested by Search Institute (Benson, 1997, 2003).

Gore's (2003; Gore & Gore, 2002) conception of family-centered community building for youths grew out of a conviction about the urgency of "bringing to a renewed level of innovation and energy . . . issues of family and human development—what I call family-centered community building" (Gore, 2003, p. vii). To provide this contribution to policy, Gore proposed a model predicated on the belief that all people should value all young people and, as well, that current social and economic circumstances require community-based efforts in support of this value. In this context, Gore contended that policy should be predicated on the fact that

> It's neither sufficient nor fair to tell overwhelmed parents that they are solely responsible for building a community and doing more for their children. Instead, it is our *shared* task to address more fundamental, systemic questions: Are communities organized in ways that support—rather than thwart—family and human development? Are community policies and institutions accessible to and trusted by families? What kinds of fundamental changes in community life must occur in order to surround families and their children with the relationships, opportunities, and supports they need to thrive? (Gore, 2003, p. vii)

In answer to these questions, Gore formulated the family-centered community building approach to the development of community policies and institutions that will be valued and available to families and the young people they are nurturing. He defined this orientation to policy by specifying that

> to address the primary family and human development issues facing our nation, the family-centered community building approach considers strategies that invest in the human and social capital of a community as well as its productive capacity. These include a range of different strategies that enhance services supporting families, youth development, family education, and parenting and skill-building activities. Family-centered community building also looks at how communities create environmental, social, and educational conditions that enhance individual relationships within families and family relationships within the community. (Gore, 2003, p. viii)

Consistent with the developmental systems theory idea that the individual plays an active role in his or her own development (Lerner, 2002), and with the centrality of the individual–context relation in promoting thriving, Gore underscored the vital role of youth participation and civic leadership in enhancing the healthy development of young people and their communities. He noted that

> ultimately, building the assets for positive youth development . . . will require engaging the human and ecological system in a manner that promotes new leadership in our nation. In particular, for family-centered community building to be sustainable, the key community members among whom leadership must be encouraged are our young people. Empowering youth assures that family-centered community building is done *with* the community and not *for* the community. It also increases the extent to which sustainable change improves the capacities and life chances of all youth and families, and ensures a legacy of contributions to civil society that will enrich all of America for generations to come. (Gore, 2003, p. viii)

In essence, Gore (2003) explained that the focus of family-centered community building for youths is on the promotion of positive youth development through enhancing the quality and quantity in communities of the mutually beneficial individual–context relations emphasized in the present theory of the development of thriving (Lerner, 2004). To illustrate this relation, we note that Gore and Gore (2002) indicated that

> the first and most important step our country can take to help families is to change our way of *thinking* about families . . . Specifically, what's required is a shift from focusing exclusively on the individual to focusing on the family as a complex system, a system whose essential meaning is found in the relationships among the individuals who are connected emotionally and committed to one another as family—those who are, as we have put it here, joined at the heart. (p. 327)

To design policies that are consistent with the principles derived from the theory of thriving we have presented (Lerner, 2004) and that Gore (2003) has suggested are involved in the family-centered community building approach to policy, society needs actions that promote thriving youth–civil society relations. In accordance with this theory, these relations should be marked by

- equity, social justice, and equal opportunity;
- sensitivity to individual differences and promotion of a goodness of fit between individually different people and contexts;
- affirmative actions to correct ontogenetic or historical inequities in person–context fit;
- efforts to recognize and celebrate diversity;
- promotion of universal participation in civic life; and hence democracy.

The social system that would be created by such community-building policies reflects liberty. It is the operationalization of the idea of America (Lerner, 2004).

CONCLUSION

Given the enormous costs to individuals, communities, and nations when hate and its behavioral concomitants are rampant, and now that, since September 11, 2001, the world has realized that the conditions that spawn hate may lead to previously unimaginable calamities that may potentially affect millions of people, we believe there is a great historical need and opportunity to capitalize on the strengths of individuals, families, and communities and to create the conditions whereby youths become thriving agents of democracy, social justice, and civil society. Indeed, given the continuous and seemingly growing threat of terrorism and conflicts based on religious and racial or ethnic hatreds, there is no time to lose in the development of asset-rich communities and empowered youths and families working collaboratively to build healthy young people and civil society and to make the thriving youth–civil society relationship normative (Lerner, 2004).

Citizens committed to civil society and social justice must become active producers of the thriving youth–civil society relation by actively engaging in the political process available to them. What society will gain from such actions are new cohorts of healthy, civically engaged youths on their way to becoming the leaders of vibrant democracies in which all people have the opportunity to contribute to their own and others' positive development. These individuals will eschew hate and social injustice; they will reject the prejudices and enmities that divide individuals and nations. Instead, they will embrace what Hawthorne (1850/2003, p. 244) described as the "intimacy and hearty knowledge" of their common humanity with the diverse peoples of the world. In the hands of such individuals, diminution of hate will occur, and there will be a new dawning of the idea of liberty.

REFERENCES

Adorno, T. W., Frenkel-Brunswik, E., Levinson, D. J., & Sanford, R. N. (1950). *The authoritarian personality*. New York: Harper.

Allport, G. W. (1954). *The nature of prejudice*. Reading, MA: Addison-Wesley.

Benson, P. L. (1997). *All kids are our kids: What communities must do to raise caring and responsible children and adolescents*. San Francisco: Jossey-Bass.

Benson, P. L. (2003). Toward asset building communities: How does change occur? In R. M. Lerner & P. L. Benson (Eds.), *Developmental assets and asset-building communities: Implications for research, policy, and practice* (pp. 213–221). Norwell, MA: Kluwer Academic.

Benson, P. L., Leffert, N., Scales, P. C., & Blyth, D. A. (1998). Beyond the "village" rhetoric: Creating healthy communities for children and adolescents. *Applied Developmental Science, 2*(3), 138–159.

Brown, R. (1965). *Social psychology*. New York: Free Press.

Cairns, R. B. (1998). The making of developmental psychology. In W. Damon (Series Ed.) & R. M. Lerner (Vol. Ed.), *Handbook of child psychology: Vol. 1. Theoretical models of human development* (5th ed., pp. 419–448). New York: Wiley.

Damon, W., Menon, J., & Bronk, K. C. (2003). The development of purpose during adolescence. *Applied Developmental Science, 7*, 119–128.

Elder, G. H., Jr. (1998). The life course and human development. In W. Damon (Series Ed.) & R. M. Lerner (Vol. Ed.), *Handbook of child psychology: Vol. 1. Theoretical models of human development* (5th ed., pp. 939–991). New York: Wiley.

Elder, G. H., Jr., Modell, J., & Parke, R. D. (Eds.). (1993). *Children in time and place: Developmental and historical insights*. New York: Cambridge University Press.

Ford, D. H., & Lerner, R. M. (1992). *Developmental systems theory: An integrative approach*. Newbury Park, CA: Sage.

Freud, S. (1949). *Outline of psychoanalysis*. New York: Norton.

Freud, S. (1961). *Beyond the pleasure principle* (J. Strachey, Trans.). New York: Norton. (Original work published 1920)

Garcia Coll, C., Bearer, E., & Lerner, R. M. (Eds.). (2004). *Nature and nurture: The complex interplay of genetic and environmental influences on human behavior and development*. Mahwah, NJ: Erlbaum.

Gore, A. (2003). Foreword. In R. M. Lerner & P. L. Benson (Eds.), *Developmental assets and asset-building communities: Implications for research, policy, and practice* (pp. vii–ix). Norwell, MA: Kluwer Academic.

Gore, A., & Gore, T. (2002). *Joined at the heart: The transformation of the American Family*. New York: Holt.

Gottlieb, G. (1997). *Synthesizing nature–nurture: Prenatal roots of instinctive behavior*. Mahwah, NJ: Erlbaum.

Gottlieb, G. (1998). Normally occurring environmental and behavioral influences on gene activity: From central dogma to probabilistic epigenesis. *Psychological Review, 105*, 792–802.

Gottlieb, G. (2004). Normally occurring environmental and behavioral influences on gene activity: From central dogma to probabilistic epigenesis. In C. Garcia Coll, E. Bearer, & R. M. Lerner (Eds.), *Nature and nurture: The complex interplay of genetic and environmental influences on human behavior and development* (pp. 85–106). Mahwah, NJ: Erlbaum.

Hawthorne, N. (2003). *The scarlet letter*. New York: Barnes & Noble Classics. (Originally published 1850)

Hirsch, J. (1997). Some history of heredity-vs-environment, genetic inferiority at Harvard(?), and the (incredible) Bell Curve. *Genetica, 99*, 207–224.

Hirsch, J. (2004). Uniqueness, diversity, similarity, repeatability, and heritability. In C. Garcia Coll, E. Bearer, & R. M. Lerner (Eds.), *Nature and nurture: The complex interplay of genetic and environmental influences on human behavior and development* (pp. 127–138). Mahwah, NJ: Erlbaum.

Leffert, N., Benson, P. L., Scales, P. C., Sharma, A. R., Drake, D. R., & Blyth, D. A. (1998). Developmental assets: Measurement and prediction of risk behaviors among adolescents. *Applied Developmental Science, 2*, 209–230.

Lerner, R. M. (1976). *Concepts and theories of human development*. Reading, MA: Addison Wesley.

Lerner, R. M. (1998). Theories of human development: Contemporary perspectives. In W. Damon (Series Ed.) & R. M. Lerner (Vol. Ed.), *Handbook of child psychology: Vol. 1. Theoretical models of human development* (5th ed., pp. 1–24). New York: Wiley.

Lerner, R. M. (2002). *Concepts and theories of human development* (3rd ed.). Mahwah, NJ: Erlbaum.

Lerner, R. M. (2004). *Liberty: Thriving and civic engagement among America's youth*. Thousand Oaks, CA: Sage.

Lerner, R. M., Brentano, C., Dowling, E. M., & Anderson, P. M. (2002). Positive youth development: Thriving as a basis of personhood and civil society. In G. Noam (Series Ed.), R. M. Lerner, C. S. Taylor, & A. von Eye (Vol. Eds.), *New directions for youth development: Theory, practice and research: Pathways to positive development among diverse youth* (Vol. 95, pp. 11–34). San Francisco: Jossey-Bass.

Lerner, R. M., Dowling, E. M., & Anderson, P. M. (2003). Positive youth development: Thriving as a basis of personhood and civil society. *Applied Developmental Science, 7*, 172–180.

McCandless, B. R. (1961). *Children and adolescents*. New York: Holt, Rinehart & Winston.

McCandless, B. R. (1967). *Children*. New York: Holt, Rinehart & Winston.

Overton, W. F. (1973). On the assumptive base of the nature–nurture controversy: Additive versus interactive conceptions. *Human Development, 16*, 74–89.

Overton, W. F. (1998). Developmental psychology: Philosophy, concepts, and methodology. In W. Damon (Series Ed.) & R. M. Lerner (Vol. Ed.), *Handbook of child psychology: Vol. 1. Theoretical models of human development* (5th ed., pp. 107–187). New York: Wiley.

Overton, W. F. (2003). Development across the life span: Philosophy, concepts, theory. In I. B. Weiner (Series Ed.), R. M. Lerner, M. A. Easterbrooks, & J. Mistry (Vol. Eds.), *Handbook of psychology: Vol 6. Developmental psychology* (pp. 13–42). New York: Wiley.

Overton, W. F., & Reese, H. W. (1973). Models of development: Methodological implications. In J. R. Nesselroade & H. W. Reese (Eds.), *Life-span developmental psychology: Methodological issues* (pp. 65–86). New York: Academic Press.

Overton, W. F, & Reese, H. W. (1981). Conceptual prerequisites for an understanding of stability–change and continuity–discontinuity. *International Journal of Behavioral Development, 4*, 99–123.

Reese, H. W. (1993). Contextualism and dialectical materialism. In S. C. Hayes, L. J. Hayes, H. W. Reese, & T. R. Sarbin (Eds.), *Varieties of scientific contextualism* (pp. 71–105). Reno, NV: Context Press.

Reese, H. W., & Overton, W. F. (1970). Models of development and theories of development. In L. R. Goulet & P. B. Baltes (Eds.), *Life-span developmental psychology: Research and theory* (pp. 115–145). New York: Academic Press.

Scales, P., Benson, P., Leffert, N., & Blyth, D. A. (2000). The contribution of developmental assets to the prediction of thriving among adolescents. *Applied Developmental Science, 4*, 27–46.

Schneirla, T. C. (1966). Instinct and aggression: Reviews of Konrad Lorenz, *Evolution and modification of behavior* and On aggression. *Natural History, 75*, 16.

Staffieri, J. R. (1967). A study of social stereotype of body build in children. *Journal of Personality and Social Psychology, 7*, 101–104.

7

HATE, CONFLICT, AND MORAL EXCLUSION

SUSAN OPOTOW

We're like two people who really hate each other. Hate. Can't stand each other. (Female middle school student, 13 years old)

Neighbors hacked neighbors to death in their homes, and colleagues hacked colleagues to death in their workplaces. Doctors killed their patients, and schoolteachers killed their pupils. Within days, the Tutsi populations of many villages were all but eliminated. (Gourevitch, 1998, p. 115)

Hate is a simple word connoting extreme enmity and, as a construct, is readily understood, even by young children. Yet its prima facie obviousness is deceptive. As the two examples above suggest, hate comes in various degrees and forms. Some hates are more powerfully felt and enduring than others. Some are socially shared, others are peculiar to an individual; some are one-way, others are mutual; some are enacted, others are not; and some are directed at individuals, others are directed at groups ranging from small family units (e.g., the Montagues and Capulets, the Hatfields and McCoys), to larger religious, ethnic, and political groups (e.g., in civil and international war). Commenting on one of these dimensions of hate—severity—Kernberg

(1992) described hate as occurring on a spectrum that includes mild, intermediate, and severe forms.

These multiple dimensions of hate are only one reason for its complexity. As Yanay (2002) observed:

> the entry of hatred into our daily speech does not help clarify the ways in which hatred works. The wide range of meanings and definitions, and the various contexts in which the concept of hatred is invoked only contribute to its opaqueness. (p. 53)

Perhaps because of hate's complexity, opacity, and range of manifestations and the diverse dimensions that define it, psychological research has tended to narrow its focus on particular kinds of hate. Psychology has, for example, scholarship on the expression of hate in hate crimes (cf. Boeckmann & Turpin-Petrosino, 2002; Cogan & Marcus-Newhall, 2002; Herek & Berrill, 1992); on its psychoanalytic sources and implications for treatment (Akhtar, Kramer, & Parens, 1995); hate among particular categories of people, such as children (Varma, 1993); and hate at a particular level of analysis, such as interpersonal hate (Goldberg, 1993) and mass hate (Kressel, 1996). As a result, the field of psychology rarely considers hate as a construct with breadth and depth and, as Sternberg (chap. 2, this volume) observes, it has generated few theories of hate. In support of his observation, psychological and social science dictionaries and encyclopedias rarely have entries for *hate* and jump from "handedness" or "hallucination" to "Hawthorne Effect," "health psychology," or "Fritz Heider" (but see Schoenewolf, 1994). Thus, the psychological study of hate has a curious centrifugality that deals with particular manifestations of hate, but offers few cross-contextual analyses that examine the core meaning of hate across contexts.

Agreeing with Kernberg's (1992) contention that mild, intermediate, and severe hate are different aspects of a unified construct, this chapter explores hate as a coherent construct that includes milder and more severe manifestations. Because I am particularly concerned with the potential of hate to foster extreme violence, I see hate as more than the emotions and cognitions that ordinarily describe it. I suspect that when hate becomes destructive, morals are likely to act as an accelerant, particularly moral justifications for harm doing, or *moral exclusion* (cf. Opotow, 1990). The first section of this chapter defines hate, moral exclusion, and their interaction. The second section uses data from interviews with middle school students and published accounts of hate radio in Rwanda to describe hate in mild and severe contexts. The third section considers the psychology of resisting hate. It does so by considering two exemplars, a middle school student and a Rwandan man, who both resisted hate when it was supported by the social context. The final section reflects on the implications of these data for the psychology of hate.

HATE

Webster's Dictionary (Gove, 1981) defines hate as:

> an intense hostility toward an object (as an individual) that has frus-
> trated the release of an inner tension (as of a biological nature); to feel
> extreme enmity toward or regard with active hostility; antonym of love;
> extreme dislike, aversion, and enmity experienced often toward an equal
> with a possible accompanying feeling of grudging respect. (p. 1038)

This definition translates easily into psychological terms in its description of
hate as relational and intrapsychic and in its emphasis on emotions and cognitions as building blocks of hate. Here, and in popular usage, hate has strong
negative connotations. Some scholars have argued for hate's constructive
potential (e.g., Fromm, 1965; Goldberg, 1993; Schoenewolf, 1994), particularly when it is a response to threats to freedom, life, or values. Responses to
injustice include righteous indignation and resistance as well as hate. When
indignation and resistance segue into hate-justified violence, they are in-
distinguishable from hate. In Guatemala's 36-year civil war, opponents of
injustice who risked their lives to oppose structural inequality and state tyr-
anny caused 6,000 deaths in 32 massacres (Comisión Para el Esclarecimiento
Histórico, 1999). These deaths accounted for only 3% of the people who
were killed or disappeared (estimated at 200,000) but nonetheless contributed to the conflict's deadliness and ultimately constrained postconflict justice
options. In peace negotiations in 1996, all parties tainted by violence had a
stake in blanket amnesties and in quashing accords calling for prosecution of
war-related violence (Popkin & Bhuta, 1999). Acknowledging that injustice
can prompt hate, this chapter focuses on hate as a negative construct (consistent with popular usage) because of its capacity to trigger destructive conflict
and violence regardless of the ideologies supporting hate.

Sources of Hate

The psychological literature and popular sources describe the genesis
of hate in humans' sociobiological makeup, in enduring between-group
animosities, and in individuals lacking an integrated sense of personhood.
Evolutionary approaches describe the emergence of hate in conditions that
protohumans might have faced. Informed by studies of animal aggression
and human groups in preindustrial societies, these approaches describe how
hate might have been adaptive as *Homo sapiens* evolved over the millennia
(cf. Waller, 2002). Intraspecific intolerance or aggression can benefit a species when it disperses members and promotes long-term species survival in
catastrophes, such as epidemics, that kill off species members in one locale.
However, dispersion results from other sources than hate, including acute
and chronic resource scarcity. Eibl-Eibesfeldt (1974) cautioned that once-

adaptive animal behaviors do not invariably remain useful. If hate was once adaptive for humans, it may not remain so and should not be viewed as an inevitable product of our evolutionary ancestry.

Some scholarly traditions and the popular media describe deadly, intransigent conflicts as emerging from deeply rooted and ancient animosities, such as between Hindus and Moslems or Catholics and Protestants (Varshney, 2001). For example, intergroup conflict in the former Yugoslavia has been depicted as originating centuries ago; in Rwanda, Tutsi–Hutu antipathy has been described as an ancient tribal conflict. Constructivist theories of ethnic conflict describe ancient animosities as a spurious explanation that covers for hate as a tactical strategy used by political elites in struggles to control resources and power. Constructivist explanations note centuries of peaceful coexistence between groups portrayed as enacting ancient antipathies (cf. Akhavan, 2001; Prunier, 1995). Like evolutionary explanations, ancient antipathies locate the emergence of hate in the distant past rather than in contemporary social arrangements and political dynamics (see Mamdani, 2001). When tested empirically among Lebanese students, ancient animosities failed as a causal explanation of conflict between Muslim and Western values; instead, antidominance explanations, including perceptions of undue Western political, economic, and military influence in Muslim contexts, support causal explanation of Islamic hatred of the West (cf. Sidanius, Henry, Pratto, & Levin, 2002).

Psychoanalytic approaches, particularly object relations theory, describe hate as emerging in the early experiences of infancy and resulting from infant dependence (Klein & Riviere, 1964; see also Glick & Roose, 1993). When an infant experiences discomfort, pain, or frustration, particularly repeatedly and over extended periods of time, he or she projects these negative feelings outward and develops a split perception as to what is good and bad and what is me and not me. With increasing maturity and adequate parenting, the infant resolves these dichotomies and comes to recognize that his or her mother is the source of both gratification and frustration. The child ultimately understands that good and bad can coexist in others and in oneself. This more tolerant and integrated perspective enables him or her to love others with an awareness that everyone has weaknesses and strengths (Deutsch, 1989).

Not all children develop in nurturing conditions that are conducive to developing an integrated perspective. Harsh circumstances, authoritarian families, and an ethnocentric, violent culture can predispose people to continue splitting between good–bad and me–not-me. When this split persists into adulthood, it offers an exonerating but delusional worldview that throws

> the responsibility for feelings of poverty and worthlessness, especially for poverty in love and goodwill, onto other people; and it brings absolution

of all guilt, greed or selfishness toward them, for *they* are the cause that one is "no good in the world." (Riviere, 1964, p. 28)

This tendency to project hate onto others makes it difficult to distinguish the hater from the hated with clarity and leads to psychological entrapment that binds the hater to those hated (Pao, 1965). The psychoanalytic literature has examined aspects of hate as self-hatred (e.g., Gruen, 1987); countertransference and therapeutic intervention (e.g., Winnicott, 1994); and psychoanalytic bases for racism, homophobia, and misogyny (e.g., Moss, 2003).

Evolutionary, cultural, and psychoanalytic explanations describe conditions that predispose individuals or groups to hate, but each of these theoretical perspectives has a dispositional slant that locates hate as part of humans' fundamental makeup at the species, cultural, or individual level. In contrast to more distal and dispositional explanations of hate, theories that highlight the proximal context describe hate as a response to immediate, ongoing, aversive circumstances in an individual's (or group's) life. MacDougall (1923) described the emergence of hate in rudimentary sentiment, especially fear, aroused by harsh experiences and punishments, often emanating from a consistent source. Fear then combines with other emotions, especially revenge, disgust, shame, and anger, to yield hate. His example illustrates this:

> After each occasion on which the father becomes the object of these emotions [in a child], they remain more ready to be stirred by him or by the mere thought of him; they all, in virtue of their repeated excitement by this one object, become associated with the object more and more intimately, until the mere idea of him may suffice to throw them all at once into a condition of sub-excitement. (pp. 169–170)

In her book *Wickedness*, philosopher Mary Midgley (1984) also described hate as a compound affective construct that results from repeated aversive experiences. Anger alone, she contended, cannot produce hate. Instead, hate emerges from strong resentment and fear interacting with anger as well as a person who comes to symbolize an element in life that one dreads or wants to kill. Similarly, Buddhist scripture describes hate as

> the deeply felt wish to harm someone else, to destroy their happiness. It is not necessarily expressed in a burst of anger. It's not expressed all the time, but it will manifest when meeting with circumstances that trigger one's animosity. It is also connected with many other related emotions, such as resentment, bearing grudges, contempt, animosity, and so on. (Ricard, quoted by Goleman, 2003, p. 78)

These explanations describe hate as a compound construct mingling anger and aggression and describe its emergence as relational, cumulative, and a response to attacks on one's personhood. Consistent with this, Allport (1992) described hate as "always a matter of frustrated affiliative desire and the attendant humiliation to one's self-esteem or to one's values" (p. 93; see also Waller, 2002). These explanations cast hate as a psychological *impasto* developing from the successive layering of emotion and cognition in conflictual, difficult relationships that are increasingly intolerable. Consistent with these descriptions, research on intergroup conflict describes the genesis of hate in Arab–Israeli relations as complex and as resulting from repeated and negative intergroup experiences (cf. D. Moore & Aweiss, 2002; Yanay, 2002).

Expressions of Hate

Expressed hate can effectively provoke social change. In Nazi Germany, "Hitler . . . made the entire nation a tool of his hatred" (von Weizsäcker, quoted in Shriver, 1995, p. 113). In the former Yugoslavia and in Rwanda, the deliberate incitement of ethnic hatred and violence allowed demagogues and warlords to elevate themselves to positions of absolute power. As Akhavan (2001) described it, "at a volatile transition stage, the calculated manipulation of fears and tensions unleashed a self-perpetuating spiral of violence in which thousands of citizens became the unwitting instruments of political elites questing after supremacy" (p. 7).

Hate, a political resource, is also a consumer of resources. In World War II, hate "mobilized huge, unprecedented technical, social, and psychological resources on both sides of this war" (Shriver, 1995, p. 143). As conflicts escalate, spiral out of control, and become increasingly violent, hate shifts from a means to achieve political ends to being an end in itself that consumes lives, businesses, communities, and societal institutions. Smaller scale hate, too, consumes energy that could be expended in more constructive pursuits. At work, employee hatred of colleagues, bosses, or the organization as a whole can become contagious; consume such organizational resources as attention, time, and energy; compromise organizational productivity; and lead to sabotage and revenge (cf. Bies & Tripp, 2001; Doherty, 1999).

Psychology has made significant contributions to a multidisciplinary (i.e., sociology, anthropology, criminal justice, and legal and policy studies) scholarship on the expression of hate in hate crimes. Psychological contributions include a focus on hate attributions, speech, and acts; legal and public policy issues; perpetrator and victim characteristics and perspectives; and the aftermath of hate crimes for individuals and communities (Boeckmann & Turpin-Petrosino, 2002; Cogan & Marcus-Newhall, 2002; Herek & Berrill, 1992). The Federal Bureau of Investigation defines hate crimes as a "preformed negative opinion or attitude toward a group of persons based on their race, religion, ethnicity/national origin, or sexual orientation" (Lawrence, 1999, p. 35). This definition and effective remedies for hate crimes remain topics of considerable controversy. From the perspective of perpetrators such as neo-Nazi or Aryan power groups, hate crimes are justified by their beliefs and values that some kinds of people are outside the scope of justice. Consequently, they see inflicting harm on representatives of these groups as a justified and worthy goal.

MORAL EXCLUSION

Whether or not we are aware of it, some kinds of people, such as family, friends, and compatriots, are within our "scope of justice," and concerns about them govern their conduct. These concerns are operationalized as distributive justice (i.e., outcomes) and procedural justice (i.e., processes) decisions intended to foster their well-being. In contrast, those outside the scope of justice are not of moral concern (Deutsch, 1985; Staub, 1990). They can be seen as expendable, undeserving nonentities who are eligible targets of exploitation (e.g., illegal immigrants, animals), or they can be seen as evil enemies who are eligible targets of violence. Whether nonentities or enemies, those outside the scope of justice are morally excluded and seen as less than human. They are not seen as deserving positive social goods, rights, or fair procedure. Distributive or procedural injustice, disadvantage, hardship, exploitation, or harm they experience can seem normal and appropriate and can fail to elicit a sense of injustice, remorse, outrage, or demands for restitution. Instead, for those viewed as evil, harm can be a cause for celebration. Religious, political, and ethnic identity and other aspects of identity, such as sexual orientation, age, gender, and mental capacity, can justify excluding people from the scope of justice (Opotow, 1990, 1995), as is evident in hate crimes, and small- and large-scale conflicts.

Antecedents of Moral Exclusion

Experimental research indicates that the scope of justice shrinks and moral exclusion increases in the context of conflict and disconnection (Opotow, 1995). Conflict, threat, and adverse social circumstances weaken prohibitions against harming others and create conditions that allow ordinary people to dehumanize and act cruelly toward others (Bandura, Caprara, Carbaranelli, Pastorelli, & Regalia, 2001; Lerner & Whitehead, 1980). These conditions include difficult life conditions, authoritarian social institutions, unstable political regimes, violence as a routine way to resolve conflict, and ineffectiveness of bystanders to the conflict (Deutsch, 1989; Staub, 1989). Moral exclusion is also likely to increase when people's feelings of connectedness to others break down. Perceiving oneself as unconnected to others can trigger negative attitudes and destructive competition, discriminatory responses, and aggressive behavior (Tajfel, 1978). In contrast, discerning threads of connection to others can create bonds of community, even among strangers (Hallie, 1979).

Expressions of Moral Exclusion

Like hate, moral exclusion takes many forms. Moral exclusion can be obvious when it is widespread and severe. It can be invisible when it is normalized as durable between-group inequalities. As depicted in Table 7.1, three dimensions that capture these diverse manifestations of moral exclusion are intensity, engagement, and extent (Opotow, 2001b). The intensity of moral exclusion can range from subtle to blatant, from rude or degrading behavior to mild injury, severe injury, torture, irreversible injuries, mutilation, and murder. Subtle forms of moral exclusion relegate some people to occupations and living conditions that undermine human health and dig-

TABLE 7.1
Dimensions of Moral Exclusion

Engagement	Subtle manifestations		Blatant manifestations	
	Narrow in extent	Wide in extent	Narrow in extent	Wide in extent
Passive	**1** Ignoring or allowing rudeness, intimidation, and derogation, such as bullying and sexual harassment	**2** Ignoring or allowing domination and structural violence such as slavery, racism, sweatshops, poverty, domestic violence	**3** Ignoring or allowing persecution and violence directed at particular subcultures, such as hate crimes, witch hunts	**4** Ignoring or allowing direct violence and rampant violations of human rights, such as ethnic cleansing, mass murder, inquisitions
Active	**5** Participating in, facilitating, executing, or devising such forms of rudeness, intimidation, and derogation as bullying, sexual harassment	**6** Participating in, facilitating, or devising domination and structural violence such as slavery, racism, sweatshops, poverty, domestic violence	**7** Participating in, facilitating, executing, or devising persecution and violence directed at particular subcultures, such as hate crimes, witch hunts	**8** Participating in, facilitating, executing, or devising such forms of direct violence and rampant violations as ethnic cleansing, mass murder, inquisitions
Perceptions of those excluded	Invisible, nonentities	Expendable, less than human	Reprehensible, vermin, a contaminating danger, a plague	

Note. From *Peace, Conflict and Violence: Peace Psychology for the 21st Century* (p. 106), edited by D. J. Christie, R. V. Wagner, and D. D. Winter, 2001, Upper Saddle River, NJ: Prentice Hall. Copyright 2001 by Prentice Hall. Reprinted with permission of Pearson Education, Inc., Upper Saddle River, NJ.

nity; blatant forms of moral exclusion include direct infliction of injury or death on individuals and groups and destruction of homes, crops, businesses, and communities. Engagement in moral exclusion can range from passive to active: from being unaware to ignoring, allowing, facilitating, executing, and devising harm. Passive engagement includes crimes of omission, when people have the social, intellectual, or financial resources to hinder harmdoing but instead remain aloof, disinterested, or uninformed. Active engagement includes crimes of commission, when people devise or enact harm. The extent of moral exclusion can range from narrowly focused to widespread. Narrowly focused moral exclusion affects smaller segments of a society, targeting marginal or deviant individuals or groups (e.g., religious or ethnic minorities). Widespread moral exclusion affects an entire society, such as in massacres or inquisitions that normalize persecution and human rights violations (R. I. Moore, 1987).

These three dimensions yield eight forms of moral exclusion (see Table 7.1). Multiple forms of moral exclusion can coexist within a society, and one form of moral exclusion can give rise to others. For example, moral exclusion characterized by passive engagement, subtle manifestation, and wide extent (cell 2) can create a social climate that tolerates more virulent forms of moral exclusion such as homophobia, misogyny, and racism (cell 7) or ethnic cleansing (cell 8). Because milder, more subtle, and narrower forms of moral exclusion more readily give way to blatant, active, and wider forms of moral exclusion than the reverse, it is quicker and easier to bring about an increasingly intolerant social climate that excludes more widely and severely than to bring about a social climate that is more tolerant, inclusionary, and peaceful (Opotow, 2001a).

Whether moral exclusion is subtle, narrow, and passive or more blatant, widespread, and active, it is a psychological orientation that

- views those excluded as psychologically distant and unconnected with oneself;
- lacks constructive obligations or responsibilities toward those excluded;
- views those excluded as nonentities, expendable, and undeserving of fairness and the community resources and sacrifices that could foster their well-being; and
- condones procedures and outcomes for those excluded that would be unacceptable for those inside the scope of justice.

Framing moral exclusion broadly makes it clear not only that it occurs in periodic widespread violence but also that it is common in everyday life. "Contemporary malignant social phenomena" (Moss, 2003, p. xxv) that change over time, from Nazism in the 1930s to homophobia, racism, and misogyny today, depend on both moral exclusion and hate. Their relationship, therefore, bears close scrutiny.

Intersections of Moral Exclusion and Hate

Descriptions of hate highlight its cognitive and emotional sources but do not describe it as explicitly moral. However, hate depends on moral judgments. Moral exclusion, attuned to who counts and who does not, can justify harmful acts directed at hated targets. Hate, in turn, provides moral exclusion with emotionally charged narrative details about particular actors in specific contexts that are capable of provoking vivid emotions. Without the justificatory framework of moral exclusion, hate might remain inchoate and unexpressed and more readily wane. Together, the emotional-cognitive logic of hate combined with the justificatory framework of moral exclusion can be sufficiently powerful to jump levels of analysis—from individually experienced hate to contagious, collectively experienced hate that has the potential to be destructive in unprecedented ways. For example, hate and moral exclusion of the Japanese enemy in World War II, which led to the atomic bombing of Hiroshima and Nagasaki, violated existing moral and military conventions of warfare:

> There were no limits here. Once the bomb had fallen, *anything* could happen. What atomic weapons meant, what the death camps in Europe had meant, was that nothing evermore was sacred. In our day, it had been revealed that human beings are capable of demolishing every imaginable boundary. (Driver, 1991, pp. 43–44)

Hate and moral exclusion together may be especially potent because they contribute drama and parsimony to our personal and social lives. In his essay *On the Pleasures of Hating*, Hazlitt (1826/1995) stated, "Without something to hate, we should lose the very spring of thought and action. Life would turn to a stagnant pool" (p. 190). Hate also contributes a practical, exclusionary ethos to social relationships, as Allport (1992) noted: "By taking a negative view of great groups of mankind, we somewhat make life simpler. Rejecting foreigners, blacks, Jews, etc. simplifies life and has an economy about it we cannot deny. Still," he observed, "it falls considerably short of the dreams men have for themselves. At bottom they still long for affiliation with life and peaceful and friendly relations with their fellow men" (p. 94). The next section presents qualitative data on mild, ordinary hate and then contrasts it with published accounts of more extreme hate. These data provide insight into the nature of hate and its enactment in relationships and how hate and moral exclusion interact.

HATE IN ADOLESCENTS' PEER CONFLICTS

To examine how hate is understood and experienced in everyday life, I consulted a set of qualitative interviews that I conducted with 40 seventh graders (i.e., 13-year-old middle school students) concerning their conflicts with peers. Student participants were volunteers who attended regular, remedial, and gifted classes in a public middle school in a northeastern U.S. city. Equal numbers of young men and young women participated; 52% of the students were Hispanic, 43% were Black, and 5% were White. I asked students to describe a conflict they had experienced with a peer and, in a semistructured interview, probed students' perceptions of the conflict, their opponent, and fairness (for details, see Opotow, 1991). Of 40 respondents, fewer than half (n = 17) spontaneously mentioned hate in their interview. These students were predominantly female (82%, n = 14). Half (50%) of the 42 mentions of hate described interpersonal hate; less than one third (29%) concerned something rather than someone they hated; other mentions disavowed the relevance of hate in their conflict (19%) or mentioned hate as a manner of speech (2%).

Defining Hate

Hate is not invariably connected with conflict. One young woman stated, "I definitely have had a lot of arguments. They're with both people I hate and like a lot." Another young woman observed that dislike is not hate: "I really don't feel that way about people, you know, you really hate a person because—you know, I disliked her. I disliked her, but I didn't hate her. I don't really use the word *hate*. It's a very negative word." Consistent with these statements, more than half of the 40 students interviewed did not mention hate, although they described emotionally charged and even physical conflicts.

Like the dictionary definition, students described hate as strong feelings and negative cognitions attached to social relationship. A young woman succinctly stated, "We're like two people who really hate each other. Hate. Can't stand each other." A young man described hate behaviorally, stating he has "seen people fighting and then they *hate* each other. They can't see each other, [or] they see each other and they want to get a punch or something." His description of hate echoed that of Martin Buber (1970): "Hatred remains blind by its very nature; one can hate only part of a being" (p. 68). The young man then stated that he and his adversary "were never like that, me and Franklin" and, perhaps because they could see more than part of each other and wanted more than to get a punch in, their relationship ultimately survived their conflict.

Students described the refusal to connect and engage as feeding hate. A classmate hated him, a student said, because "I play around with his girlfriend":

> And now every time he walks by me he used to push me. And I didn't wanna start nothing 'cause I don't even know him yet. So I try to, every

time I try to see him, I try to stop him to talk to him about it, but I can't. I try to talk to him about it. I told his girl I want to talk to him about it. He says he hates me. So, I don't know what else to say.

Students also described connection and engagement as feeding hate. To avoid feeling hated, a young woman sought to disengage herself from two peers. She said, "Every day I was going to school they would just do everything they could do to be mean." So she cut off the focus, emotion, and energy flow that repeatedly got her upset: "I don't think of them anymore, and I just don't take the energy to hate them." Another young woman described her effort to contain the distress induced by hate by disconnecting herself from the thoughts that feed hate: "I hated her, for what she did. Sometimes when I think about her, I—I still hate her, but it doesn't really matter, 'cause I don't think about her that much anymore."

Interpersonal Hate

Most hate mentions (50%) referred to interpersonal hate, including students' hate for an adversary ("I hate him"), the adversary's hate for the student ("She hates me!"), and hate among peers ("My friend hated this girl's guts"). Students who described hate for an adversary expressed frustration, anger, dislike, disgust, and disappointment with the adversary (see Table 7.2). Students justified their feeling of hate by describing an adversary's irritating behavior, including bothering people, making up things, asking stupid questions, and taking advantage of them. As a consequence, students had strong negative feelings for their adversary and sought to act on them by trying to get the adversary off a team, feeling the desire to hurt him, or wanting to beat her up.

Students who described being hated by an adversary emphasized the adversary's dispositional flaws, such as being antisocial, erratic, and stuck-up:

- "[He'd] hit people and like pull their hair and hit them in the head including hitting people on the head and pulling their hair."
- "Her whole attitude just changes; all of a sudden she just got this anger."
- "She think she all light [i.e., light-skinned]."

Two students saw the adversary's hate of them as simple dislike. "She really doesn't like me," stated one student. "I don't know what's the matter with her but she got an attitude with me," stated another. Students described a third basis for adversary hate in their own behavior. One young man surmised that a peer hated him because "I play with his girlfriend." Students responded to adversary hate several ways:

TABLE 7.2
Middle School Students' Descriptions of Interpersonal Hate

Interpersonal dynamic	Bases of hate	Consequences of hate
One's hate for an adversary	I hated her for what she did. He liked to bother people too much. He used to make up things. He would ask stupid questions. He used to go around his block and tell people I was his girlfriend. She took advantage of me.	I always tried to get him off [the volleyball team]. I just want to hurt them. She makes me just want to beat her up.
An adversary's hate for oneself	When we talk to her, her whole attitude just changes. All of a sudden she just got this anger. She really doesn't like me. [He'd] hit people and like pull their hair and hit them in the head. She think she all light. I play with his girlfriend. I don't know what's the matter with her but she got an attitude with me.	[She]makes me feel bad. I try to talk to him about it. We can't [have her on our committee].
Between other parties	She felt that way sometimes because she thinks of what they [people talking to her] do to her. . . . She was getting beaten with a stick. Now I understand why she acts that way. My friends were real nice, but . . . they hated when they see me with each other because they weren't friends.	First she's, like, happy; then, like, when we talk to her, her whole attitude just changes. They started fighting. They were always fighting for me.

- avoidance ("See, my committee, it's full. And then they [committee members] want her in my committee but I said, 'We can't because it's too full, and we can't have nobody'");
- affective discomfort ("She . . . makes me feel bad"); and
- efforts to resolve conflict ("I try to talk to him about it").

In describing hate in which they were bystanders rather than the hater or target of hate, students' descriptions were especially sensitive and complex. One young woman described the connection between friendship, jealousy, and hate in her relationship with two classmates: "They were real nice, but they were always fighting for me. They hated when they see me with each because they weren't friends." As a result, she experienced such logistical challenges as finding a satisfactory venue for lunch and apportioning her time:

> They were arguing over whether we should go to McDonald's or Burger King or Wendy's. It was getting me really mad. I said, "Look, why don't

we do this? Mondays, Wednesdays, and Fridays, I stay with you, and Tuesdays and Thursdays I stay with you." And they go, "How come she gets two days?" "How come she gets to three days?" "OK. Tuesdays, Thursdays, and Saturdays I stay with you. Mondays, Wednesdays and Fridays [I go with you]. And I'll stay alone on Sunday." "OK," they said, "but where do we eat lunch?"

Her account clarifies that her friends' mutual hate led to small-scale but chronic distributive and procedural justice dilemmas for her.

Another young woman saw hate between her friend and another girl as irrational, futile, and ultimately destructive:

> My friend hated this girl's guts. They started fighting. "It's not gonna be right if you hate somebody's guts and then you wanna fight them. For what? They didn't do nothing back to you." My friend wanted to do the same thing. She wanted to fight this boy, she hated too much his guts. I don't know why. I told her, "Don't fight."

Perhaps intuitively attuned to the potential of behavior to change attitudes, this young woman urged her friend not to fight.

A third young woman who described a friend's hate did not take her friend's explanation for hate at face value. Instead, she saw its genesis as deep and tragic:

> First she's like happy, then like when we talk to her, her whole attitude just changes. All of a sudden she just got this anger, you know, it's just hate all over her. It's very funny. I don't know. She said, she felt that way sometimes to the people that's talking to her because she thinks of what they do to her. I don't really think of it that way because I saw—when we went to the subway one night, her mother caught her going to the subway and she said, "D.—You hear me talking to you?" and she slapped her in the street, and she was cursing at her and she was hitting her up the street, like all of this was happening and she was yelling at her in the street and she was just cursing, and she was like, "Yeah," and like, she told me, she said, "If she beat me with that stick, I'm gonna hit her back." I never knew that she was getting beaten with a stick. Now I understand why she acts that way—'cause her mother acts that way toward her.

This student described how hate in one social context can spill over and affect others. Her description recalls psychoanalytic theories of hate, and it also echoes the psychological *impasto* that builds up layers of fear, revenge, disgust, shame, and anger to ultimately yield hate. It also suggests how hate, sensitively understood, can prompt understanding and caring between friends.

Hating Something, Not Someone

The second category of hate mentioned, accounting for almost one third (29%) of students' descriptions, is hate associated with something rather than someone: "I hate being ignored," "I hate fighting," "I hate . . . the way he used to joke around, like hit people and like pull their hair and hit them in the head and stuff," "I don't do anything in gym; I hate it," "I hate people hitting my [younger] brother," "I hate going to Burger King." *Hate*, used this way, emphasizes detestation and asserts one's personal preferences and individuality. "I hate" makes a statement about who one is, operationalized as strong, negative, unconcealed preferences: I am the sort of person who does not tolerate being ignored, or reckless fooling around, or seeing my kid brother victimized. *Hate*, described this way, reflects a role of hate overlooked in popular and scholarly definitions: "I hate" as the public assertion of personal identity. When one moves from the individual to collectives, hate becomes categorical rather than particularistic. That is, rather than hate in the first person singular, it is asserted "in the first person plural . . . not as 'I' alone, but as a white person, a straight person, a man" (p. xviii), as Moss (2003) described it. It is this shared, collective hate that has the potential to be active, widespread, blatant, and murderous, as it was in Rwanda in 1994.

RADIO TELEVISION LIBRE MILLE COLLINES: HATE RADIO IN RWANDA

Radio is an inexpensive and widely available communication technology that is especially influential where illiteracy rates are high, income is low, and hilly topography prevents transmission of television signals. In Rwanda, a hilly country, more than 60% of the population cannot read or write. People depend on radio broadcasts for information, and radios are among the first items purchased when people obtain a job. Radio Television Libre Mille Collines (RTLM or RTLMC) has been accused of calling for and directing the genocide directed at Tutsis and moderate Hutus by the International Criminal Tribunal for Rwanda (Agence France Presse, 2002; Hirondelle News Agency, 2002). Hate radio is not unique to Rwanda. It has functioned in the United States for decades (Rimer, 1995; Warren, 1996), as well as in wars in Angola (Windrich, 2000), Yugoslavia (Akhavan, 2001), and throughout the world (http://www.rnw.nl/realradio/dossiers/html/definitions.html).

Background

Before the 1994 genocide, Rwanda was a linguistically and culturally homogeneous society. When Europeans arrived (ca. 1826), Tutsi and Hutu people lived side by side and often intermarried. The Hutu majority, largely peasants, cultivated the soil; the Tutsi, a strikingly tall, thin people, were cattle herders. Traditional Rwandan political administration was complex and included both Tutsi and Hutu chiefs. Tensions in this arrangement primary pitted the center of control against the harder-to-control periphery, rather than Tutsi against Hutu. As Prunier (1995) described it, "although Rwanda was not a land of peace and bucolic harmony before the arrival of the Europeans, there is no trace in its precolonial history of systemic violence between Tutsi and Hutu" (p. 39).

Under colonialism, particularly under Belgian rule (1926–1962), Rwanda was administratively modernized and simplified. Tutsis, perceived to be racially superior and of foreign origin, were elevated politically. By 1959, they controlled most chiefdoms, and Hutus were excluded from the political sphere. Influenced by Europeans' racial assumptions, Hutus saw themselves as indigenous and Tutsi as invaders. The Belgians eventually understood that the Hutu majority chafed under this arrangement. Hutus were then elevated politically while Tutsis were excluded from political life. Riots in 1959 killed more than 20,000 Tutsis and resulted in a Tutsi exodus from Rwanda. In 1990, Tutsis' determination to return to Rwanda led to an invasion as a show of force and serious intent. Rwandan media then stoked fears that the Tutsis sought to control all of Rwanda as before. From 1991 to 1993, periodic battles occurred between the Rwandan army and the Rwandan Patriotic Front (RPF), the political arm of a guerilla force of Tutsis in exile. More Tutsi deaths in this period led to another Tutsi exodus from Rwanda. The Arusha peace accords, signed on August 4, 1993, set up a power sharing arrangement between the Hutu-led government and the RPF. Hutu Power extremists were outraged by the accords.

Radio Television Libre Mille Collines

On July 8, 1993, less than a month before the Arusha accords were signed, RTLM began broadcasting. Before then, Radio Rwanda, a government-owned station, was the sole radio station in Rwanda. RTLM introduced an attractive talk radio alternative to government radio that broadcast in Kinyarwandan, the common language in Rwanda spoken identically by Hutu and Tutsi people (Prunier, 1995), and featuring reggae, hip hop, and shock jocks. Its mixture of rousing oratory with songs by Hutu Power pop stars made it widely popular. It also introduced relentless Tutsi-bashing broadcasts that harped on Tutsis' evil role in Rwandan history, aimed to convince unsophisticated, poor, and unemployed Rwandans that their woes resulted from past Tutsi domination (Gourevitch, 1998; Prunier, 1995; Temple-Raston, 2002). Tutsis were routinely referred to as *inyensi* (cockroaches), snakes, and traitors who deserved to die (Afflito, 2000; McCullum, 1997). Moderate Hutus were similarly vilified and labeled "accomplices of the cockroaches" (Gourevitch, 1998, p. 96). Music by popular singer Simon Bikindi[1] was repeatedly played on RTLM and emphasized this slanted perspective (Temple-Raston, 2002). His song *I Hate These Hutus*[2] described politically moderate Hutus as "de-Hutuized Hutus," imbeciles, and scornful braggarts who deserve to die (Gourevitch, 1998).

Just before the genocide began in April 1994, RTLM repeatedly reminded its listeners that Tutsi were evil and "soon one would have to reach for the top part of the house" (Prunier, 1995, p. 211), traditionally where weapons were hung. Days before the airplane carrying Rwanda's President Habyarimana (a Hutu considered too moderate by Hutu Power extremists) was shot down as it landed in Kigali, an RTLM broadcast hinted that something was about to happen: "On the 3rd, 4th and 5th, heads will get heated up. On 6 April, there will be a respite, but 'a little thing' might happen. Then on the 7th and the 8th and the other days in April, you will see something" (Prunier, 1995, p. 223). The genocide began on April 6, 1993, within the hour that President Habyarimana's airplane went down. Immediately

> RTLMC started to broadcast direct incitements to deliberately murder "to avenge the death of our President." Within the next few hours the calls turned into hysterical appeals for ever greater quantities of blood. It was difficult to credit that normal people could broadcast such things as "You have missed some of the enemies in this or that place. Some are still alive. You must go back there and finish them off." Or "The graves are not yet quite full. Who is going to do the good work and help us fill them completely?" (Prunier, 1995, p. 224).

In one man's recollection of the events of April 1994, he recounts that "all of a sudden everything on the radio was anti-Tutsi . . . When we heard about the violence, at first we thought it would last just a day or two. But then it kept going, day after day." People throughout Rwanda, regardless of their ethnicity or ideology, listened to RTLM with a

> stupefied fascination, incredulous at the relaxed joking way in which it defied deeply cherished human values. The fascination extended

---

[1]Simon Bikindi was indicted by the International Criminal Tribunal for Rwanda for inciting genocide with song lyrics. He defended himself, saying that he is an artist whose songs don't advocate killing (Temple-Raston, 2002).

[2]I hate these Hutus, these arrogant Hutus, braggarts, who scorn other Hutus, dear comrades . . .
I hate these Hutus, these de-Hutuized Hutus, who have disowned their identity, dear comrades.
I hate these Hutus, these Hutus who march blindly, like imbeciles,
this species of naïve Hutus who are manipulated, and who tear themselves up, joining in a war whose cause they ignore.
I detest these Hutus who are brought to kill,
to kill, I swear to you,
and who kill the Hutus, dear comrades.
If I hate them, so much the better . . . (Gourevitch, 1998, p. 100)

to the RPF [i.e., Tutsi] fighters in the battle who preferred listening to it rather than to Radio Huhabura, their own 'politically correct' and rather preachy station. (Prunier, 1995, p. 189; see also http://www.rnw.nl.realradio/dossiers/html/rwanda-h.html for a brief audio clip of RTLM).

As the massacres spread, RTLM broadcast hiding places and license plate numbers of Tutsis to help killers find victims (Temple-Raston, 2002). As a senior UN peacekeeper described it, the generally illiterate population "listens very attentively to broadcasts in *Kinyarwanda*; they hold their cheap little radio sets in one hand and their machetes in the other, ready to go into action once the signal is given" (McCallum, 1997).

Incendiary broadcasts continuously called for the total extermination of Tutsis, and radio announcers reminded listeners not to take pity on women and children (Gourevitch, 1998). As genocide became a way of life, RTLM became "vampire radio," openly calling for more blood and massacres:

> "One hundred thousand young men must be recruited rapidly," Habimana[3] declares. "They should all stand up so that we kill the *Inkotanyi* and exterminate them. Look at the person's height and his physical appearance. Just look at his small nose and then break it." Maniacal laughter erupts. "Haa haa haa yaa yaa." (Temple-Raston, 2002)

> One Tutsi hiding in a church and listening to RTLM

> heard the radio announcers' gentle encouragements to leave no grave half full, and the more urgent calls for people to go here or go there because more hands were needed to complete this or that job. He heard the speeches of potentates from the Hutu Power government, as they traveled around the country, calling on the people to redouble their efforts. And he wondered how long it would be before the slow but steady massacre of refugees in the church where he was hiding caught up with him. On April 29 RTLM proclaimed that May 5 was "cleanup" day for the final elimination of all Tutsis in Kigali. (Gourevitch, 1998, p. 134)

COMPARING MILD AND SEVERE HATE

The RTLM and adolescent peer conflict are clearly different in degree of severity, extent, and the active pursuit of hate. These two cases sample extremes, but comparing them (see Table 7.3) offers provocative insights into the nature of hate and identifies how hate is experienced and understood psychologically.

---

[3]Kantano Habimana, one of the RTLM's most popular newscasters, was later indicted by the International Criminal Tribunal for Rwanda.

TABLE 7.3
Comparing Mild and Severe Hate

Element of hate	Mild hate	Severe hate
Targets of hate	A particular person or particular characteristics or actions of that person	A group of people or their characteristics or behavior ascribed to them
Perceiving hated people	Personal experience emphasized as primary; prevailing norms are less important	Prevailing norms emphasized as primary; personal experience de-emphasized
Emergence of hate	Spontaneous	Calculated and encouraged
Communicating hate	Face-to-face, direct, and low- or no-tech	Communication technology required (e.g., radio) to foster coordination
Rationalizing hate	Cause-and-effect relationships, however illogical, made explicit and particular	Cause-and-effect relationships, however illogical, supplied, normalized, and made implicit and universal
Outcomes of hate	Dislike, discomfort, avoidance	Encouragement and celebration of harmdoing
Scope of hate	Small scale, individual; dislike, indignation	Large scale, categorical; morally condemnatory

Targets of Hate

Adolescents who mentioned hate in their conflict descriptions emphasized particular individuals or characteristics. They were explicit about their dislike for a particular person and—even more precisely—for that person's disliked characteristics or actions. For example, when talking about their own hate, students said, "I hated her for what she did," "He liked to bother people too much," "He used to make up things," "He would ask stupid questions," "He used to go around his block and tell people I was his girlfriend," and "She took advantage of me." In each of these instances, however petty, students were specific about a particular person's action or characteristic that they found objectionable.

In the RTLM case, hate was categorical rather than focused on a specific person or particular actions or characteristics of that person. RTLM descriptions of hate essentialized, stereotyped, and dehumanized the targets of hate, which were categories of people, rather than individuals. Tutsis were called "cockroaches," "snakes," and "traitors"; moderate Hutus were called "arrogant imbeciles" and "accomplices to cockroaches" (Gourevitch, 1998).

When RTLM named individuals, it did so pragmatically to direct the *interahamwe*, the genocide foot soldiers, to apprehend and often murder them.

Perceiving Hated People

Adolescents' mentions of hate in their descriptions of peer conflicts emphasized their personal experience as primary and relied on their own rather than on others' perceptions of the hated person or his or her behavior. They rarely referred to prevailing social norms or mores to support their observations about the hated person. In the RTLM case, descriptions of hated persons sought to displace personal experience with new perceptions of hated targets provided by hate radio. Doing so was essential because before the genocide, individual Tutsis and Hutus were friends, neighbors, coworkers, and family members (from intermarriage). To supplant these close relationships with hate required submerging personal experience with perceptions consistent with the prevailing ideology of hate. Continually repeated derogatory stereotypes, packaged along with music, jokes, and innuendo, served to replace individual experience, perceptions, and morals with the logic of hate.

The Emergence of Hate

The adolescents' mentions of hate in their descriptions of peer conflicts indicate that their hate was spontaneous and arose from events in their lives. Often the hate was passing and diminished over time, or if it was more sustained, the students described active efforts to reduce it, ignore it, or work around it so that it did not negatively affect their lives. In the RTLM case, hate emerged from a calculated, prepackaged effort. Violence, although described as spontaneous and uncontrollable, was continually cultivated by RTLM to ensure that it remained sustained.

Communicating Hate

The adolescents either did not discuss their hate with its target or, if they did, their discussions were face to face. Their hate was low- or no-tech; they did not depend on technology to explain or broadcast their feelings of hate. RTLM depended on communication technology—radio, in this case, because it was a widely available, inexpensive, and credible technology—to quickly and efficiently nurture hate and to urge and coordinate its expression.

Rationalizing Hate

The adolescents' descriptions of hate in their relationships with peers spontaneously offered a causal relationship (however illogical) that specified causes and consequences of hate. For example, one young woman explained hate in her relationship with another student because "she got an attitude with me." As a result, she didn't want that student on her committee. In the RTLM case, ideology supplied by RTLM specified a causal relationship between ethnic hate and murder. Statements such as "traitors who deserved to die," "cockroaches and snakes which should be stamped out," and filling "not yet quite full" graves repeatedly normalized this cause-and-effect relationship on the airwaves. As the result of repetition, this causal relationship became implicit, beyond logic, and rooted in the prevailing culture. Unlike adolescent peer conflicts, this logic was applied wholesale rather than particularized.

Outcomes of Hate

The adolescents identified outcomes they experienced because of hate in peer conflicts, including dislike for the person hated, personal discomfort, and avoidance of that person whenever possible. Students also described outcomes they wanted as a result of hate: "I always tried to get him off [the volleyball team]," "I just want to hurt them," and "She makes me just want to beat her up." Students did not necessarily follow up on their desires. Although the logic they specified is subjective, they nevertheless delineated a cause-and-effect relationship that was particular to the circumstances as they understood them. RTLM continually advocated, encouraged, and celebrated extreme harmdoing, which included abuse, torture, looting, rape, and murder, directed toward those hated or suspected of being in hated categories.

In sum, these contrasts between mild and severe hate suggest that mild hate remains contained and relatively benign because it is limited to a particular person or, even more specifically, to particular characteristics or actions of that person. Students emphasized their own experience and their own contact with the hated person. When students experienced dislike or discomfort, they sought to reduce it, ignore it, or work around it so that interpersonal hate did not negatively affect their lives. Rather than focus on particulars, severe hate was categorical rather than individual, emphasized shared over individual norms and experiences, and once elicited was not allowed to ebb; instead, it was continually cultivated and encouraged.

Comparing mild and severe hate indicates that severe hate not only changes cognitions and emotions, but also changes one's moral orientation and identity vis-à-vis the hated others. Students describing conflicts with peers expressed dislike or indignation, but they did not become obsessed with moral condemnation. Quite the contrary, they sought to reduce contact with the others as much as possible and stop seeing or thinking about them to get on with their lives.

In contrast, RTLM proffered blatant moral condemnation of targets of hate and effectively replaced the normal moral code that fosters coexistence in everyday life with a shared, primitive, and simplistic cause-and-effect logic that justified mob violence. Hate was a means to elicit collectively felt emotions and collectively perceived cognitions about hated categories of people. Moral exclusion supplied the rationalization for hate and generated enthusiasm for its extraordinarily destructive outcomes: the mutilation and death of 500,000 to 1 million people in 100 days in brutal face-to-face slaughters, largely with machetes, the most rudimentary of weapons.

The RTLM case clarifies that in the context of widespread, blatant hate, active and passive moral exclusion work together. Whether the victims of hate are seen as evil enemies or invisible nonentities, they are seen as less than human and the violence visited on them as not of concern. Hutu Power advocates demonized Tutsis and moderate Hutus as evil enemies, while the outside world apathetically saw them as invisible nonentities. This mix of active and passive moral exclusion is what made the widespread butchery of the Rwandan genocide possible. International Red Cross President Cornelio Sommaruga described the attitude of the outside world as desertion (Prunier, 1995; see also Dallaire, 2003). The refusal of the community of nations both to name what was occurring *genocide* and to send troops or equipment emboldened those promoting and engaging in genocide to act with impunity. The Rwandan genocide, through the lens of moral exclusion, indicates that passive moral exclusion is neither mild nor innocuous. Joined with active moral exclusion, it can justify and allow previously unimaginable violence.

RESISTING HATE

Given the potential of hate to negatively influence attitudes and social behavior, it is important to identify factors capable of preventing, interrupting, and undoing hate. To identify these factors, one may find it instructive to consider cases in which hate could have triumphed but did not. The next section describes two people, one Rwandan and one middle school student, who did not fall prey to hate when doing so would have been consistent with prevailing social norms.

Resisting Hate During Genocide

In the book *We Wish to Inform You That Tomorrow We Will Be Killed With Our Families*, journalist Philip Gourevitch (1998) described the Rwandan genocide in several personal accounts. Paul Rusesabagina, a Hutu, was an independent-minded critic of the Habyarimana regime and a hotel director in Kigali at the time of the genocide. His responses to personal and collective dangers posed by the normalization of hate and violence are instructive.

Rusesabagina's hotel was selected by the genocidal Hutu Power government as its headquarters. They dispatched a military convoy to his home to bring him to Kigali to open the hotel for their use. Along with family, friends, and neighbors who had taken refuge at his home, Rusesabagina proceeded with the convoy toward the hotel. After a mile, the soldiers pulled over:

> "Mister," said one of the soldiers, "Do you know that all the managers of businesses have been killed? We've killed them all. But you're lucky. We're not killing you today, because they told us to look for you and get you for the government." I'm telling you I was sweating. I started negotiating, telling them, "Listen, killing won't gain you anything. There's no profit from that. If I give you some money, you profit, you go and get what you need. But if you kill someone—this old man, for instance, he's now sixty years old, he has finished his life in this world—what are you gaining from that?" (Gourevitch, 1998, p. 116)

Rusesabagina negotiated for over an hour and ultimately was allowed to proceed after he had given away more than $500.

After 3 days, the genocidal government, bombarded by the RPF, decided to leave Kigali for safer ground. The European manager of the premier Hôtel des Milles Collines in Kigali was being evacuated and asked Rusesabagina to care for the hotel in his absence (both hotels were owned by Sabena, a Belgian corporation). When the heavily armed genocidal government convoy moved out of Rusesabagina's hotel, he, along with family and friends, tagged along, as if part of the convoy, and peeled off as it passed the Hôtel des Milles Collines.

Telephone lines to the hotel had been cut, and the hotel was occupied by foreign journalists (evacuated 2 days later), some officers of the United Nations Assistance Mission in Rwanda,[4] and hundreds of (eventually close to 1,000) Tutsis and moderate Hutu refugees packed into rooms and corridors. The hotel was undefended. Those who came and went included political and military personnel involved in the genocidal government. In this edgy context, Rusesabagina worked through middlemen to keep liquor well stocked and to arrange for enough sweet potatoes and rice to keep his guests from starving. This required dealing with the military command, and Rusesabagina took advantage of his contacts:

> "I was using drinks to corrupt people," he told me, and laughed, because the people he was corrupting were Hutu Power leaders, and what he

---

[4]Prunier (1995) described the University National Assistance Mission to Rwanda (UNAMIR) as "the powerless UN military force which watched the genocide without being allowed to lift a finger" (p. 377). Force Commander Lieutenant-General Dallaire (2003) soberly concurred: "That mission, UNAMIR, failed" (p. 6). The role of bystanders to widespread and deadly hate, described in detail by Dallaire, clearly warrants study.

meant by corrupting them was feeding them liquor so they wouldn't kill the refugees under his roof. "I gave drinks and sometimes I even gave money," he said. Major General Augustin Bizimungu, the commander of the Forces Armées Rwandaises (the Rwandese armed forces of the Habyarimana and interim governments, heavily involved in the genocide; Prunier, 1995), was one of many unsavory visitors of the hotel whom Paul kept well lubricated. "Everybody came," Paul said. "I had what they wanted. That was not my problem. My problem was that nobody should be taken out of my hotel." (Gourevitch, 1998, p. 127)

Rusesabagina also found a way to connect to the outside world. He had previously worked at the Hôtel des Milles Collines and recalled that a telephone line had been installed to support its first fax years ago. Although the government had cut service to the hotel's switchboard,

> Paul discovered that—"miraculously," as he said—the old fax line had a dial tone. Paul regarded this line as the greatest weapon in his campaign for the protection of his guests. "We could ring the King of Belgium," Paul told me. "I could get through to the Ministry of Foreign Affairs of France immediately. We sent many faxes to Bill Clinton himself at the White House." As a rule, he said, he would stay up until four in the morning—"sending faxes, calling, ringing the whole world." (Gourevitch, 1998, p. 132)

Rusesabagina guarded his phone carefully but allowed access to refugees with useful foreign contacts. His determination to protect his charges faced many challenges:

> Shortly before dawn one morning, Lieutenant Apollinaire Hakizimana from military intelligence walked up to the reception desk, rang Paul in this room, and said, "I want you to get everyone out of this hotel within thirty minutes." Paul had been asleep, and he woke up negotiating. "I said, 'Mister, do you know these people are refugees? What security do you guarantee? Where are they going? How are they going? Who's taking them?'" Lieutenant Hakizimana said, "Did you hear what I said? We want everyone out, and within half an hour." Paul said, "I'm still in bed. Give me thirty minutes. I'll take my shower, and then get everybody out." Paul quickly sent for several of the refugees he trusted most, who were well connected with the regime—including François Xavier Nsanzuwere, the former Attorney General of Rwanda, a Hutu who had once investigated Hakizimana as a leader of Hutu Power death squads. Together, Paul and his friends began working the phone, calling General Bizimungu, various colonels, and anyone else they could think of who might pull rank on the lieutenant. Before the half hour was out, an army jeep arrived at the hotel with orders for Hakizimana to leave. (Gourevitch, 1998, p. 128)

Another time, a military intelligence officer turned up at the hotel and told Rusesabagina that everybody would be killed that night:

Paul rallied all of his connections in the government and abroad, and called on every refugee with plausible contacts to do the same. Paul remembers speaking with the director-general of the Ministry of Foreign Affairs in Paris, and telling him, "Mister, if you want these people to be saved, they will be saved. But if you want them to die, they will die today, and you French people will pay in one way or another for the people who are killed in this hotel today." Almost immediately after this conversation, General Bizimungu of the FAR high command and General Dallaire of UNAMIR came to Paul to assure him that the hotel would not be touched. (Gourevitch, 1998, p. 143)

Gourevitch described Rusesabagina as a mild-mannered and ordinary-looking man who regarded himself as a person who did nothing extraordinary in refusing to cave in to the insanity that swirled around him. "I wasn't really strong," Rusesabagina said. "I wasn't. But maybe I used different means that other people didn't want to use . . . During the genocide, I didn't know. I thought so many people did as I did, because I know that if they'd wanted to they could have done so" (p. 141). Gourevitch explained as follows:

> Paul had devoted all his diverse energies to avoiding death—his own and others'—but what he feared even more than a violent end was living or dying as what he called a "fool." . . . The riddle to Paul was that so many of his countrymen had chosen to embrace inhumanity. "It was more than a surprise," he told me. "It was a disappointment." (p. 141)

Evident in this account of Rusesabagina's creative and tireless efforts to preserve the hotel as a safe haven and protect its thousand refugees is his enduring obligation to play the hand he was dealt as well as possible. I see two important lessons in this account. First, Rusesabagina's sense of morality remained unshakable, and it clarified his obligations, responsibilities, and behavior toward victims, perpetrators, and bystanders. His relative isolation at the hotel protected him from a contagious weakening of moral standards. As a result, his scope of justice extended beyond his family and friends to include refugees. He operationalized his concern for those in danger by maintaining close contact with bystanders, including Belgium's king, France's Ministry of Foreign Affairs, and the United States' President Clinton, explicitly pointing out that they had power to make a difference and therefore bore responsibility for negative outcomes. He also maintained contact with the perpetrators of genocide and skillfully used their needs, power, and foibles as resources to protect his charges. His orientation toward all who were involved—for better or worse—was of moral inclusion (Opotow, 2001b).

Second, Rusesabagina fully used resources at his disposal. These resources not only included "a liquor cabinet, a phone line, an internationally famous address, and his spirit of resistance," as Gourevitch (1998, p. 142) aptly described it, but his resources also included his formidable and gutsy negotiation skills. In the face of threats to himself, family, and refugees, he took stock of what was ultimately at stake—death—and decided that an even worse fate was to live or die as a "fool" (Gourevitch, 1998, p. 141):

> "People became fools. I don't know why," he said to me. "I kept telling them, 'I don't agree with what you're doing,' just as openly as I'm telling you now. I'm a man who's used to saying no when I have to. That's all I did—what I felt like doing. Because I never agree with killers. I don't agree with them. I refused, and I told them so." (Gourevitch, 1998, p. 127)

Like the adolescent respondents who reported something (rather than someone) they hate to signify their identity, in the face of genocide Rusesabagina was able to delineate his identity in his statement, "I never agree with killers." This not only told others who he is, but it also may have helped him remain who he is, with his morals, his sense of identity, and his capabilities intact. He was able to look danger in the face, avoid denial, understand humanity in all its weakness, consider his options, and act.

It is significant that in this account of the Rwandan genocide, all key protagonists are male. Space precludes a consideration of gender in facing off hatred, particularly when it is severe and widespread. Clearly, the relationship between gender and power needs to be considered, along with the capacity of power to marshal material and nonmaterial resources (but see Gourevitch's [1998] account of Odette Nyiramilimo).

Resisting Hate in Peer Conflict

When Marcus (a pseudonym), a seventh-grade student, mentioned hate in his description of a peer conflict with his best friend, he said, "[I've] seen people fighting and then they *hate* each other, they can't see each other, they see each other and they want to get a punch or something. We were never like that, me and Franklin." Here is his description of the conflict:

> There were a lot of people that would always tease on him and everything, and I would feel bad about him. It was like a lot of pressure on me, and they'd make me pick on him, and I didn't like it. So then, out of nowhere, he started getting mad at me, so we had an argument. I felt really bad 'cause he just came out of nowhere with a bad attitude, thinking that I did something wrong. He was telling me that I did, that I was doing something, I don't remember exactly what it was, but it was something that got him real mad. I tried to keep, like, down, I tried not to come out with things to hurt him. I let him hurt me, but I wouldn't hurt him, 'cause I knew he wasn't really mad, he was just, he didn't know what he was thinking. [I decided not] to hurt him, to tell him things that he did. I wouldn't do that. I talked to him a little, I'm sorry to him for what I did, and I told him what he did wrong, and he said sorry, and then after that we just became friends again. It was real hard. [I was afraid] that he

was going to scream at me or do something, but I knew he wouldn't do something like that to me 'cause he's real…he doesn't like to fight much. Afterwards, we were friends again. Every time we'd have an argument, we'd always be friends again.

In this conflict, Marcus specifically sought to avoid hate. Faced with coercive social circumstances, poor communication, and the potential for distrust, Marcus focused on the larger picture rather than the immediate context. He focused on the friendship and its importance to him, his sense of his adversary as a friend who is "an easy person to hurt" and who is "real sensitive," and his sense of himself as a loyal person who does not harm a friend. Therefore he "tried to keep, like, down, I tried not to come out with things to hurt him, to tell him things that he did." He was willing to withstand his friend's wrath and perhaps seem like a wimp to others. He offered and accepted an apology, guided by his conviction that a friendship of value to him should survive rough times. Like Paul Rusesabagina, Marcus was guided by a moral code and a sense of personal and social identity and inclusiveness that withstood demands of social conflict and social context. He resisted excluding Franklin from his scope of justice.

CONCLUSION

What do these two cases suggest about ways to deter, resist, and reduce hate? The following sections describe some ways.

Communicate With Enemies Without Attempting to Annihilate Them

In *An ethic for enemies*, Shriver (1995) proposed that to

> demonstrate that one can confront and oppose enemies without attempting to annihilate them is a political gain in any civic culture. To educate the enemy in the justice of one's cause and to persuade that enemy to consent to that justice is a still greater gain. (pp. 199–200)

Paul Rusesabagina was effective because he was able to keep the channels of communication open to bystanders and even to the perpetrators of the genocide. Doing so allowed him to argue his cause—not the grand causes of war and peace, but the immediate crises that he faced and was able to resolve without violence. Marcus, too, was able to remain connected with and concerned about his friend in spite of conflict and was able to avoid the need for personal validation and victory that can lead to justifications for annihilating relationships and people. Describing the effects of the civil rights movement in its fight against racism and violence, Shriver (1995) explained that in opposition, confrontation, and education, "a certain measure of forgiveness comes to birth along with beginnings of a new social covenant . . . Such gain," he warned, "is fragile among fractious humans" (pp. 199–200). Paul Rusesabagina and Marcus offer examples of creating the social-psychological space in which this can be done.

Face Our Own Hate

Goldberg (1993) argued that seeking to avoid hate is counterproductive. Instead, people need to come face to face with hate without fear:

> Coming face-to-face with hatred can indeed be frightening, particularly if we have been taught all our lives that hate is evil. However, once we acknowledge hate, we find that it need not be destructive—that in fact it can be our psychological ally and defender. The more attuned we are to aggression in its various forms, the more adept we become at managing hate and rage constructively. By emptying the caldron of bitterness that boils in our unconscious, we free ourselves to better enjoy the present. (p. 243)

Although Goldberg's description focuses on hatred in interpersonal relations, the example of Paul Rusesabagina indicates that when hate has the potential to be extremely destructive, attunement provides a reality check that can be more effective than denial. Rusesabagina was not incapacitated by the violence and hatred swirling around him. Instead of cringing in fear or wallowing in bitterness, he focused on what he could do and chose positive ends. Marcus, too, was aware of the potential for hate in peer conflict, remained attuned to his own and his adversary's feelings, and was able to manage conflict in constructive ways.

Avoid Lowering Standards of Justice

Paul Rusesabagina and Marcus were able to "look truth in the eye," grapple with the messiness and complexity of social and political living, and act in ways that were consistent with their inner standards of justice. Shriver (1995) described the complex balance that is needed to thwart hate and foster constructive social change: "A society changes for the better," he says, "by a certain balance between realism and hope, trust and mistrust of power, justice and compassion, remembering and forgiving . . . [by] people determined to live together as neighbors in one political community in spite of all the pulls of history to the contrary" (pp. 198–199).

Encourage Constructive Conflict

Shriver (1995) asserted that American democracy is sustained by conflict coupled with respect and interdependence:

Negative relations are only tolerable when they are sustained by respect for the humanity of the "others" and a reverence for their very lives. One does not argue long with people whom one deems of no real importance. American democracy is at its best when people of clashing points of view argue far into the night because they know that next day they are gong to count and encounter each other as residents of the neighborhood. (p. 230)

In social relations, conflict is inevitable (Deutsch, 1973), and as Shriver made clear, conflict is not only an occasion for perspective taking and social change but also an occasion that can test oneself, one's moral principles, and one's ability to argue and negotiate for what one believes, as Paul Rusesabagina did. Marcus too noted that potential of conflict to test and strengthen friendship. Disability activist Harriet McBryde Johnson (2003) described the importance of struggle because it can loosen social strictures and change the perspective of people who neither understand nor experience the world as she does:

> As a disability pariah, I must struggle for a place, for kinship, for community, for connection. Because I am still seeking acceptance of my humanity . . . My goal isn't to shed the perspective that comes from my particular experience, but to give voice to it. I want to be engaged in the tribal fury that rages when opposing perspectives are let loose. (p. 79)

In sum, dealing with and deterring hate should not be considered an extraordinary effort, although, clearly, it can be heroic when hate is coupled with blatant, active, and widespread moral exclusion. Hate has less potential for destructiveness when it is contained, allowed to ebb, and remains relatively free of moral exclusion. A key resource in deterring and undoing hate is people's capacity for moral inclusion that remains steadfast and whole and does not wither in the face of danger. Humans' individual and collective capacity to address hate, and to do so with openness that is unimpeded by complicity, fear, denial, destructive conflict, and violence, is a fundamental skill in the craft of productive, happy, and just social living.

REFERENCES

Afflito, F. M. (2000). Victimization, survival and the impunity of forced exile: A case study from the Rwandan genocide. *Crime, Law and Social Change, 34,* 77–97.

Agence France Presse. (2002, September 26). *Founder of Rwandan "hate radio" tells court he lost control.* Paris: Author.

Akhavan, P. (2001). Beyond impunity: Can international criminal justice prevent future atrocities? *American Journal of International Law, 95,* 7–31.

Akhtar, S., Kramer, S., & Parens, H. (Eds.). (1995). *The birth of hatred: Developmental, clinical, and technical aspects of intense aggression*. Northvale, NJ: Jason Aronson.

Allport, G. (1992). The nature of hatred. In R. M. Baird & S. E. Rosenbaum (Eds.), *Hatred, bigotry, and prejudice: Definitions, causes, and solutions* (pp. 91–94). Buffalo, NY: Prometheus. (Original work published 1979)

Bandura, A., Caprara, G. V., Carbaranelli, C., Pastorelli, C., & Regalia, C. (2001). Sociocognitive self-regulatory mechanisms governing transgressive behavior. *Journal of Personality and Social Psychology, 80*, 125–135.

Bies, R. J., & Tripp, T. M. (2001). A passion for justice: The rationality and morality of revenge. In R. Cropanzano (Ed.), *Justice in the workplace: From theory to practice* (Vol. 2, pp.197–208). Mahwah, NJ: Erlbaum.

Boeckmann, R. J., & Turpin-Petrosino, C. (Eds.). (2002). Understanding the harm of hate crime [Special issue]. *Journal of Social Issues, 58*(2).

Buber, M. (1970). *I and thou* (W. Kaufmann, Trans.). New York: Touchstone Books.

Cogan, J. C., & Marcus-Newhall, A. (2002). Hate crimes: Research, policy, and action [Special issue]. *American Behavioral Scientist, 45*(12).

Comisión Para el Esclarecimiento Histórico. (1999, February). *Guatemala, memory of silence: Report of the Commission for Historical Clarification: Conclusions and recommendations*. Retrieved May 29, 2001, from http://hrdata.aaas.org/ceh/report/english/

Dallaire, R. (2003). *Shake hands with the devil: The failure of humanity in Rwanda*. Toronto, Canada: Random House.

Deutsch, M. (1973). *The resolution of conflict*. New Haven, CT: Yale University Press.

Deutsch, M. (1985). *Distributive justice: A social-psychological perspective*. New Haven, CT: Yale University Press.

Deutsch, M. (1989, March 19). *Hate and love: Destructive and constructive conflicts*. Paper presented at the Anatomy of Hate seminar, Boston University, Boston, MA.

Doherty, S. (1999). *From betrayal to revenge: Exploring the development of employer/employee disputes*. Unpublished master's thesis, University of Massachusetts, Boston.

Driver, T. F. (1991). *The magic of ritual*. San Francisco: HarperCollins.

Eibl-Eibesfeldt, I. (1974). *Love and hate: The natural history of behavior patterns* (G. Strachan, Trans.). New York: Schocken.

Fromm, E. (1965). *Man for himself: An inquiry into the psychology of ethics*. New York: Fawcett Premier.

Glick, R. A., & Roose, S. P. (Eds.). (1993). *Rage, power, and aggression*. New Haven, CT: Yale University Press.

Goldberg, J. G. (1993). *The dark side of love: The positive role of our negative feelings—anger, jealously, and hate*. New York: Putnam.

Goleman, D. (2003). *Destructive emotions: How can we overcome them? A scientific collaboration with the Dalai Lama.* New York: Bantam Dell.

Gourevitch, P. (1998). *We wish to inform you that tomorrow we will be killed with our families: Stories from Rwanda.* New York: Farrar, Straus, & Giroux.

Gove, P. B. (Ed.). (1981). *Webster's third new international dictionary of the English language, unabridged.* Springfield, MA: Merriam-Webster.

Gruen, A. (1987). *The insanity of normality: Realism as a sickness, toward understanding human destructiveness* (H. & H. Hannum, Trans.). New York: Grove Weidenfeld.

Hallie, P. P. (1979). *Lest innocent blood be shed: The story of the village of Le Chambon, and how goodness happened there.* New York: Harper & Row.

Hazlitt, W. (1995). On the pleasures of hating. In P. Lopate (Ed.), *The art of the personal essay: An anthology from the classical era to the present* (pp. 189–198). New York: Anchor Books. (Original work published 1826)

Herek, G. M., & Berrill, K. T. (Eds.). (1992). *Hate crimes: Confronting violence against lesbians and gay men.* Newbury Park, CA: Sage.

Hirondelle News Agency. (2002, October 15). Our journalists did make mistakes, admits founder member of "Hate-Radio." *Africa News.* Retrieved July 14, 2004, from LexisNexis database.

Kernberg, O. F. (1992). The psychopathology of hatred. In T. Shapiro & R. N. Emde (Eds.), *Affect: Psychoanalytic perspectives* (pp. 209–238). Madison, CT: International Universities Press.

Klein, M., & Riviere, J. (1964). *Love, hate and reparation.* New York: Norton.

Kressel, N. J. (1996). *Mass hate: The global rise of genocide and terror.* New York: Plenum Press.

Lawrence, F. M. (1999). *Punishing hate: Bias crimes under American law.* Cambridge, MA: Harvard University Press.

Lerner, M. J., & Whitehead, L. A. (1980). Procedural justice viewed in the context of justice motive theory. In G. Mikula (Ed.), *Justice and social interaction.* New York: Springer-Verlag.

MacDougall, W. (1923). *Social psychology* (15th ed.). Boston: John W. Luce.

Mamdani, M. (2001). *When victims become killers: Colonialism, nativism, and the genocide in Rwanda.* Princeton, NJ: Princeton University Press.

McBryde Johnson, H. (2003, February 16). Unspeakable conversations. *The New York Times Magazine,* pp. 50–55, 74, 78–79.

McCullum, H. (1997, April). Death by radio: The media's malignancy and neglect in Rwanda. *Track Two,* 6(1). Retrieved July 30, 2003, from http://ccrweb.ccr.uct.ac.za/two/2/p29.html

Midgley, M. (1984). *Wickedness: A philosophical essay.* London: Routledge & Kegan Paul.

Moore, D., & Aweiss, S. (2002). Hatred of "others" among Jewish, Arab, and Palestinian students in Israel. *Analyses of Social Issues and Public Policy,* 2(1), 151–172.

Moore, R. I. (1987). *The formation of a persecuting society*. Oxford, England: Basil Blackwell.

Moss, D. (Ed.). (2003). *Hating in the first person plural: Psychoanalytic essays on racism, homophobia, misogyny, and terror*. New York: Other Press.

Opotow, S. (1990). Moral exclusion and injustice: An introduction. *Journal of Social Issues, 46*(1), 1–20.

Opotow, S. (1991). Adolescent peer conflicts: Implications for students and for schools. *Education and Urban Society, 23*, 416–441.

Opotow, S. (1995). Drawing the line: Social categorization, moral exclusion, and the scope of justice. In B. B. Bunker & J. Z. Rubin (Eds.), *Conflict, cooperation, and justice* (pp. 347–369). San Francisco: Jossey-Bass.

Opotow, S. (2001a). Reconciliation in times of impunity: Challenges for social justice. *Social Justice Research, 14*(2), 149–170.

Opotow, S. (2001b). Social injustice. In D. J. Christie, R. V. Wagner, & D. D. Winter (Eds.), *Peace, conflict and violence: Peace psychology for the 21st century* (pp. 102–109). Upper Saddle River, NJ: Prentice Hall.

Pao, P. N. (1965). The role of hatred in the ego. *Psychoanalytic Quarterly, 34*, 257–264.

Popkin, M., & Bhuta, N. (1999). Latin American amnesties in comparative perspective: Can the past be buried? *Ethics and International Affairs, 13*, 99–122.

Prunier, G. (1995). *The Rwanda crisis 1959–1994: History of a genocide*. Kampala, Uganda: Fountain.

Rimer, S. (1995, April 27). New medium for the far right. *The New York Times*, pp. A1, A22.

Riviere, J. (1964). Hate, greed, and aggression. In M. Klein & J. Riviere (Eds.), *Love, hate and reparation* (pp. 3–53). New York: Norton.

Schoenewolf, G. (1994). Hate. In V. S. Ramachandran (Ed.), *The encyclopedia of human behavior* (pp. 501–508). New York: Academic Press.

Shriver, D. W. (1995). *An ethic for enemies: Forgiveness in politics*. New York: Oxford University Press.

Sidanius, J., Henry, P. J., Pratto, F., & Levin, S. (2002, April). *Why do they hate us so? The clash of civilizations or the politics of dominance?* (Working Paper 187). New York: Russell Sage Foundation.

Staub, E. (1989). *The roots of evil: Origins of genocide and other group violence*. New York: Cambridge University Press.

Staub, E. (1990). Moral exclusion, personal goal theory, and extreme destructiveness. *Journal of Social Issues, 46*(1), 47–64.

Tajfel, H. (Ed.). (1978). *Differentiation between social groups: Studies in the social psychology of intergroup relations*. New York: Academic Press.

Temple-Raston, D. (2002, September/October) Radio hate. *Legal Affairs*. Retrieved April 1, 2003, from http://www.legalaffairs.org/issues/September-October-2002/toc.html

Varma, V. (Ed.). (1993). *How and why children hate*. London: Jessica Kingsley.

Varshney, A. (2001). Ethnic conflicts and ancient hatreds: Cultural concerns. In N. J. Smelser & P. B. Baltes (Eds.), *International encyclopedia of the social and behavioral sciences* (pp. 4810–4813). Amsterdam: Elsevier.

Waller, J. (2002). *Becoming evil: How ordinary people commit genocide and mass killing*. New York: Oxford University Press.

Warren, D. (1996). *Radio priest: Charles Coughlin, the father of hate radio*. New York: Free Press.

Windrich, E. (2000, August). The laboratory of hate: The role of clandestine radio in the Angolan war. *International Journal of Cultural Studies, 3*(2), 206–218.

Winnicott, D. W. (1994). Hate in the countertransference. *Journal of Psychotherapy Practice and Research, 3*, 350–356.

Yanay, N. (2002). Understanding collective hatred. *Analyses of Social Issues and Public Policy, 2*(1), 53–60.

8

ON HATE AND ITS DETERMINANTS: SOME AFFECTIVE AND COGNITIVE INFLUENCES

LEONARD BERKOWITZ

hate: intense hostility and aversion usually deriving from fear, anger, or sense of injury . . . (*Merriam-Webster's Collegiate Dictionary*, 1993)

Those who are fear'd, are hated. (Benjamin Franklin, *Poor Richard's Almanack*, 1744)

Hate is no stranger to humankind. Most (or maybe all) people are capable of experiencing the "intense hostility and aversion" toward some entity that is characteristic of this emotion. Nevertheless, rather than deal with the various forms and full range of this all-too-common feeling, this chapter is concerned largely with what Gaylin (2003) termed "true" or "raw" hatred: "True haters," he observed, "live daily with their hatred. Their hatred is a way of life . . . They are obsessed with their enemies, attached to them in a paranoid partnership" (pp. 4–5). In Gaylin's view, the hatred they feel is a long-lasting enmity focused on some person or group that seeks the destruction of this target, more for the pleasure this will bring than for purposes of advantage, material gain, or revenge (see Gaylin, 2003, chap. 2).

But even more narrowly, I focus much of my attention on hate crimes, especially on the more extreme cases in which someone is deliberately killed because of his or her membership in a hated group. Hate crimes are typically differentiated from other types of crimes on the basis of the victim's group membership; the offense probably would not have occurred if he or she had not belonged to that particular group (see Steinberg, Brooks, & Remtulla, 2003). In this chapter I speculate about the factors that promote these assaults, including anger and its determinants, disinhibitory influences, and the personal characteristics (including the self-conceptions) of the bigots. In carrying out this task I try to show that ideas based to a considerable extent on experimental laboratory research can provide a valuable supplement to conceptions growing out of more naturalistic observations in helping us understand serious hate crimes.

I illustrate many of my points by looking at two horrendous instances of hate killings. I cannot say how representative these incidents are of other brutal hate-motivated murders, but they furnish concrete examples of the forces that may be at work in many of these violent crimes. Because of insufficient information about the personality characteristics of the people involved in these two incidents, much of my discussion of the personal qualities of "true haters," to use Gaylin's (2003) term, is based on observations of racism made in the United States.

TWO EXAMPLES OF HATE KILLINGS

The Murder of James Byrd Jr.

Early one morning in June 1998, in the small town of Jasper, Texas, three young White men gave a hitchhiker, James Byrd Jr., a middle-aged Black man, a ride in their pickup truck. Evidently spurred by one of them, the three Whites soon overpowered Mr. Byrd, beat him up, chained him to the back of the truck, and "dragged him three miles down a country road until his flayed and battered body was torn apart" (Lyman, 1999, p. 1).

The killers were friends and all from the bottom rungs of their east Texas society. Others who knew them described them "alternately as good boys and small-time criminals" (Bragg, 1998, p. 12). One of the three, 23-year-old Shawn Berry, a part-time mechanic and unsuccessful burglar, claimed that he had been forced to participate in the crime. The real instigator, he said, was John King, also 23 years of age, his partner in the failed burglary. Both King and the third killer were members of the "Confederate Knights of America, a racist group linked to the Ku Klux Klan" (Bragg, 1998, p. 12), but King apparently had been the one most determined to act on his hatred. The county prosecutor, noting that King was so full of racial hatred that his body was festooned with racist tattoos, maintained that the young man had been motivated partly by hostility toward Blacks and also by his desire to attract attention. He "had dreamed of forming his own chapter of a White supremacist group but felt he needed some dramatic event to catapult him into the limelight" and draw members (Lyman, 1999, p. 1).

The killing was so widely denounced that the Texas klaverns of the Klan insisted they had no connection with the three men. All were found guilty, and John King was sentenced to death.

Jedwabne

> JEDWABNE, Poland [Mar. 11, 2001]—The rough stone monument in this farming village shocks with its terse language: "Site of a massacre of Jews. Gestapo and Nazi soldiers burned 1,600 people."
>
> Now all Poland is being jolted awake to the awful reality: The Jews of Jedwabne were locked in a barn and burned to death on July 10, 1941, not by Nazis, but by their neighbors—fellow Poles" (Pasek, 2001, ¶ 1, 3).

Using eyewitness accounts and other evidence, Jan T. Gross, a Polish émigré and professor of Politics and European Studies at New York University, has laid out the grim details of this massacre in his 2001 book *Neighbors*. The story he tells is highly disturbing. According to Gross, "when the Nazi commanders moved into the eastern Polish village, they 'easily reached agreement' with town officials on what to do about the Jews" (cited by Pasek, 2001, ¶ 10). The newly occupying German army evidently had not compelled the massacre, but the local Poles were quick to seize the opportunity presented by their entry into the village. "Hundreds, including women and children, were soon brought into the town square. They were beaten with clubs and stones, then herded into a barn, which was locked and set ablaze" (cited by Pasek, 2001, ¶ 10). "The 1,600 Jedwabne Jews were murdered not by the Nazis or Soviets," Gross wrote, "but by the society" (cited by Pasek, 2001, ¶ 12). All but seven of the town's Jews were killed; the seven were saved by a Polish woman.

ISSUES TO BE DISCUSSED

These two incidents have some resemblance to other violent assaults on minority groups. Most hate crimes in the United States, like the murder of James Byrd Jr., are offenses against a person, often by multiple perpetrators who are apt to be young and male. The victim is attacked not as an individual, but because of his or her membership in a group that typically cannot be altered. The majority of these assaults target racial minorities, usually African Americans. And moreover, hate-motivated aggression is more likely to injure the victim seriously than are other attacks on a person (see Steinberg et al., 2003, for the statistics on which all these statements are based).

The Jedwabne killings unfortunately are also similar to other mass murders in which the victims are slaughtered because of their ethnic group membership. Most of these instances stem from religious differences, such as that between (to take only some examples) Shiite Muslims and Sunni Muslims in Iraq and Pakistan, Muslims and Hindus in India and Kashmir, Jews and Palestinians in the Mideast, Catholics and Protestants in Northern Ireland, and Christians and Muslims in the Balkans.

The two incidents I have singled out differ in a number of respects, of course, but it is worth considering their apparently common elements. The perpetrators in both cases obviously hated their victims. But why did they kill them? People commonly want to avoid those they say they hate, to want to have nothing further to do with them (Fitness & Fletcher, 1993), but in these—and many other—instances, the actors' intense feelings evidently impelled them to seek out and hurt, or even destroy, the objects of their emotion.

My supposition is that the brutal killings were impelled by a paroxysm of rage. Every hate crime is not necessarily spurred by anger, of course. In their review of bigotry-motivated offenses, Levin and McDevitt (1993) maintained that a great many of these crimes in the United States are actually efforts at thrill-seeking prompted by boredom. As several writers have pointed out (e.g., Baumeister, 1997; Waller, 2002), the offenses could also be acts of instrumental aggression brought about by considerations of self-interest. John King, who seemed to be primarily responsible for the Texas killing, could have believed that the murder would help him gain adherents to his White supremacy movement. On the basis of the FBI's investigation of skinhead groups in Southern California, Schafer and Navarro (2003) distinguished between instrumentally oriented and noninstrumental skinhead groups. Although both kinds of groups engaged in antiminority activities, at times at least some of them were primarily interested in for-profit criminal endeavors, whereas other groups were decidedly more strongly motivated by hate.

Nevertheless, murders such as those I have highlighted might well be propelled by intense anger, at least to some extent. It apparently is not uncommon for people belonging to extreme hate groups, especially the younger members, to display strong anger when they speak of racial and ethnic minorities and talk of how they would like to assault them brutally (see Ezekiel, 1995). One of my central tasks in this chapter is to suggest why this anger can be so intense in some instances that lives are taken.

But writers on hate (e.g., Fitness & Fletcher, 1993; Gaylin, 2003) typically maintain that this emotion is more than transitory anger or even temporary rage. According to Gaylin, "Rage, even murderous rage, is . . . short of hatred . . . Rage explodes; hatred festers and may also then explode" (pp. 61–62). Quoting Allport (1954), Gaylin held "that it is the sustained nature of hatred that distinguishes it from the volatile and often passing nature of anger" (p. 36). I suggest here that there is a strong but latent disposition to anger in the "festering" hatred. True haters, to use Gaylin's term, are not always emotionally aroused but can be easily and strongly angered when they encounter even the slightest of cues associated with the despised minority group. I also suspect they may be especially aroused by stimuli having to do with the relationship between this disliked out-group and their own in-group.

More than this, cognitive processes are obviously also involved in hatred. What role do these thoughts and beliefs have in generating and directing anger? Then, too, there is the question of the perpetrators' individual characteristics. Racism, by all reports, was pervasive in Jasper, but it was only the three young White men who carried out the racial crime; they evidently differed in important ways from the other White residents of the community. What about the people in Jedwabne who beat and then burned their Jewish neighbors? Social psychology as a discipline is very inclined to assume that the surrounding situation exerts an exceedingly powerful influence on one's conduct and that therefore, if the circumstances are right, almost anyone can become a bigoted persecutor of "different" others (Waller, 2002; see also Berkowitz, 1999). Was this the case in Jedwabne? Were the perpetrators, presumably like so many other people contributing to the Holocaust, only "ordinary men" (Browning, 1992)? What about the cultural context within which all of these persons were embedded? Broader societal attitudes and values undoubtedly can also contribute to intergroup hostility, at least by permitting—or at times inhibiting—their aggression, and something should be said about this kind of general influence.

The discussion in this chapter is in some respects in accord with Smith's conceptualization of prejudice (Smith, 1993; also see Mackie, Devos, & Smith, 2000), although I place greater emphasis on individual-level determinants. The present formulation views prejudice (in its negative sense, of course) as a disposition to react with a negative emotion, largely anger, to the thought or sight of a particular group or its symbols. The negative beliefs and attitudes regarding this entity are presumably a concomitant of the anger, sometimes facilitating the development of the group's ability to evoke anger-related feelings and ideas and sometimes an outgrowth of the elicited anger. Pettigrew and Meertens (1995) highlighted the importance of intense negative feelings in strong prejudice. Distinguishing between "blatant" (very strong) and "subtle" (much weaker) forms of prejudice against immigrants in several western European countries, they found that the extreme prejudice was accompanied by intense negative affect, whereas the much milder bigotry was generally associated only with the absence of positive feelings.

The particular group is hated, I suggest, when it has acquired the capacity to elicit intense anger and when the beliefs accompanying this feeling maintain that this strong negative feeling is warranted. This sense that an assault on the despised group is justified is at least partly due to the haters' hostility in itself. Feeling angry, wanting to hurt the people who disturb them so much, the haters, as Allport (1954) observed, almost inevitably fault the target of their enmity. For Gaylin (2003), the true haters have a paranoid-like view of those they detest. Whatever harm is done to people in this group, the haters think the group deserves it (see also Smith, 1993; Mackie et al., 2000).

A primary task in the present analysis of hate, then, is to account for the reasons why a particular collection of people generates such strong anger. The exposition I offer will look at a number of affective and cognitive influences that can contribute to the development of such an intense feeling. These two classes of determinants are considered somewhat separately, even though, of course, I realize such a distinction between affect and cognition is frequently highly artificial.

SOME AFFECTIVE INFLUENCES
ON AGGRESSION AND HATE KILLINGS

Guiding Formulation

My analysis in this discussion of affective influences generally assumes that the true haters' strong latent disposition to anger is partly a function of their relatively frequent past exposure to aversive occurrences. I also suggest that one can profitably understand some of the consequences of these often-encountered negative events in terms of my cognitive–neoassociationistic (CNA) model of anger arousal (e.g., Berkowitz, 1993, 2003). CNA basically proposes that any strong negative affect, usually experienced as great distress, initially gives rise to feelings, thoughts, memories, and motor impulses associatively linked together in an anger–affective aggression syndrome, as well as a set of affective and cognitive reactions associated with a fear–flight syndrome (perhaps among other syndromes). A host of factors—genetic, learned, and situational—govern the relative dominance of these different emotional constellations. The model also maintains that several syndromes can be activated at the same time, although to different degrees. In this mixture, fear would be dominant over anger when there is the sense of overwhelming danger, whereas anger is apt to be the prominent emotion in the absence of clear signs of great danger to the person. Appraisals, as well as one's interpretive schemes, social rules, and anticipated costs and benefits, presumably come into play quickly after these relatively "primitive" reactions, but only to the extent that the persons engage in higher-order cognitive processing.

For me, one of the intriguing, and challenging, aspects of this formulation has to do with the effects of fear arousal. CNA suggests that even when fear is clearly the dominant emotion and the frightened person is mainly oriented toward escaping from the dangerous situation, the anger–affective aggression syndrome has also been activated to some degree, though it is "submerged" by the stronger fear–flight constellation of reactions. The anger–affective aggression syndrome can become apparent when the danger seems to lessen—or often, as the cornered rat phenomenon indicates, when escape is no longer possible. I return to this presumed effect of fear arousal in my discussion of the affective contributors to hate.

All in all, then, CNA proposes that a wide variety of aversive occurrences can promote anger and contribute to hate, even when these incidents have little if any bearing on the person's self-concept. I have reviewed research consistent with this contention elsewhere (e.g., Berkowitz, 2003), but unfortunately there's little direct evidence that non-self-threatening negative affect can enhance prejudice and hate. Still, my general assumption here, as I said earlier, is that the inclination to react with strong anger to a relevant cue is a positive function of the frequency with which one has previously experienced decidedly unpleasant events.

Selection of a Minority as a Target for Hate

The first question in any analysis of antiminority hatred has to be why certain groups are the target for intense hostility rather than others. In the United States, African Americans, Jews, gays, and nowadays Muslims are much more likely to be victimized by hate crimes than, for example, people from Scotland or Russia. Gaylin (2003) held that true hatred involves "an obsessive extended relationship to a perceived enemy" (p. 62). Why does this particular relationship come about?

Various theories have been offered to account for this selectivity (e.g., see Adorno, Frenkel-Brunswick, Levinson, & Sanford, 1950; Allport, 1954; Brewer & Brown, 1998; Burleigh, 1997; Dovidio & Gaertner, 1986; Gaylin, 2003; Naimark, 2001; Wistrich & Jordan, 1991). Although these accounts provide many important insights, in my view most of the points they make can be subsumed under one significant general principle: They all provide reasons why the particular group is greatly disliked. Put another way, these formulations indicate why that minority acquired a strongly negative cue value. Whatever else might result from this decidedly unpleasant group quality, I suggest that it facilitates the generalization of hostility aroused by other sources to that particular collection of people.[1]

A number of experiments have reported findings consistent with this last-mentioned proposition. In one of the earliest of these studies (Berkowitz

---

[1]This suggestion, that particular groups are selected as targets for displaced hostility because they are disliked, obviously runs the risk of being a great oversimplification and even a tautology. Comprehensive analyses of anti-Semitism, and of bigotry in general, surely must go well beyond such a general proposition (e.g., see Burleigh, 1997; Gaylin, 2003; Naimark, 2001; Wistrich & Jordan, 1991).

& Holmes, 1960), the female participants were first induced to either dislike or have a neutral attitude toward a peer and then were either insulted or treated in a neutral manner by the experimenter. When all of the women were then given an opportunity to deliver electric shocks to their peer, supposedly as an evaluation of her work on a task, those who had been provoked by the experimenter administered the severest punishment to the person they had earlier learned to dislike. This latter individual's negative cue value apparently had enhanced her ability to draw the hostility engendered by the provocateur.

Other examples of this kind of hostility generalization are provided by Pedersen and Miller's studies of "triggered" hostility displacement. In one experiment (Pedersen, Gonzales, & Miller, 2000), some of the research participants first were provoked (or not) by one individual and then encountered another person who acted in a slightly annoying (or neutral) manner. Where the mildly bothersome second person evoked only a relatively low level of hostility from the nonprovoked participants, those who had been deliberately angered by the provocateur earlier directed a comparatively high level of hostility to this slightly annoying person. According to Pedersen and his colleagues, this latter target's mildly negative quality had triggered the aggression elicited just before by the provocation. (Or to look at this another way, the hostility evoked by the previous strong insults had generalized to the person having a negative cue value.) In keeping with CNA, the enmity toward the annoying second person was a direct function of the displeasure he had evoked rather than of the participants' appraisal of his behavior as "wrong."

SOME SOURCES OF NEGATIVE AFFECT

Fear as a Possible Contributor to Hate

The two quotations given at the beginning of this chapter both reflect that people frequently come to hate those they fear. Gaylin (2003) also made this point in his discussion of hatred. After observing that fear and anger are usually "inextricably intertwined" (p. 38), he maintained that "rage is the public face of fear in most men and many women. The two can be considered as opposite sides of the same coin" (p. 46). My CNA model of anger arousal takes a basically similar position, as I said earlier. Unfortunately, there is little direct evidence from research with humans indicating that frightening events can also instigate aggression, although findings obtained in animal experiments on pain-elicited aggression appear suggestive (e.g., Hutchinson, 1983; Ulrich, 1966). Research with animals also supports the occurrence of the cornered rat phenomenon: Although pained animals frequently prefer to avoid or escape from the aversive situation rather than attack an available target, they are especially apt to assault a suitable target when they do not know how to get away from the pain source (Hutchinson, 1983).

However inadequate any direct support for the notion that fear and anger are "inextricably intertwined," there is still some reason to believe that at least two of the most frequently hated minorities in the United States, African Americans and Jews, are often considered dangerous and thus may well be feared by those who despise them. The idea of Blacks as dangerous appears widespread in U.S. society,[2] and racists could well be especially inclined to think of Blacks as a fearful enemy. In his interviews with the members of a Detroit neo-Nazi group, Ezekiel (2002) gained a definite impression of their underlying fear: "At an unspoken but deep level, the members seemed to feel extremely vulnerable, that their lives might be snuffed out at any time like a match flame in the wind" (p. 58). These people tended to enter the White supremacist group with an existing prejudice against Blacks, but the group's ideology strengthened this enmity by, among other things, telling them that Black men wanted to rape White women and that the extremist movement represented Whites in a struggle against Blacks (Ezekiel, 2002). White supremacist ideology pictures Jews as even more threatening. Because of their control of the media, their great influence on government, their money, and their communism, Jews are seen as the ones leading the effort to destroy the White race (Ezekiel, 2002). Nazi ideology was even more relentless. For Hitler and his adherents, as one historian put it, "The 'Jew' was a force of almost cosmic malevolence" who "stood behind such diverse modern phenomena as capitalism or Russian Bolshevism" (Burleigh, 1997, p. 158). Jews were even biologically dangerous, according to Nazi ideology. They "directly threatened the survival of German men and women" by seducing and impregnating "innocent German girls . . . spreading syphilis and other sexually communicated diseases wherever they went" (Naimark, 2001, p. 59). With so much evil power at their disposal, the stereotypic Jews were to be feared—and destroyed.

Unpleasant Physical Conditions

As I indicated earlier, my guiding theoretical analysis (e.g., Berkowitz, 1993, 2003) maintains that intensely disturbing negative affect can activate anger-related feelings, thoughts, and actions even when the persons affected do not attribute their displeasure to an external agent's malevolence and they have little reason to think their self-value has been diminished. There

---

[2]Suggesting the pervasiveness of the underlying view that Blacks could be dangerous, Donnerstein and Donnerstein (1976, p. 137) found that when White college students were individually paired with a Black student and could receive electric shocks from this person, they typically expected that the Black would shock them more severely than a White student would and, furthermore, that the Black's punishment of them would be more severe than the punishment they would give the Black.

is some suggestive evidence of such an effect in the studies of the race riots of almost two generations ago. Following up on some earlier investigations (see Berkowitz, 1993, p. 52), Carlsmith and Anderson (1979) ascertained what the temperatures had been during the many instances of collective violence in the United States between 1967 and 1971. Presumably because even illegal mob actions by Blacks seemed to be legitimated both by the protests many African Americans were voicing at that time and by the other racial disorders that had taken place around the country, quite a few urban disorders broke out in Black neighborhoods during this period. But this rioting was especially likely to erupt on unpleasantly hot days, whereas the end of the heat waves apparently helped "cool things off," literally and figuratively, so that the riots then came to an end. Somehow, with the social conditions right for this to happen, the unusually uncomfortable weather evidently activated assaults on the established societal order.

Social psychology has provided quite a few other demonstrations of hot temperature–evoked anger and aggression (see Anderson & Anderson, 1998). If further corroboration is required, it can be found in Shakespeare's *Romeo and Juliet*, when Romeo urges his friend to withdraw from a potentially dangerous situation:

> I pray thee, good Mercutio, let's retire;
> The day is hot, the Capulets abroad.
> And, if we meet, we shall not 'scape a brawl,
> For now, these hot days, is the mad blood stirring.

(3.1.1–4)

Hostility Displacement

Hostility displacement, which undoubtedly has some role in the development of many instances of prejudice and hatred (Berkowitz, 1959, 1993; Hovland & Sears, 1940), can also be seen as an example of negative affect–induced enmity toward people not responsible for the affect arousal. The previously cited findings obtained by Pedersen et al. (2000) can also be looked at this way.

Other research suggests that characteristically highly prejudiced persons are especially apt to exhibit this kind of hostility generalization. One of my early experiments (Berkowitz, 1959) took advantage of the relative freedom many Midwestern college students felt at that time to express prejudiced opinions openly. After the female participants had been deliberately derogated by the experimenter, those who had highly anti-Semitic attitudes tended to be the most hostile toward a neutral woman nearby.

A somewhat different kind of affective generalization conceivably could have operated in the two cases I am giving special attention to. Maybe the perpetrators had been greatly aroused by what was happening around them at the time (the Texas killers by a night of drinking, the villagers in

Jedwabne by the war and the German army's victorious sweep into their community). This excitation (Bower, 1981) might have then intensified the anger primed by the sight of the hated minority (e.g., Mr. Byrd in the former instance and the Jews in the latter case) so that there was an explosion of violence. The assaults might also have been fueled by an undercurrent of anger and resentment growing out of the economic privations and resulting humiliations the attackers had experienced over the past years.

The Possible Role of Economic Frustrations

The aversive experiences linked to economic hardships obviously can do serious damage to the affected persons' self-concepts. Those who have been laid off, are underemployed in one way or another, or have a low income may come to see themselves as undervalued and as held in low regard by the others around them—and this often hurts, at least psychologically. The consequence can be an inclination to aggression and other forms of antisocial behavior, especially if no punishment for this behavior is anticipated (e.g., Catalano, Novaco, & McConnell, 1997). Although a number of studies indicate that the persons who commit hate crimes are not especially likely to be economically frustrated or even doubtful about their future financial well-being (American Psychological Association, 1998; Steinberg et al., 2003), this does not mean that economic privations have no role in crime generally. Economic troubles and other social stresses and strains can help generate a proclivity to a range of antisocial actions (Berkowitz, 2003; see also Wilson & Herrnstein, 1985, for another view). Emotionally aroused people having such a readiness to engage in antisocial conduct might then assault a hated minority under the right circumstances—for example (as could have happened in the murder of James Byrd), when a helpless member of that group is before them, alcohol has dissolved their inhibitions, and they believe their action will not be punished.

A classic investigation approximately 6 decades ago even suggested that financial difficulties can lead to brutal hate killings under some circumstances. In their test of the generality of the frustration–aggression analysis, Hovland and Sears (1940) reported that during the period covered by their data, sudden drops in the market value of cotton in the U.S. South were often closely followed by a rise in the number of Blacks lynched in that part of the country. With their well-being seriously hurt by the unexpected decline in the cotton market, the Whites dependent on this crop for their livelihood had presumably become very resentful, even angry, and they apparently had displaced their hostility onto Blacks who they believed had seriously violated their communities' norms. However, a later close examination of these data highlights a very important qualification. Green, Glaser, and Rich (1998) showed that the cotton price–lynching relationship held only for the time up to the Great Depression, but not afterward. And moreover, on extending their investigation to the effects of economic difficulties on nonlethal hate crimes, Green et al. (1998) found that unemployment rates in New York City in the decade before their study had no relationship to the number of reported hate crimes against homosexuals, Jews, Blacks, and Asians during that period. All in all, it could be that when people experience economic frustrations and other social stresses, they openly direct their resulting aggressive urges onto disliked minority groups only if they think that others important to them, their in-groups, will not disapprove of these assaults. Such widely shared attitudes condoning the lynching of Blacks might have diminished sufficiently in the rural South by the late 1930s so that angered Whites felt less free to take the law into their own hands, and only a relatively few New Yorkers might have possessed such aggression-approving attitudes in the 1980s and 1990s.

Perceived Injustice

A deep feeling of injustice frequently contributes to the hate purveyors' abiding resentments. As Gaylin (2003) saw it, a number of White working-class persons were drawn to White supremacy movements in the last half of the 20th century as they increasingly came to believe that traditional values were changing rapidly and that old rules were somehow no longer appropriate. "Members of this group began to feel deceived and treated unfairly" (Gaylin, 2003, p. 49; see also Steinberg et al., 2003, p. 983). Even worse, Gaylin believed, the Great Society legislation of the 1960s creating welfare programs and affirmative action policies on behalf of minorities led the resentful Whites to think that these minorities were receiving benefits they did not deserve. Some investigators of racist groups (e.g., Ezekiel, 2002) have reported that White supremacists tend to have a more general sense of injustice and threat. In their perception of the world, according to Ezekiel (2002), Whites "are losing ground [relative to Jews and Blacks], the world is changing, and [they themselves] may not do well in the world" (p. 54).

Anti-Semitism clearly is often grounded in a sense of injustice. The archetypical example of the charge that Jews were engaged in illegitimate, even immoral, conduct was the infamous forgery, The Protocols of the Elders of Zion, promulgated by the Russian secret service at the start of the 20th century. Here, dramatically, was the indictment that Jews were wrongly and secretly seeking world domination. The same conspiracy theory was a central feature of the Nazis' anti-Semitic ideology (e.g., Koch, 1975, p. 117). "International Jewry," it was stridently maintained, was trying to enslave the German people. The "money power" of the banks, of "international financiers"—of Jews—wanted to push "true Germans" against the wall and control them. Polish anti-Semitism expressed a very similar view, especially during the period between the two World Wars (Orlet, 2001). Quite a few Poles (although perhaps mostly in the rural areas such as Jedwabne) insisted that Jews caused the war and that even though "most Jews were Communist sympathizers," they had become "rich by taking advantage of poor, hard-working peasants" (Orlet, 2001).

Because of this deep sense of injustice, almost paranoid-like in their ideation (according to Gaylin, 2003), the haters believe they are entitled to rectify the wrong done to them and "their kind" by striking at the offending minority. In their minds, this aggression is even morally proper (Steinberg et al., 2003). The neo-Nazis and Ku Klux Klan members interviewed by Ezekiel (2002) exemplified this kind of thinking by insisting that the White race was in a struggle for supremacy with Blacks, Jews, and other minorities, that they were the only Whites who really understood this, and that they had to fight the enemy to maintain the White people's position in the social order. Orlet (2001) quoted an old Polish peasant voicing a similar senti-ment by maintaining that Poles had to fight Jews because Jews were trying to rule them.

Threats to the Self-Concept

Threats to one's self-concept are usually very wounding and are there-fore especially likely to produce an angry reaction. This is, of course, a fre-quent theme in appraisal accounts of anger generation. Lazarus (1991), for example, held that people are angered when they appraise an occurrence as a "demeaning offense" against some significant aspect of themselves.

I go into this proposition more intensively later when I give greater at-tention to cognitive influences on hate and hateful behavior, but it is worth noting here one version of this general line of thought: Explanations of the relatively high rate of homicides in the U.S. South that attribute the vio-lence to a "culture of honor" (e.g., Nisbett & Cohen, 1996[3]) basically also see the aggression as a response to a threatened self-concept. As a case in point, Nisbett and Cohen (p. 31) found that Southerners were more likely than their Northern counterparts to say that a person would not be "much of a man" if he did not seriously attack someone who had endangered his or his family's honor. Southern culture somehow leads many of its White men to regard their honor as closely linked to their conception of themselves as tough, manly, and well able to protect themselves, their families, and others of their own kind. A challenge to their honor, to their image of themselves as a person not to be trifled with, is evidently apt to induce anger. They also are very likely to believe that the most appropriate recourse is to show how manly they are by attacking the offender (Nisbett & Cohen, 1996, pp. 50–

---

[3]The Nisbett and Cohen (1996) thesis of a Southern "culture of honor" is one variation of the concep-tion, well known in criminology and sociology, of "subcultures of violence" (e.g., Wolfgang & Ferracuti, 1967), maintaining that some segments within the larger society possess attitudes and values that prescribe violence as the appropriate response to a demeaning offense.

53).[4] As one manifestation of this set of beliefs, Nisbett and Cohen (p. 31) additionally found that Southern Whites also tended to think that sexual affronts by another man were a particularly grievous challenge to one's honor and demanded a "manly" violent reaction. It is not surprising, then, that quite a few of the Blacks who were lynched in the pre-World War II South were accused of having sexually assaulted a White woman.

Some discussions of hate also bring up the idea of a damaged self-concept by speaking of the perpetrators' felt humiliation. In Fitness and Fletcher's (1993) investigation of emotions in close relationships, hate was frequently elicited by the sense of having been betrayed or humiliated by one's partner. Gaylin's (2003) analysis of hatred places particular emphasis on the importance of this felt humiliation and suggests that the perception of having been betrayed leads to hate only to the extent that the betrayal is regarded as a humiliation.

This notion of hate arising from a feeling of humiliation and a perceived threat to one's self-concept does not necessarily mean that the hater is generally low in self-esteem. A recent flurry of research, largely prompted by Baumeister and Bushman (e.g., Baumeister, Smart, & Boden, 1996; Bushman & Baumeister, 1998), has seriously questioned the widespread belief that many highly aggressive people are easily provoked to violence because of their characteristically poor image of themselves. These investigations indicate that it is the threat to a grandiose self-concept (narcissism or what Baumeister and Bushman termed "egotism"), and not a further reduction of already low self-esteem, that produces the aggressive reaction. This conception is discussed more fully later when I take up the matter of the personality characteristics linked to persistent hatred.

SOME COGNITIVE INFLUENCES

I now turn to clearly cognitive influences on prejudice and hate. In this section I discuss some factors that enhance enmity and then look briefly at several psychological conditions that can lower biased people's restraints against engaging in an attack on the hated minority.

Categorization and In-Group Centrism

As psychologists are well aware, people readily use salient cues to classify those they encounter into comparatively few categories, particularly if

---

[4]Although Nisbett and Cohen (1996) had expected a public affront to be more upsetting than a private one, because they thought the humiliation would then be more of a blow to the person's public reputation, their research findings indicated that a nonpublic insult was just as bothersome as a clearly open affront (p. 53). The threat known only to the person himself obviously challenged that individual's "manly" conception of himself.

these others are not familiar as distinct individuals (Brewer & Brown, 1998; Fiske & Taylor, 1991). Research initiated by Tajfel several decades ago (see Tajfel, 1981) has demonstrated that people are particularly likely to use whatever information is available to categorize themselves and those around them into "our kind," those similar to them—their in-group—and those different from them—an out-group. Perhaps because persons highly prejudiced against a particular out-group are often quick to think about that group, if situational cues indicate that this group might be present, these bigoted people are especially likely to believe that the unknown and ambiguous nearby individuals could well belong to that negative out-group (Brewer & Brown, 1998, especially pp. 557–558).

More than this, highly prejudiced persons might also exhibit yet another exaggerated aspect of the categorization process. Generally speaking, in establishing the different categories, the perceivers often accentuate the differences they believe exist among these groupings: Those placed together, say, as the in-group, are regarded as having many similar qualities; those classified as the out-group are also seen as alike in important respects, and—what is especially significant—the in-group is viewed as very different from these "other people" (Fiske & Taylor, 1991). And so extremely bigoted persons often automatically think that those strangers they place together in the same disliked social grouping have the unfavorable qualities they stereotypically associate with that category (Fiske, 2002),[5] and that these others have comparatively little in common with their own in-group. For anti-Black racists, African Americans are very apt to be lazy, ostentatious, and dangerously animal-like, whereas anti-Semites generally view Jews as intelligent, shrewd, and unscrupulous. White supremacists typically regard Jews as far more dangerous than Blacks or Hispanics because of these particular "Jewish" characteristics (Ezekiel, 1995). The Polish stereotype, evidently prevalent in Jedwabne, maintained that Jews were also God-killers, rich, Communists, and exploiters of the poor (Orlet, 2001). Nazi ideology was even more extreme, insisting that "the Jew was a liar, a dissembler, a sponger, and a parasite . . . and no amount of assimilation could alter the eternal, fundamental evil carried in the blood of the Jewish race" (Naimark, 2001, pp. 58–59).

Adding to the potential difficulties in the relations between in-group and out-group, self-serving attributions frequently lead to a favorable interpretation of one's fellow group members' behavior whereas the other peoples' conduct is often viewed less kindly (Brewer & Brown, 1998). From the perceivers' perspective, as Fiske and Taylor (1991) put it, "Our group's failures are due to external circumstances beyond our control [such as the unscrupulous actions of Jews]; their group's failures [for example, the high

---

[5]Fiske (2002) noted that people with little prejudice against a particular minority group, in comparison to their more bigoted peers, can more readily "compensate for their automatic associations [to that category] with . . . conscious effort" (p. 124).

rate of poverty among Blacks] show how incompetent they really are" (p. 134). For those persons with a strong dislike for a particular minority, negative attributions disparaging that out-group can then easily operate (Fiske, 2002). If many Blacks are poor or unemployed, the racists blame them; "it's their own fault; they're lazy." When Jewish homes and stores were vandalized by street gangs before the war, the Polish anti-Semites said they had brought this on themselves. (It is interesting, perhaps partly because of their relatively great need to lessen the perceived uncertainty in the world about them [Jost, Glaser, Kruglanski, & Sulloway, 2003], that political conservatives seem to be more likely than their liberal counterparts to contend that victims of unfortunate circumstances, such as poverty or theft, are themselves largely responsible for their condition [see Quist & Wiegand, 2002, for citations].)

In-group centrism (ethnocentrism in many cases) can also produce a pervasive inclination to favor the in-group over the out-group in the distribution of valued resources (Tajfel, 1981), and this can occur, furthermore, even when the perceiver and in-group will not benefit from the favoritism (Turner, Brown, & Tajfel, 1979). It is not altogether clear why this kind of pro–own group bias arises (see Brewer & Brown, 1998). Extending the original conception of personal self-identity that had been advanced by Tajfel (e.g., 1981) and Turner (e.g., 1985), I suggest that people often regard their in-group as closely tied to their personal image of themselves so that in discriminating in favor of their "own kind," they essentially are favoring themselves (see also Fiske & Taylor, 1991). However, more recent theoretical conceptions, offered by Tajfel and Turner (1986) and also favored by writers such as Smith (1993), give greater emphasis to group attachments and intergroup relations. Tajfel and Turner proposed that the discrimination in favor of one's in-group is prompted by a desire to establish an advantage for one's own kind over the others—to make one's in-group "positively distinctive" relative to the out-group.

Nazi ideology essentially sought an extreme version of such a positive distinctiveness for Germany. Based in large part on a primitive Darwinism, this doctrine insisted on the reality of relatively sharp racial differences and held that the "Aryan race"—Germans—deserved far more than did inferior groups such as the Slavs (Burleigh, 1997, p. 156; Naimark, 2001) and could even properly expel these latter people from lands they had occupied for centuries.[6] More pertinent to my present interests, White supremacists, such as James Byrd's three killers, evidently desire this kind of positive distinction for what they regard as their "race." Ezekiel (2002) noted that quite a few of the neo-Nazis and Klansmen he interviewed maintained that "Whites

---

[6]M. Mann (2000) cited statistics attesting to the atrocities visited on the supposedly racially inferior Slavs: The Germans were estimated to have killed 3 million Polish and 7 million Soviet noncombatants, as well as 3.3 million Soviet prisoners of war (p. 332).

are civilization builders who have created our modern world" and that God had intended Whites to dominate and rule the other races (p. 53). Only they, Ezekiel also observed, understood that Whites were losing their "true" position in society (p. 54). In Runciman's (1966) terminology, one could say that these White racists experienced a fraternal relative deprivation—they believed that their own kind was not doing as well, relative to the out-groups, as they deserved. They themselves, as individuals, were undervalued and deprived of many of the good things of life, but much more than this, their in-group, Whites in general, were losing out in competition with the undeserving (and even, in the case of Jews especially, malevolent) out-groups. Fixing responsibility on these other people for the various deprivations they were suffering, their prejudice and bigotry became even more intense (see also Gaylin, 2003).

Disinhibitory Influences

Social Norms

The anger-instigating conditions I have discussed in this chapter obviously do not always lead directly to an open attack on hated individuals. Even highly aroused persons can restrain themselves and turn away rather than assault the one who had provoked them. These inhibitions frequently arise because of widespread cultural or group attitudes frowning on aggression. Just as the Southern "culture of honor" evidently calls on its adherents to react violently to offenses they view as demeaning, people in other parts of the United States (and the world) apparently have widely shared attitudes and values that discourage the use of aggression in altercations. Nisbett and Cohen (1996, p. 16) showed, for example, that the homicide rate for Whites residing in the smaller cities (populations below 200,000) of New England is much lower than the rate for their White counterparts living in the same-size cities in other regions of the country, especially the South. The culture in these smaller New England communities seems to be especially strong in restraining assaults on others with whom one has an interpersonal difficulty.

Of course, other parts of the country, including the South, also possess such aggression-inhibiting attitudes and values in some degree, and nowhere is it legally permissible for private persons to deliberately inflict serious physical harm on another individual with whom one has a dispute. Yet these aggression-discouraging legal and cultural restraints do not always govern what people actually do.

The killers involved in the two crimes I have singled out could have believed that their murderous actions would not be condemned by their peers. In the Texas case, not only was racism pervasive in the community (Bragg, 1998), but John King, the main instigator of the brutal slaying, knew of another instance in which Whites charged with murdering a Black man had been acquitted by an all-White jury (Lyman, 1999). He could have thought that many of the people in his community would accept his action, tacitly anyway. The American Psychological Association's (1998) online report on hate crimes noted that quite a few persons committing these offenses believe they have societal permission to assault the minorities they despise. And similarly, observers have acknowledged that a far-reaching and even obsessive anti-Semitism in Poland between the two World Wars, particularly in nationalistic circles, probably contributed to the Jedwabne atrocity (Majman, 2001; Orlet, 2001) by telling the Polish villagers that Jews were largely to blame for their troubles and by allowing them to assault their Jewish neighbors.

Anonymity and Deindividuation

Violence-inhibiting social norms and laws are backed up to a considerable extent by the threat of public disapproval and, in some cases, the possibility of legal punishment. Circumstances that minimize this likelihood of retribution can then allow angry people to act on their aggressive urges. One such condition, obviously, is *anonymity*, the person's sense that he or she is not known to any onlookers and the public at large. Social scientists have long noted how people in crowds, each believing that he or she cannot be individually identified in the midst of so many others, can depart from socially approved standards of conduct. This feeling of anonymity arising from immersion in a group may be one reason why, as I mentioned before, so many hate crimes are carried out by multiple offenders (Steinberg et al., 2003).

Clothing can also help produce a sense of anonymity; uniforms cloak individual differences and create the impression that everyone in the situation is alike, and of course masks and hoods literally prevent individual identification. In social psychology, Zimbardo (1969) provided the best-known illustration of how this latter type of anonymity can permit the expression of aggressive inclinations. Using small groups of ordinarily well-mannered female undergraduates as his participants, Zimbardo greatly heightened some of the groups' sense of anonymity by dressing each member in identity-hiding baggy white coats and hoods and having them carry out their assignment in the dark. The women in the other groups, by contrast, were made to feel individually highly conspicuous by giving them large name tags, requiring them to use each others' first names in their conversations, and having them work under bright lights. When the people in both "treatments" were asked to give a fellow student electric shocks, those administering the shocks in the anonymity condition were more punitive than were their individually identifiable peers. What we have here, in a way, is a simulation of a Ku Klux Klan nighttime assault on an innocent victim. Klan members, feeling safe from detection and punishment because of their protective hoods and gowns and the cover of darkness, may also feel freer to attack those they hate.

All of this is quite commonsensical. But when social psychologists, including Zimbardo (1969) and others (e.g., Diener, 1980), looked closely at this state of anonymity, they concluded that the reduced inhibitions may be due to more than the lowered possibility of being publicly identified. Speaking of *deindividuation* and extending the research into the consequences of self-attention (e.g., Wicklund, 1975), growing numbers of investigators now propose that the disinhibition may also reflect a lack of self-regulation caused by the diversion of attention away from the self. According to the theorizing advanced by Prentice-Dunn and Rogers (1982, 1989), as an example, emotionally aroused persons in the midst of, say, a large crowd will be affected by two types of cues: those defining their level of accountability and attention modifiers. The former cues indicate that these persons are anonymous—not identifiable by the others around them.

Theoretically, the consequence is that their public self-awareness would then be low so that they would give little if any consideration to how their actions look to others. Attention modifiers, on the other hand, affect the extent to which the persons focus on themselves and their personal attitudes and values. If they are submerged in a large crowd with lots of things happening around them, their attention could well be drawn outward, away from themselves, so that they do not regulate their behavior in terms of their personal values and beliefs. In this deindividuated state, they may even follow the crowd in engaging in illegal or antisocial conduct. Consistent with this analysis, when Prentice-Dunn and Rogers (1982) manipulated both accountability cues and attention modifiers in a laboratory experiment, they found that both the participants' low level of concern about their public image and their low level of self-attention led to relatively strong attacks on a neutral target person (also see L. Mann, Newton, & Innes, 1982, for supporting evidence).

Much the same kind of reasoning could contribute to an understanding of lynch mobs. Mullen (1986) proposed that when emotionally aroused people in a crowd encounter one or more individuals who might be a target for their aggressive inclinations, the degree of restraining self-attention experienced by each crowd member is an inverse function of the "Other–Total Ratio"—the number of possible victims relative to the total number of people in the situation (i.e., potential victims plus crowd members). An example would be an angry mob of Whites in a rural community in the U.S. South before World War II facing a few Black men who they believe had raped a White woman. The smaller the number of Black men and the larger the number of Whites, the less likely it would presumably be that each person in the mob would consider his or her personal standards and ideals (usually in opposition to antisocial behavior). The lower this Other–Total Ratio, then, the more deindividuated the aroused Whites would be and thus the greater the chances that they would assault the Blacks, even when the attack was illegal.

To test this formulation, Mullen (1986) used a collection of newspaper reports of the lynching of Blacks by Whites in the period between 1899 and 1946 to calculate the Other–Total Ratios in 60 of these cases and also to establish an index of the savagery of the lynching (based on whether the victims were mutilated, dismembered, tortured, and the like). He found that the greater the presumed level of deindividuation in the mob (i.e., the smaller the ratio), the more atrocious was the killing, even when the analysis employed only the number of lynchers or only the number of victims.

The slaughter of the Jews of Jedwabne could conceivably have been facilitated by a similar deindividuation process. Each of the Polish villagers in the crowd attacking their Jewish neighbors could have been so carried away by the sights and sounds of what was happening, and especially by their own frenzied excitement, that they failed to think about their humane values and Christian beliefs calling for love and compassion toward others. Hate and the actions of the others around them controlled their behavior. James Byrd's Texan killers may also have experienced a decreased behavior-regulating self-attention as they assaulted their victim. Shortly after the men picked up Mr. Byrd, they stopped their truck at a clearing, drank a great deal of beer, and then beat up the helpless Black man and tied him to the truck bumper (Lyman, 1999). The alcohol they had consumed could well have lessened their self-consciousness (Hull, Levenson, Young, & Sher, 1983) to the point that they not only did not think of whatever values they possessed opposing murder, but also failed to realize they were leaving a great many self-incriminating clues at the death scene (Lyman, 1999).

Dehumanization

Less subtle than the deindividuation process, but perhaps more important, a dehumanization effect undoubtedly also contributed to the mass killings in Jedwabne and maybe to the Texas murder as well. Kelman and Hamilton (1989, cited in Waller, 2002, p. 245) believed that this dehumanization occurred in two steps: first, robbing the persons of their individual identities by defining them solely in terms of their membership in an ethnic or racial category—only as "Jews" or "Blacks"—and second, excluding them from the community of humans. Both of these steps had been applied to the Jewish citizens of Poland as well as Germany (as well as elsewhere in Europe) before World War II (Orlet, 2001). Extremely nationalistic and even strongly Catholic groups in Poland were almost obsessively preoccupied by the so-called Jewish issue before the onset of World War II and were quick to label even some of the most distinguished people in their country as Jews or non-Jews (Majman, 2001). The anti-Semites also frequently characterized Jews as outside the pale of normal civilized society, as nonhuman "devils," "degenerates," a "plague," an "alien species." With Jews being seen as so very different from their own kind, the anti-Semites, and others who listened to them, were less likely to empathize with the Jewish victims of anti-Semitic actions. Seeing them brutalized or even killed did not arouse the guilt or sympathy that otherwise might have arisen when a "fellow human" was mistreated.

White supremacists are also apt to dehumanize Blacks in this manner. For them, people of color are the "mud people," products of the mating of Whites with animals, and largely animal-like themselves (Ezekiel, 2002). John King and his two friends apparently did not think of James Byrd as another human being with feelings and desires like their own. Rather, as an animal devoid of human qualities, he could be beaten up and dragged along the road much as they might pull an animal carcass behind their truck.

There is a lesson here even for ordinarily well-behaved and relatively nonracist people. As Bandura (1999) demonstrated, many people find it easier to punish a stranger, than otherwise would be the case, merely as a consequence of that person's being labeled an animal and thus dehumanized.

THE PERSONALITIES OF BIGOTS

Ordinary People?

That ill effects may result from merely thinking of an out-group member as an animal does not necessarily mean that any ordinary person will engage in the kind of brutal behavior exemplified by the murder of James Byrd Jr. and the slaughter of the 1,600 Jews of Jedwabne. Although several historians of the Holocaust (see M. Mann, 2000), as well as many social psychologists (see Berkowitz, 1999; see also Waller, 2002), have maintained that virtually anyone will act in a bigoted and cruel manner toward innocent victims in response to authoritative commands, mounting scholarship has seriously questioned whether the mass killings of the Nazi era can adequately be understood as a mere compliance to social pressures (M. Mann, 2000; Berkowitz, 1999).

M. Mann (2000), as a notable example, examined the biographies of 1,500 persons actively involved in the Nazis' atrocities and concluded that the great majority of them were not "ordinary people" and, indeed, were likely to have come from the "core Nazi constituencies." The Jedwabne Poles who took the most active part in the slaughter of their Jewish neighbors apparently were also somewhat special. Although anti-Semitism was pervasive throughout Polish society, the most brutal perpetrators tended to come from the lower socioeconomic rungs of the Jedwabne community (Gross, 2001). James Byrd Jr.'s three White killers were also far from representative of their town; they were fairly low in the area's social status hierarchy. John King and his two followers were not uncommon in this respect. Men convicted of the most serious forms of hate crimes are especially likely to have had a prior criminal history, much like John King and Shawn Berry and, more to the point, are also apt to be economically marginalized (Steinberg et al., 2003; see also Ezekiel, 2002, regarding American neo-Nazis' low social status[7]).

The Self-Concept of "True Haters"

In this last part of this chapter, I speculate about the personalities of extreme racists and bigots, basing my discussion largely on observations made in the United States. These brief sections are far from comprehensive and certainly do not claim that the true haters' actions are governed primarily by their personal qualities. Just as psychologists have long noted that any individual's behavior arises from the interaction of personality and situation, the highly prejudiced people's assaults on members of hated groups derive not only from their personal characteristics but also from their social setting and the circumstances surrounding them.

The Sense of Vulnerability

I spoke earlier of the possible effects of the racists' economic deprivations on their images of themselves. Being at the lower levels of their community's socioeconomic totem pole, they could well, in Gaylin's (2003) words, "feel less whole, less powerful, less useful, and less valued" (p. 55). Ezekiel's (2002) observation that the neo-Nazis he interviewed felt "extremely vulnerable, that their lives might be snuffed out at any time like a match flame" (p. 58) also points to this sense of having little control over what happens and of being devalued. Ezekiel believed that the picture Ackerman and Jahoda (1950, cited in Ezekiel, 2002, p. 62) had drawn of anti-Semites fit the neo-Nazi youths he had interviewed "to a startling degree" (p. 62). The most important of these characteristics were "a vague feeling of fear, linked to an inner picture of the world around them that appears to be hostile, evil, and difficult to master"; and "a shaky self-image, identity problems, and fluctuations between overestimation of self and self-derogation" (Ezekiel, 2002, p. 63).

As Ezekiel (2002), Gaylin (2003), and Beck (1999, cited in Steinberg et al., 2003, p. 984) emphasized, true haters apparently attempt to defend themselves against the threats and dangers they see around them by taking on a cloak of macho toughness. Thus, citing research into authoritarian

---

[7]I should acknowledge, however, that Ezekiel (2002) was uncertain about the linkage between economic factors and membership in racist groups in part because of the previously cited research by Green et al. (1998). My own guess is that although low economic status might not lead to membership in such groups, this low status and the humiliations it engenders might promote a proclivity to extreme, even violent, actions against people they despise. It is also worth noting that high levels of ethnic prejudice are often associated with relatively low levels of formal education (e.g., Wagner & Zick, 1995), apparently partly because the lesser education is apt to be linked to a sense of fraternal relative deprivation and political conservatism. This low level of education can also, of course, be the result of low socioeconomic status.

personalities, Ezekiel (2002) believed that authoritarian movements typically possess "an ideology of pseudomasculinity, an ideology that glorifies toughness and fears tenderness or nurturance as weakness" as a way of buttressing the members' shaky egos (p. 62). These three writers also agreed that the extreme racists and bigots characteristically regard their hostility toward the despised minorities as right and proper, especially given the injustices they have suffered. In Gaylin's (2003, pp. 136–137) analysis, as an illustration, the true haters' powerful rage impels them to blame the out-group as the cause of their troubles.

My sense is that one can gain additional insight into the personalities of these highly prejudiced people by considering a number of recent investigations of the role of the self-concept in producing highly aggressive reactions to perceived threats. The true haters appear to have at least some of the characteristics of those persons who are greatly offended by challenges to the way they want to see themselves.

Low Self-Esteem or Narcissism?

It is easy to view the extreme bigots' intense hostility to minority groups as a product of their low self-esteem. They supposedly are angry largely because they think very poorly of themselves. However, as I remarked earlier in this chapter, a recent spurt of studies dealing with the relationship between the self-concept and aggression, initiated to a great extent by Baumeister and Bushman (e.g., Baumeister, Bushman, & Campbell, 2000; Baumeister et al., 1996; Bushman & Baumeister, 1998), indicates that the true nature of this relationship is somewhat more complicated. Ezekiel (2002) pointed to such a complication in the proposition that the neo-Nazis' self-image fluctuated between an "overestimation of self and self-derogation" (p. 63). For Baumeister and Bushman (e.g., Baumeister et al., 1996), it is the "overestimation of self" that is the key to this aggression. Violent men, these researchers contend, "have a strong sense of personal superiority, and their violence often seems to stem from a sense of wounded pride. When someone else questions or disputes their favorable view of self, they lash out in response" (Baumeister et al., 2000, p. 26).

Baumeister and his colleagues (e.g., 2000) insisted that the strong self-pride these aggressive persons possess is not "simply a superficial form of bluster that is put on to conceal deep-rooted insecurities and self-doubts" (p. 28). They do not have low self-esteem. Rather, in the terminology favored by Baumeister and his associates, the aggression is a reaction to a "threatened egotism"(see also Bushman & Baumeister, 1998). Generalizing from the analyses of narcissism in the psychoanalytic and psychological literatures, these writers proposed that narcissistic personalities are especially likely to experience such a threatened egotism when they think they have been disparaged in some way. They have a grandiose view of themselves, Bushman and Baumeister (1998) said, and care passionately about being superior to others. Threats to this inflated self-regard presumably then infuriate them.[8] Thus, in the research by Bushman and Baumeister, after their participants had been deliberately insulted by a peer, those persons scoring high on a measure of narcissism were the ones who retaliated with the highest levels of aggression. Self-esteem, however, did not predict the strength of the assault on the provocateur. In addition, the narcissists displayed strong aggression only after the insult, but not if they had received a favorable treatment from the "other person."

Twenge and Campbell (2003) reported supporting findings. In their experiments with undergraduates, narcissists led to think they had been socially rejected were highly aggressive to the person who had spurned them as well as to an innocent third party[9] but did not exhibit any particularly strong aggression after learning they had been accepted socially. Also in accord with Baumeister and Bushman's thesis, a self-esteem measure did not predict the degree of aggression exhibited after the social rejection. Yet other research has examined the narcissism–aggression relationship. Extending the Baumeister and Bushman model (Baumeister et al., 1996; Bushman & Baumeister, 1998), Stucke and Sporer (2002) showed that it is not the grandiosity of the narcissists' self-conception in itself that produces the strong aggressive reaction to an ego threat. Instead, in their experiments it was the most narcissistic people with unclear images of themselves who were most strongly angered by negative feedback and who were also most hostile to the purveyor of the critical information. The narcissists with clear ideas of themselves tended to be only moderately hostile to the person who gave them the negative feedback.

One obviously can only speculate as to what these research findings say about racists and bigots in general and James Byrd Jr.'s killers in particular. My sense is that the Baumeister–Bushman analysis, especially as modified by Stucke and Sporer (2002), resembles Ezekiel's (2002) conception of the personalities of the neo-Nazis he studied. And I also suspect that John King, the man who evidently was primarily responsible for Mr. Byrd's murder, might well have had the grandiose but shaky self-image described by the investigators I have just cited.

---

[8]Stucke and Sporer (2002) offered a slightly different conception of the narcissistic personality in quoting from the American Psychiatric Association's (1994) *Diagnostic and Statistical Manual of Mental Disorders* (4th ed., *DSM–IV*). This widely used manual holds that "narcissists display self-aggrandizement and fantasies about unlimited ability and power, and they react with rage, shame or humiliation when their self-esteem is threatened." According to the *DSM–IV*, the grandiosity is "used to bolster and enhance a rather fragile self-esteem" (p. 510). At any rate, whatever the exact nature of this narcissism, there is evidence that people having this kind of personality are likely to react with strong anger when they encounter a threat to their grandiose image of themselves (Rhodewalt & Morf, cited in Stucke & Sporer, 2002, p. 511).

[9]Bushman and Baumeister (1998) did not obtain any indications of hostility displaced onto an innocent bystander in their research.

CONCLUSION

The interpretations I have offered in this chapter present a somewhat pessimistic view of those persons likely to engage in serious antiminority violence. My analysis suggests that the inclination to assault (and not only hate) particular minority groups grows to a considerable degree out of frequent exposure to decidedly unpleasant situations, particularly conditions that interfere with the development of a stable and secure self-concept. In common with other theoretical formulations, I have also proposed that conditions causing people to view themselves and their in-groups as being on the lower rungs of a status hierarchy relative to certain out-groups, especially out-groups they had previously learned to dislike, are among the major determinants of such a troubled self-image. Although this argument might perhaps reflect an undue complacency on my part, I wonder if invidious comparisons of this kind are not inevitable in societies such as our own. Differences in opportunities, talents, and motivations are bound to result in some people doing less well than others. Our cultural assumptions and values tell us that we are individually greatly responsible for what happens to us, that we are "masters of our fate, captains of our souls," so that it is all too easy to believe it is our own fault that we have not done better in life. Combining such a self-doubt with the aggressive proclivities arising from other frequent aversive experiences, some persons are all too likely to blame the despised minorities for their failures and difficulties.

And yet, there is some reason for hope. Cultural norms can and do change. Blatant discrimination against racial and ethnic minority groups is lower these days than it was, say, in the 1950s (Dovidio & Gaertner, 1986). And there probably has also been a concurrent decline in those attitudes and values that permit frustrated people to displace their hostility onto minority group members (Green et al., 1998). Vigilant legal actions against those perpetrating hate crimes, together with sophisticated hate-prevention programs (e.g., American Psychological Association, 1998; Ezekiel, 2002; Steinberg et al., 2003), could do much to lessen antiminority violence and promote social harmony.

REFERENCES

Adorno, T., Frenkel-Brunswik, E., Levinson, D., & Sanford, R. (1950). *The authoritarian personality.* New York: Harper.

Allport, G. W. (1954). *The nature of prejudice.* Reading, MA: Addison-Wesley.

American Psychiatric Association. (1994). *Diagnostic and statistical manual of mental disorders* (4th ed.). Washington, DC: Author.

American Psychological Association. (1998). *Hate crimes today: An age-old foe in modern dress.* APA Online-Public Affairs. Retrieved July 4, 2003, from http://www.apa.org/pubinfo/hate

Anderson, C. A., & Anderson, K. B. (1998). Temperature and aggression: Paradox, controversy, and a (fairly) clear picture. In R. G. Geen & E. Donnerstein (Eds.), *Human aggression: Theories, research, and implications for social policy* (pp. 247–298). San Diego, CA: Academic Press.

Bandura, A. (1999). Moral disengagement in the perpetration of inhumanities. *Personality and Social Psychology Review, 3,* 193–209.

Baumeister, R. F. (1997). *Evil: Inside human cruelty and violence.* New York: Freeman.

Baumeister, R. F., Bushman, B. J., & Campbell, W. K. (2000). Self-esteem, narcissism, and aggression: Does violence result from low self-esteem or from threatened egotism? *Current Directions in Psychological Science, 9,* 26–29.

Baumeister, R. F., Smart, L., & Boden, J. M. (1996). Relation of threatened egotism to violence and aggression: The dark side of high self-esteem. *Psychological Review, 103,* 5–33.

Berkowitz, L. (1959). Anti-Semitism and the displacement of aggression. *Journal of Abnormal and Social Psychology, 59,* 182–187.

Berkowitz, L. (1993). *Aggression: Its causes, consequences, and control.* New York: McGraw-Hill.

Berkowitz, L. (1999). Evil is more than banal: Situationism and the concept of evil. *Personality and Social Psychology Review, 3,* 246–253.

Berkowitz, L. (2003). Affect, aggression, and antisocial behavior. In R. J. Davidson, K. R. Scherer, & H. H. Goldsmith (Eds.), *Series in affective science: Handbook of affective sciences* (pp. 804–823). New York: Oxford University Press.

Berkowitz, L., & Holmes, D. S. (1960). A further investigation of hostility generalization to disliked objects. *Journal of Personality, 28,* 427–442.

Bower, G. H. (1981). Mood and memory. *American Psychologist, 36,* 129–148.

Bragg, R. (1998, June 17). Unfathomable crime, unlikely figure. *The New York Times,* p. 12.

Brewer, M. B., & Brown, R. J. (1998). Intergroup relations. In D. T. Gilbert, S. T. Fiske, & G. Lindzey (Eds.), *Handbook of social psychology* (4th ed., Vol. 2, pp. 554–594). New York: McGraw-Hill.

Browning, C. R. (1992). *Ordinary men: Reserve Police Battalion 101 and the final solution in Poland.* New York: HarperCollins.

Burleigh, M. (1997). *Ethics and extermination: Reflections on Nazi genocide.* Cambridge, England: Cambridge University Press.

Bushman, B., & Baumeister, R. F. (1998). Threatened egotism, narcissism, self-esteem, and direct and displaced aggression: Does self-love or self-hate lead to violence? *Journal of Personality and Social Psychology, 75,* 219–229.

Carlsmith, J. M., & Anderson, C. A. (1979). Ambient temperature and the occurrence of collective violence: A new analysis. *Journal of Personality and Social Psychology, 37,* 337–344.

Catalano, R., Novaco, R., & McConnell, W. (1997). A model of the net effect of job loss on violence. *Journal of Personality and Social Psychology, 72,* 1440–1447.

Diener, E. (1980). Deindividuation: The absence of self-awareness and self-regulation in group numbers. In P. B. Paulus (Ed.), *Psychology of group influence* (pp. 209–242). Hillsdale, NJ: Erlbaum.

Donnerstein, E., & Donnerstein, M. (1976). Research in the control of interracial aggression. In R. G. Geen & E. C. O'Neal (Eds.), *Perspectives on aggression* (pp. 133–168). New York: Academic Press.

Dovidio, J. F., & Gaertner, S. L. (Eds.). (1986). *Prejudice, discrimination, and racism*. Orlando, FL: Academic Press.

Ezekiel, R. S. (1995). *The racist mind: Portraits of neo-Nazis and Klansmen*. New York: Viking Press.

Ezekiel, R. S. (2002). An ethnographer looks at neo-Nazi and Klan groups. *American Behavioral Scientist, 46,* 51–71.

Fiske, S. T. (2002). What we know now about bias and intergroup conflict, the problem of the century. *Current Directions in Psychological Science, 11,* 123–128.

Fiske, S. T., & Taylor, S. E. (1991). *Social cognition*. New York: McGraw-Hill.

Fitness, J., & Fletcher, G. J. O. (1993). Love, hate, anger, and jealousy in close relationships: A prototype and cognitive appraisal analysis. *Journal of Personality and Social Psychology, 65,* 942–958.

Gaylin, W. (2003). *Hatred: The psychological descent into violence*. New York: Public Affairs.

Green, D. P., Glaser, J., & Rich, A. (1998). From lynching to gay bashing: The elusive connection between economic conditions and hate crime. *Journal of Personality and Social Psychology, 75,* 82–92.

Gross, J. T. (2001). *Neighbors: The destruction of the Jewish community in Jedwabne, Poland*. Princeton, NJ: Princeton University Press.

Hovland, C., & Sears, R. (1940). Minor studies in aggression: VI. Correlation of lynchings with economic indices. *Journal of Psychology, 9,* 301–310.

Hull, J. G., Levenson, R. W., Young, R. D., & Sher, K. J. (1983). Self-awareness reducing effects of alcohol consumption. *Journal of Personality and Social Psychology, 44,* 461–473.

Hutchinson, R. R. (1983). The pain–aggression relationship and its expression in naturalistic settings. *Aggressive Behavior, 9,* 229–242.

Jost, J. T., Glaser, J., Kruglanski, A. W., & Sulloway, F. J. (2003). Political conservatism as motivated social cognition. *Psychological Bulletin, 129,* 339–375.

Koch, H. W. (1975). *The Hitler youth: Origins and development, 1922–45*. London: MacDonald and Jane's.

Lazarus, R. S. (1991). *Emotion and adaptation*. New York: Oxford University Press.

Levin, J., & McDevitt, J. (1993). *Hate crimes: The rising tide of bigotry and bloodshed*. New York: Plenum Press.

Lyman, R. (1999, February 17). Dragging death is called signal for racist plan. *The New York Times,* p. 1.

Mackie, D. M., Devos, T., & Smith, E. R. (2000). Intergroup emotions: Explaining offensive action tendencies in an intergroup context. *Journal of Personality and Social Psychology, 79,* 602–616.

Majman, S. (2001). Jedwabne. *The Warsaw Voice*. Retrieved March 4, 2001, from http://www.warsawvoice.pl/old/v645/viewpoint00.html

Mann, L., Newton, J. W., & Innes, J. M. (1982). A test between deindividuation and emergent norm theories of crowd aggression. *Journal of Personality and Social Psychology, 42,* 260–272.

Mann, M. (2000). Were the perpetrators of genocide "ordinary men" or "real Nazis"? Results from fifteen hundred biographies. *Holocaust and Genocide Studies, 14,* 331–366.

Merriam-Webster's collegiate dictionary. (10th ed.). (1993). Springfield, MA: Merriam-Webster.

Mullen, B. (1986). Atrocity as a function of lynch mob composition: A self-attention perspective. *Personality and Social Psychology Bulletin, 12,* 187–197.

Naimark, N. M. (2001). *Fires of hatred: Ethnic cleansing in twentieth century Europe.* Cambridge, MA: Harvard University Press.

Nisbett, R. E., & Cohen, D. (1996). *Culture of honor: The psychology of violence in the South.* Boulder, CO: Westview Press.

Orlet, C. (2001). Small steps: The 60th anniversary of the Jedwabne pogrom. *Central Europe Review*. Retrieved July 3, 2003, from http://www.ce-review.org/01/14/orlet14.html

Pasek, B. (2001). *Poles face truth of Jedwabne: 1,600 Jews slain by neighbours—not Nazis.* Retrieved July 3, 2003, from http://www.canoe.ca/CNEWSFeatures0103/11_nazi-ap.html

Pedersen, W. C., Gonzales, C., & Miller, N. (2000). The moderating effect of trivial triggering provocation on displaced aggression. *Journal of Personality and Social Psychology, 78,* 913–927.

Pettigrew, T. F., & Meertens, R. W. (1995). Subtle and blatant prejudice in Western Europe. *European Journal of Social Psychology, 32,* 57–75.

Prentice-Dunn, S., & Rogers, R. W. (1982). Effects of public and private self-awareness on deindividuation and aggression. *Journal of Personality and Social Psychology, 43,* 503–513.

Prentice-Dunn, S., & Rogers, R. W. (1989). Deindividuation and the self-regulation of behavior. In P. B. Paulus (Ed.), *Psychology of group influence* (2nd ed., pp. 87–100). Hillsdale, NJ: Erlbaum.

Quist, R. M., & Wiegand, D. M. (2002). Attributions of hate: The media's causal attributions of a homophobic murder. *American Behavioral Scientist, 46,* 93–107.

Runciman, W. G. (1966). *Relative deprivation and social justice.* Berkeley: University of California Press.

Schafer, J. R., & Navarro, J. (2003, March 1). The seven-stage hate model: The psychopathology of hate groups. *FBI Law Enforcement Bulletin*. Retrieved July 25, 2003, from http://www.rickross.com/reference/hate_groups355.html

Smith, E. R. (1993). Social identity and social emotions: Toward new conceptualizations of prejudice. In D. M. Mackie & D. L. Hamilton (Eds.), *Affect, cognition, and stereotyping* (pp. 297–315). San Diego, CA: Academic Press.

Steinberg, A., Brooks, J., & Remtulla, T. (2003). Youth hate crimes: Identification, prevention, and intervention. *American Journal of Psychiatry, 160,* 979–989.

Stucke, T. S., & Sporer, S. L. (2002). When a grandiose self-image is threatened: Narcissism and self-concept clarity as predictors of negative emotions and aggression following ego threat. *Journal of Personality, 70,* 509–532.

Tajfel, H. (1981). *Human groups and social categories: Studies in social psychology.* Cambridge, England: Cambridge University Press.

Tajfel, H., & Turner, J. C. (1986). The social identity theory of intergroup behavior. In S. Worchel & W. G. Austin (Eds.), *Psychology of intergroup relations* (pp. 7–24). Chicago: Nelson.

Turner, J. C. (1985). Social categorization and the self-concept: A social cognitive theory of group behavior. In E. J. Lawler (Ed.), *Advances in group processes* (Vol. 2, pp. 77–121). Greenwich, CT: JAI Press.

Turner, J. C., Brown, R. J., & Tajfel, H. (1979). Social comparison and group interest in ingroup favoritism. *European Journal of Social Psychology, 9,* 187–204.

Twenge, J. M., & Campbell, W. K. (2003). "Isn't it fun to get the respect that we're going to deserve?" Narcissism, social rejection, and aggression. *Personality and Social Psychology Bulletin, 29,* 261–272.

Ulrich, R. E. (1966). Pain as a cause of aggression. *American Zoologist, 6,* 643–662.

Wagner, U., & Zick, A. (1995). The relation of formal education to ethnic prejudice: Its reliability, validity, and explanation. *European Journal of Social Psychology, 25,* 41–56.

Waller, J. (2002). *Becoming evil: How ordinary people commit genocide and mass killing.* New York: Oxford University Press.

Wicklund, R. A. (1975). Objective self-awareness. In L. Berkowitz (Ed.), *Advances in experimental social psychology* (Vol. 8, pp. 233–275). New York: Academic Press.

Wilson, J. Q., & Herrnstein, R. J. (1985). *Crime and human nature.* New York: Simon & Schuster.

Wistrich, R. S., & Jordan, F. (1991). *Antisemitism: The longest hatred.* New York: Pantheon Books.

Wolfgang, M. E., & Ferracuti, F. (1967). *The subculture of violence.* London: Tavistock.

Zimbardo, P. G. (1969). The human choice: Individuation, reason and order versus deindividuation, impulse and chaos. In W. J. Arnold & D. Levine (Eds.), *Nebraska Symposium on Motivation: Vol. 17. Current theory and research in motivation* (pp. 237–307). Lincoln: University of Nebraska Press.

9

GENOCIDAL HATRED:
NOW YOU SEE IT,
NOW YOU DON'T

DAVID MOSHMAN

People kill, one might think, because they hate. Thus, it is natural to assume that groups destroy other groups because of genocidal hatred. But people kill for other reasons too, and they may have other reasons for committing genocide. In this chapter, after defining genocidal hatred, I examine its role in five genocides. Genocidal hatred, I conclude, is not necessary for genocide, and not as important as one might think. Some of the perpetrators of some genocides do indeed appear to be motivated, at least in part, by genocidal hatred, but it is far from clear that genocidal hatred is the usual or primary cause of genocide. Although genocides usually appear at first glance to be intrinsically hateful, closer examination of the beliefs, motives, and social contexts of individual perpetrators shows genocidal hatred to be a more elusive phenomenon than might have been expected.

Genocides, I conclude, are not caused by genocidal hatred. Like other complex historical phenomena, they have no single cause. A plausible account of any genocide must consider multiple interacting ideologies, identities, motivations, and social contexts (Browning, 1998; Chalk & Jonassohn,

1990; Chirot & Seligman, 2001; Chomsky, 2003; Eidelson & Eidelson, 2003; Fein, 1993; Hinton, 2002; Moshman, 2004a, 2004b; Staub, 2003; Waller, 2002). We resist such accounts, however, because they explain acts of genocide in the same terms that we use to explain our own behavior, and thus raise the specter that we are not as different as we think from the perpetrators of genocide.

GENOCIDAL HATRED

We normally do not hate tornadoes, no matter how much damage they do. In fact, we do not even get angry at them. We see tornadoes as forces of nature, not as agents responsible for their actions. If we learn that the destruction caused by a tornado was due to shoddy construction or inadequate emergency procedures, we may be angry at those responsible, but anger at the tornado itself would generally be seen as misplaced, and an enduring hatred for it would likely be deemed pathological.

We would be more likely to get angry at a dog or a young child than at a tornado, even for damage on a far lesser scale. Dogs and young children, unlike tornadoes, are seen as agents responsible, to some degree, for their own actions, and thus an attitude of anger seems more justified. Even in the case of a dog or young child, however, an attitude of hatred would normally seem misplaced. To hate, we must see the other not just as an agent, but as an enduring rational agent—that is, as a being that acts on the basis of enduring beliefs and values of its own such that it can be held responsible, in a deep and ongoing sense, for what it has done. Defining a person as an enduring rational agent (Moshman, 2004a, 2004b, 2005), it follows that whereas anger may be a momentary reaction to a particular behavior, hatred is, at least prototypically, an enduring attitude directed at persons.

Hatred, then, is perhaps more an attitude than an emotion, and a highly cognitive attitude at that, requiring a conception of others as persons in a strong sense—as enduring rational agents. Very young children not only cannot be hated but also cannot hate. Young children may react with anger to the actions of others, but to hate those others requires an ability to conceive of them as agents who are causally and morally responsible, in an ongoing sense, for their actions. With the development of increasingly sophisticated conceptions of personhood, children become increasingly able to form enduring attitudes toward persons and, thus, to hate.

What, then, is genocidal hatred? Following Churchill (1997), I define *genocide* as the extermination, entirely or in part, of an abstractly defined group of people (for definitional alternatives and analysis of the associated conceptual issues, see Moshman, 2001). By genocidal hatred, then, I mean a murderous hatred that is directed at a racial, ethnic, national, religious, cultural, linguistic, political, economic, sexual, or other abstract group.

Genocidal hatred may be directed at individuals, but it is directed at them not on the basis of their unique characteristics, but rather on the basis of their affiliation with the hated group.

It is tempting to suggest at this point that genocidal hatred is what causes genocide, in which case reducing genocidal hatred should be central to any effort to prevent genocide. Rather than uncritically accepting such a claim, however, consider, at a more general level, the relation of hatred to violence. An individual may hate another but not engage in violence, and he or she may even feel murderous hatred but not commit murder. Alternatively, an individual may engage in violence, and even murder, for reasons such as financial gain unrelated to hatred. Thus, it is clear that hatred is neither a necessary nor a sufficient condition for violence or murder, though it surely plays a role in some murders and other acts of violence.

Similarly, it is plausible that an individual may harbor an attitude of genocidal hatred without engaging in violence or murder, much less genocide, or may participate in genocide for political, religious, economic, or professional reasons unrelated to hatred. Thus, although the notion that genocidal hatred is the cause of genocide may seem at first a truism, it is in fact an empirical claim and could well be false.

With these conceptions and questions in mind, I now proceed to five case studies: (a) the 1994 genocide in Rwanda; (b) the Nazi death camp Treblinka; (c) Argentina's "Dirty War"; (d) the 1981 massacre at El Mozote, El Salvador; and (e) the 1890 massacre at Wounded Knee, South Dakota. At first we see genocidal hatred everywhere we look. In each case, however, a detailed examination of particular individuals shows a network of beliefs, commitments, and motives in which genocidal hatred, if present at all, played a surprisingly minor role.

The present five cases are only a very small subset of the many genocides throughout human history and were not randomly selected. It is worth noting, however, that the five cases were not chosen to confirm or disconfirm any particular point of view; they are simply five cases about which I have some knowledge on the basis of previous work (Moshman, 2001, 2004a, 2004b, in progress). Although we must be cautious about generalizing across genocides, the present five cases suffice to illustrate the diversity and complexity of genocidal motivations and warn against simplistic explanations in which genocidal hatred, or some other single force, is deemed the fundamental cause of genocide.

THE 1994 GENOCIDE IN RWANDA

On April 6, 1994, President Juvenal Habyarimana of Rwanda was killed when the plane in which he was returning to Kigali, Rwanda's capital, was shot down over the presidential palace. This spectacular assassination was quickly overshadowed by a 100-day genocide in which members of the Hutu majority, armed with government-issued machetes and homemade nail-studded clubs, killed approximately 800,000 Rwandans, 10% of the population, mostly members of the Tutsi minority:

> Neighbors hacked neighbors to death in their homes, and colleagues hacked colleagues to death in their workplaces. Doctors killed their patients, and schoolteachers killed their pupils. Within days, the Tutsi populations of many villages were all but eliminated, and in Kigali prisoners were released in work gangs to collect the corpses that lined the roadsides. Throughout Rwanda, mass rape and looting accompanied the slaughter. Drunken militia bands, fortified with assorted drugs from ransacked pharmacies, were bused from massacre to massacre. Radio announcers reminded listeners not to take pity on women and children. (Gourevitch, 1998, p. 115)

Many of the killings were exceptionally brutal. Victims were physically tortured, often by having parts of their bodies cut off and then being left to die of their wounds. Some of the assaults were psychological:

> Assailants tortured Tutsi by demanding that they kill their own children and tormented Hutu married to Tutsi partners by insisting that they kill their spouses . . . Assailants often stripped victims naked before killing them, both to acquire their clothes without stains or tears and to humiliate them. In many places, killers refused to permit the burial of victims and insisted that their bodies be left to rot where they had fallen. (Des Forges, 1999, p. 216)

Tens of thousands of Tutsi women were raped, often multiple times, and in many of these attacks the genocidal hatred was clear:

> Generally esteemed as beautiful, Tutsi women were . . . said to scorn Hutu men whom they found unworthy of their attention. Many assailants insulted women for their supposed arrogance while they were raping them . . .
>
> Assailants sometimes mutilated women in the course of a rape or before killing them. They cut off breasts, punctured the vagina with spears, arrows, or pointed sticks, or cut off or disfigured body parts that looked particularly "Tutsi," such as long fingers or thin noses. (Des Forges, 1999, p. 215)

Western accounts of the genocide called up an image of ancient tribal animosities erupting into uncontrollable mass killings, a prime example, it would seem, of genocidal hatred causing genocide. On closer examination, however, it turns out that the hatreds associated with the Rwandan genocide were neither ancient nor tribal. The Hutu and Tutsi have never been distinct tribes or even ethnic groups; for centuries before European colonization, they lived interspersed among each other, speaking the same language, sharing the same religious beliefs, participating in the same society, intermarrying, and moving across generations from one category to another, distinguishable only in that the Tutsi, having traditionally been herdsman, tended to be of a higher socioeconomic status than the Hutu, who were traditionally cultivators. The sharp and fixed distinction between Hutu and Tutsi, and the associated genocidal hatreds, were legacies of 20th-century European colonialism (Berry & Berry, 1999; Des Forges, 1999; Gourevitch, 1998; Mamdani, 2001; Moshman, 2004b).

These hatreds, moreover, were themselves manipulated for political purposes. Rwanda's progress toward independence in the early 1960s was marked by a dramatic reversal in the fortunes of the Hutu and Tutsi. Belgium had controlled Rwanda for decades by supporting the Tutsi, who constituted about 15% of the population, in their increasing subjugation of the Hutu. With independence the majority Hutu took control of the new government and struggled for 3 decades with the question of how to deal with the Tutsi. By the early 1990s, the Hutu Power movement, which sought to permanently establish Rwanda as a Hutu nation, was threatened by the Rwandan Patriotic Front (RPF), a Tutsi-dominated army of Rwandan refugees that was invading Rwanda from the Uganda border, and by ongoing peace talks that might lead to a new government including Tutsi representation. Hutu Power responded by inciting Hutu hatred of the Tutsi.

Even if genocidal hatred played a proximate role in the killings, then, the genocidal hatred was a legacy of colonialism that was encouraged and manipulated by a political movement for political reasons. Far from being the inevitable result of genocidal hatred, the Rwanda genocide was in large part political:

> It is true that the perpetrators of genocide within the Rwandan political and security apparatus propagated ethnic hatred, and such an appeal resonated with the fears of some Rwandans. So ethnicity *was* important in the violence, but one should not infer from this that all Hutu hated all their Tutsi neighbors and wished to kill them. Nevertheless some accounts in the international media implied that Hutu and Tutsi were programmed to hate each other. Such a view is misleading . . . (Newbury & Newbury, 2003, p. 139)

One strong indication of the political nature of the genocide is the fact that tens of thousands of its victims were politically moderate Hutu who opposed the Hutu Power ideology and the genocide. Popular singer Simon Bikindi, who was employed by the government, excoriated such traitors in "I Hate Hutus," one of his best-known songs:

> I hate these Hutus, these de-Hutuized Hutus, who have renounced their identity, dear comrades.
> I hate these Hutus, these Hutus who march blindly, like imbeciles.

This species of naive Hutus who join a war without knowing its cause.

I hate these Hutus who can be brought to kill and who, I swear to you, kill Hutus, dear comrades.

And if I hate them, so much the better. (McNeil, 2002, p. 59)

Bikindi's songs were played by the government's quasi-official radio station constantly throughout the genocide and were sung by the killers as they carried out their killings. Even if the hatred was politically manipulated, the connection of genocidal hatred to genocide seems clear.

Bikindi himself, however, subsequently facing charges of genocide, claimed that he opposed killing and never advocated it in his lyrics but that it was his job to entertain at government rallies with songs that supported government policy. This claim may be in part a matter of legal strategy, but there is some corroboration for the view that Bikindi himself, at least, was not motivated by genocidal hatred:

> His former mistress, Angeline Mukabanana, says he hated no one. She points out that she is a Tutsi herself and that Bikindi adopted her first son, who had a Tutsi father, and defended their Tutsi neighbors against Hutu thugs before the genocide.
>
> She sees him as a romantic opportunist, too eager to please. "After he wrote 'I Hate Hutus,'" she said, "I asked him: 'Why did you write that? What if the R.P.F. wins the war?' He said: 'The government obliges me to write these songs. If I hear the R.P.F. is coming to Kigali next month, I'll write a song for them.'" (McNeil, 2002, p. 59)

Bikindi, then, may have been motivated neither by hatred nor by politics, but rather by professional advancement. Other Hutu were no doubt motivated by a genuine fear of the return of Tutsi domination or by terror induced by Hutu Power propaganda about RPF atrocities. Some of the killings, moreover, no doubt reflected various local, personal, and sexual animosities. Some were motivated at least in part by economic considerations—the opportunity to claim the property of those murdered. And for many, the process was facilitated by the systematic portrayal of the Tutsi as *inyenzi*—cockroaches.

In sum, without denying an important role for genocidal hatred in the Rwanda genocide, such hatred is just one factor among many. The various factors, moreover, cannot be sharply isolated and no doubt played intersecting and interacting roles. An overemphasis on genocidal hatred, then, may deflect attention from other important bases for genocide and hinder the formulation of more complex and comprehensive theories of genocidal motivation.

TREBLINKA

Arguably the core of what has come to be called the Holocaust was Operation Reinhard, the Nazi plan to kill all the Jews in the so-called

General Government, the major portion of occupied Poland (Arad, 1987). It encompassed three death camps—Belzec, Sobibor, and Treblinka—and the largest of these was Treblinka.

Treblinka was constructed in the middle of 1942 in the northeast section of the General Government not far from Malkinia, a town and station on the main railway from Bialystok to Warsaw. It began operation, while still under construction, in July 1942. By November 1943, when it was closed and demolished, approximately 900,000 Jews had been killed there, nearly all of them within hours of arrival. The camp consisted of a Reception Area, an Extermination Area, and an Administrative Area (Donat, 1979; Glazar, 1995; Willenberg, 1989).

The Reception Area included the platform where the trains arrived, a large barrack in which the men undressed, and a large barrack in which the women undressed and had their hair cut off. The Jews, who had just spent days crammed into airless freight cars without food, water, or sanitary provisions, were told they were headed for showers and disinfection. After the forced separation of families, the public undressing and humiliating searches for valuables, and the cutting off of the women's hair, they were brutally directed through "The Tube" to the Extermination Area. In addition to the platform and undressing barracks, the Reception Area included the Sorting Square, where clothing and other belongings taken from the Jews were sorted into immense piles, and storerooms for these belongings. Finally, across the Sorting Square from the undressing barracks, was the *Lazarett*, a hidden execution site for special cases and a large, permanently burning pit of dead bodies.

The Extermination Area included the gas chambers, burial pits for the dead bodies, and living quarters for the Jewish slave laborers. Naked Jews arriving by the hundreds through The Tube were driven with whips into the gas chambers, which were then sealed shut. They were then killed with carbon monoxide gas from a diesel engine, a process that typically took 20 to 25 minutes, after which the bodies were taken to the burial pits. Beginning in March 1943, there were also railroad rails known as "The Roasts" on which dead bodies were burned.

In addition to the Reception and Extermination Areas, Treblinka also included an Administrative Area with a variety of structures in which the camp staff lived and worked. Notwithstanding its demonic presence, Treblinka was, we must keep in mind, a human institution designed and run by human beings. It is the beliefs, motivations, and social contexts of those persons that we must understand if we are to account, to whatever extent this can be done, for Treblinka. We must see Treblinka from their perspective.

Perspective taking is always a challenge, however, and taking the viewpoint of the perpetrators of a genocide is especially difficult for at least two reasons. First, we feel that it is the victims, not the perpetrators, who merit our empathy. There seems something morally indecent about the very act of trying to see the genocide from the perpetrators' points of view. But this is what we must do if we wish to understand a genocide.

Second, it is crucial to our self-conceptions to see ourselves as fundamentally different from the perpetrators of genocide. Thus we are reassured by simplistic theories that present the perpetrators as evil beings in the grip of genocidal hatred. Because they show the perpetrators as qualitatively different from us, we are inclined to accept such theories uncritically.

In fact, the perpetrators of genocide at Treblinka were diverse and complex figures whose attitudes toward Jews were, in general, closer to indifference than to hate (Sereny, 1983, p. 178; see also Glazar, 1995; Willenberg, 1989). Much is known, in particular, about the senior officer, Commandant Franz Stangl, who after being convicted of genocide and sentenced to life in prison agreed to a series of interviews with the journalist Gitta Sereny (1983). Stangl's recollections should not be taken at face value, of course. Even under the best of circumstances, remembering is a constructive process that actively makes sense of the past. Memories of one's role in important events, moreover, not only are reconstructed, but are highly likely to be influenced by self-serving biases—especially if one has been the commandant of a death camp.

It does not appear, however, that Stangl intended through his participation in these interviews to present a false picture of himself or his role, nor is there evidence that he was lying about specifics. Sereny, moreover, appears to have been a critical and knowledgeable interviewer who repeatedly challenged evasions and questionable claims and persistently pressed Stangl to acknowledge and confront his own behavior. Although one cannot be sure of Stangl's original motivation in agreeing to these interviews, there is reason to think that, for the most part, he was collaborating with Sereny in a genuine, and excruciatingly difficult, search for the truth about how he came to do what he did.

There is nothing special in Stangl's childhood goals, activities, or experiences to explain how he grew up to be a genocidal mass murderer. Born in 1908 in Altmunster, a small Austrian town, he left school at age 15 to become an apprentice weaver in a local textile mill. Although he attained the status of master weaver over the next few years, he came to see his work in the mill as a professional dead end and applied to join the police. By the time of the Anschluss—Germany's March 1938 annexation of Austria—Stangl was a senior officer with specialized training and experience in political investigations.

In November 1940 Stangl was ordered to report to Berlin for a new assignment in the General Foundation for Institutional Care. In Berlin he was told

"that it had been decided to confide in me the very difficult and demanding job of police superintendent of a special institute which was administered by this Foundation, the HQ of which was Tiergartenstrasse 4 in Berlin."

"Did you know then what Tiergartenstrasse 4 was?"

"I had no idea. I had heard it vaguely referred to now and then as T4, but I didn't know what their specific function was."

This was no doubt true at that time. For Tiergartenstrasse 4 was the hub of what was for years the most secret operation in the Third Reich: the administration first of the "mercy-killing" of the mentally and physically handicapped in Germany and Austria, and later of the "Final Solution": the extermination of the Jews. (Sereny, 1983, p. 49; italics in original indicate the interviewer's question)

Stangl was subsequently assigned to Operation Reinhard and later appointed Commandant of Treblinka, where he arrived in September 1942. Each step of the way he could have chosen not to accept the next assignment, but someone else would have been assigned in his place, and he would have received an unspecified alternative assignment. Each time, despite what seems to have been genuine personal horror, he accepted the next level of responsibility as a professional challenge:

> Stangl regarded his job as commander of a death camp as he would have viewed any other job. He wanted to succeed at the task and mission that had been assigned to him, that is, to eliminate the people who had been sent to the camp and to dispose of their property in accordance with the directives that he had received from his commanders, and to make certain that this be carried out quickly and efficiently. (Arad, 1987, pp. 184–186)

On the assumption that genocidal hatred is the primary basis for genocide, one might expect the Commandant of Treblinka to manifest a fanatical hatred of Jews. There is no evidence that Franz Stangl hated Jews at all, however. On the contrary he saw them as "cargo," as like a herd of cows.

"Would it be true to say [asked Sereny] *that you finally felt they weren't really human beings?"*

"When I was on a trip once, years later in Brazil," he said, his face deeply concentrated, and obviously reliving the experience, "my train stopped next to a slaughterhouse. The cattle in the pens, hearing the noise of the train, trotted up to the fence and stared at the train. They were very close to my window, one crowding the other, looking at me through that fence. I thought then, 'Look at this; this reminds me of Poland; that's just how the people looked, trustingly, just before they went into the tins . . .'"

"You said 'tins'," I interrupted. *"What do you mean?"* But he went on without hearing, or answering me.

". . . I couldn't eat tinned meat after that. Those big eyes . . . which looked at me . . . not knowing that in no time at all they'd all be dead."

He paused. His face was drawn. At this moment he looked old and worn and real.

"*So you didn't feel they were human beings?*"

"Cargo," he said tonelessly. "They were cargo." He raised and dropped his hand in a gesture of despair. (Sereny, 1983, pp. 200–201; italics in original)

The primary motive for the extermination of Jews, Stangl apparently believed, was financial: "They wanted the Jews' money" (quoted in Sereny, 1983, p. 232).

"That racial business," said Stangl, "was just secondary. Otherwise, how could they have had all those 'honorary Aryans'? They used to say General Milch was a Jew, you know."

"*If the racial business was so secondary, then why all that hate propaganda?*"

"To condition those who actually had to carry out these policies; to make it possible for them to do what they did."

"*Well, you were part of this: did you hate?*"

"Never. I wouldn't let anybody dictate to me who to hate. Anyway, the only people I could ever hate would be those who were out to destroy me—like Prohaska [a personal enemy]."

"*What is the difference to you between hate, and a contempt which results in considering people as 'cargo'?*"

"It has nothing to do with hate. They were so weak; they allowed everything to happen—to be done to them. They were people with whom there was no common ground, no possibility of communication—that is how contempt is born. I could never understand how they could just give in as they did. (Sereny, 1983, pp. 232–233; italics in original)

Stangl was right that dehumanization is different from hate. From his point of view, Jews were so contemptible as to lie outside the universe of moral obligation. But this is not hate. On the one occasion where Stangl expressed what might be considered a genocidal hatred, he spoke not as a Nazi but as an Austrian recalling the Anschluss: "'I hate . . . I hate the Germans,' he suddenly burst out with passion, 'for what they pulled me into. I should have killed myself in 1938'" (Sereny, 1983, p. 39).

Research on other perpetrators of the Nazi Judeocide, from Arendt's (1963/1994) classic "report on the banality of evil" to Browning's (1998) detailed account of "ordinary men," suggests that Stangl was not atypical. No doubt there were Nazis who hated Jews, but there were many like Stangl who saw Jews as subhuman, which is different. Hatred makes it possible to kill those we see as persons. Dehumanization makes it possible to kill without hating, as you would kill a cow.

THE DIRTY WAR IN ARGENTINA

Through most of the 1970s and 1980s, Latin America was marked by extraordinary programs of government-sponsored terror and genocide that targeted persons and communities suspected of political subversion and resulted in the deaths of hundreds of thousands of innocent individuals. In Argentina, Chile, and other South American countries, the central phenomenon of these "dirty wars" was what came to be called "disappearances."

In the late 1970s, after a military junta took control of Argentina, some 30,000 people were "disappeared" (Bouvard, 1994; Fisher, 1989; Guest, 1990; Mellibovsky, 1997). The typical victims were college students and other young adults who had worked with the poor or supported social justice or had been named by others of this sort and were thus deemed to be subversives. Armed military squads would arrive in Ford Falcons, search and ransack their homes, and take them away to secret detention centers dispersed across Argentina, never to be seen again by anyone who had known them before they were disappeared.

Prisoners in the detention centers were required to wear hoods over their heads at all times, covering their faces, and were periodically taken for torture sessions where they would be shocked with electric cattle prods or have their heads immersed under water or their fingers and toes severed or their eyes removed. Sometimes whole families were arrested; children were tortured in front of their parents and parents in front of their children. Finally, after months of such physical and psychological degradation, the victims would be killed and buried in secret graves or have their bodies tossed onto dark streets, or they would be sedated and dropped alive from airplanes into the Atlantic Ocean.

"In order to achieve peace in Argentina," General (and soon to be military President) Jorge Rafael Videla had advised his officers, "all the necessary people will die" (quoted in Fisher, 1989, p. 18). And they would not just cease to exist; they would never have existed. On April 22, 1976, the junta decreed the following:

> As from today it is forbidden to comment or make references to suspects connected with subversive incidents, the appearance of bodies and the deaths of subversive elements and/or members of the armed or security forces in these incidents, unless they are reported by a responsible official source. This includes the victims of kidnappings and missing persons. (Quoted in Fisher, 1989, p. 25)

The government denied any responsibility for or knowledge of disappeared persons, suggesting that the missing men had joined subversive groups and that the women had gone off to become prostitutes. There were no *desaparecidos*, and there was nothing further to be said about people who had never existed.

In 1983, disgraced by its loss to Great Britain in the war over the Malvinas (Falkland Islands), the military ceded power to a civilian government. After early promises of justice and some initial trials, the government pardoned most of the convicted and put a stop to further prosecutions.

Not long after, in a subway in Buenos Aires, Adolfo Francisco Scilingo approached the renowned journalist Horacio Verbitsky (1996) with an offer to discuss his experiences at the Navy School of Mechanics, the most notorious of the secret detention centers. He had, it turned out, participated in two flights in which he and others threw drugged individuals from an airplane into the Atlantic Ocean. In deciding to talk, Scilingo appears to have been motivated by anger that senior officers of the military government, who were denying the disappearances, were denying having given the orders that, in Scilingo's view, justified what he and many others had done. It was time, he thought, to set the record straight on behalf of those who had followed such orders. This was, in a real sense, a concern for truth and justice, though it was not, at least initially, a concern for the disappeared, nor for the Mothers of the Plaza de Mayo, who marched weekly on their behalf.

In genocidal situations, genocidal hatred, at least if one is looking for it, is rarely hard to find. Scilingo specifically referred at one point in a later interview to "the hatred I felt for subversives" (Feitlowitz, 1998, p. 196). This was a hatred for an abstract category of persons and for all individuals affiliated with that category and is thus potentially genocidal. In context, however, this reference to hatred may indicate little about the basis for Scilingo's behavior. Scilingo was recounting an episode in which he unexpectedly came upon a group of female prisoners at the Navy School of Mechanics:

> I opened a door and out came a young woman in an advanced state of pregnancy, dressed in a nightgown, slippers, and robe. She stopped in front of me, looked at me with sad eyes, then continued on to the bathroom. There were other pregnant women in that room . . . It was unnerving to see future mothers in these circumstances, in spite of the hatred I felt for subversives . . . This was the war I had asked to fight, but did it have to be like this? . . . It was a scene out of the Middle Ages (Scilingo, quoted in Feitlowitz, 1998, p. 196; ellipses in original)

Even genocidal hatred, it appears, can be dampened by empathy for individual persons. But this does not rule out participating in genocide, because such participation is a function of multiple factors, including patriotism:

> Today I'm telling you that it was a barbaric thing. At that time we were totally convinced of what we were doing. The way we had internalized it, with the situation we were living through in this country, it would be a total lie if I told you that I wouldn't do it again under the same conditions. I would be a hypocrite. When I did what I did I was convinced

they were subversives. What happens is that, as I tell you about this right now—and I'm telling you about it in detail, since you ask me to and I believe the truth must be known—don't think that it makes me very happy or that it makes me feel very good. Right now I can't say that they were subversives. They were human beings. We were so deeply convinced that no one questioned it . . . It was something that you had to do. I don't know what executioners go through when they have to kill, to drop the blade or pull the switch on the electric chair. No one liked to do it, it wasn't a pleasant thing. But it was done, and it was understood that this was the best way. It wasn't discussed. It was something supreme that was done for the sake of the country. A supreme act. (Scilingo, quoted in Verbitsky, 1996, pp. 23–24)

Participation in these supreme acts of patriotism, moreover, was a responsibility rotated across members of the navy from throughout Argentina. It was, in Scilingo's words, "a kind of communion" (quoted in Verbitsky, 1996, p. 23). The genocide was thus due, at least in part, to powerful political identities rooted in a shared ideological commitment. Together with other patriotic Argentine officers, Scilingo was, in his own mind, doing what needed to be done for the future of Argentina.

Scilingo's immediate social context is also a crucial consideration. As a lieutenant he was expected to follow orders without question, including orders to kill. As he later explained, "If the armed forces are what they must be, you have to have total confidence in your superior officer." You can't "stop and analyze every single order" (quoted in Verbitsky, 1996, p. 29). And even if the orders were extraordinary, "all of us were convinced that we were involved in a different kind of war, for which we were not prepared, and that we were using the means we had at hand" (quoted in Verbitsky, 1996, pp. 29–30).

Thus, Scilingo followed orders during what he saw as an unprecedented sort of war to save his nation from subversion. Even so, there were moral qualms. For him, like many, these qualms were put to rest by the Catholic Church:

"From the religious point of view, talked over with chaplains, it was accepted."

"The chaplains approved of the method?"

"Yes. After my first flight, despite everything I'm telling you, it was very hard for me to accept it on a personal level. After returning, although I might coldly have thought everything was fine, that was not the reality inside me. I believe all human beings have this problem; if I had had to shoot someone, I would have felt the same way. I don't think any human being takes pleasure in killing another. The next day I didn't feel very good and I was talking with the chaplain of the school, who found a Christian explanation for it. I don't know if it comforted me, but at least it made me feel better."

"What was the Christian explanation?"

"I don't remember very well, but he was telling me that it was a Christian death, because they didn't suffer, because it wasn't traumatic, that they had to be eliminated, that war was war and even the Bible provided for eliminating the weeds from the wheat field." (Verbitsky, 1996, p. 30; italics in original indicate the interviewer's questions)

Hatred was absent in the Christian explanation. Just as Hutu Power represented the Tutsi as cockroaches and Commandant Stangl saw the Jews as cows, the chaplains portrayed the subversives as weeds, even less subject to hatred than an animal, but no less subject to elimination.

Scilingo saw his fellow perpetrators as much like himself. Far from exulting in victory over a hated foe, they had done what they thought needed to be done and now wanted nothing more than to forget:

"At heart, all of us were disturbed."
"But you talked among yourselves?"
"It was taboo."
"You went, threw twenty living people into the ocean, came back, and didn't talk about it among yourselves?"
"No."
"You picked up where you had left off, as if it hadn't existed."
"Yes. Everyone wants to erase it from their minds. I can't." (Verbitsky, p. 30; italics in original)

Accounts of other perpetrators are consistent with Scilingo's picture of himself and his colleagues as motivated by patriotic, moral, and religious commitments, with genocidal hatred of the subversives, if present at all, a secondary consideration (Osiel, 2001). Even Julio Simón, the notorious torturer known as Julián the Turk, said on television, "What I did I did for my Fatherland, my faith, and my religion. Of course I would do it again" (quoted in Feitlowitz, 1998, p. 212). In a subsequent interview he added, "I am not repentant. I'm no crybaby like that sorry Scilingo . . . This was a war to save the Nation from the terrorist hordes" (quoted in Feitlowitz, 1998, p. 212). Perceptions such as this may be accompanied by genocidal hatred, but such hatred, it once again appears, is not necessary for participation in genocide.

THE MASSACRE AT EL MOZOTE

In Central America during the same period, the dirty wars included genocidal massacres in Guatemala, El Salvador, and elsewhere. One case that has been especially well documented is the 1981 massacre in El Mozote, a mountain village of several hundred people in the northern part of the province of Morazán in northeastern El Salvador (Danner, 1994). Northern

Morazán was widely known as the Red Zone because it was largely under the control of left-wing Salvadoran guerrillas attempting to overthrow the right-wing government of El Salvador. Most of El Mozote's inhabitants, and probably most people in most of the Red Zone, tried to live their lives as best they could without antagonizing either side in the war going on around them. For days after they heard that the Atlacatl Battalion was conducting a sweep of northern Morazán, they debated whether it was riskier to leave or to stay. Most finally stayed, and as the sounds of mortars, small arms, and aircraft drew closer, the village swelled with people from surrounding areas who thought El Mozote would be safer than where they lived.

On December 10th at twilight, after a morning of strafing and bombing by the Salvadoran Air Force, the people of El Mozote were hiding in their houses when the Atlacatl Battalion arrived. The soldiers yelled for everyone to come out and forced them all to lie face down in the street. Soon it was dark, with more than a hundred children crying, and the soldiers went up and down the rows, shouting, kicking, beating, taking jewelry and crucifixes, taking names, and demanding information about guerrillas and weapons.

Later that evening, the soldiers sent everyone back to their homes. In alternating terror and relief, hoping that the worst was over, they spent the night waiting. Before dawn the next morning they were ordered out to the Plaza, the men were separated from the women and children, and they stood for hours. Finally, the men were herded into the church and the women and children into a small home nearby, as a helicopter landed in the Plaza and military officers emerged. In the church, men were bound, blindfolded, and brutally interrogated, and then, after an hour, the soldiers began to decapitate them with machetes. In the nearby house, the women and children could hear them screaming, and from a small window could see other men, their husbands, their fathers, and their sons, led in small groups, bound and blindfolded, to be killed in the forest with a shot to the head. Children became hysterical. Their mothers cried and hugged each other.

About midday, the soldiers came for the young women and the older girls, wresting them from their mothers to take them up to the hills, where their screams could be heard in the house. Then they came back for the mothers and took them in groups, one group at a time, until only the crying children remained in the house. The women were taken to another house and forced inside, where they were shot. The later groups, seeing the carnage through the doorway, refused to enter. But they too were forced inside, screaming and begging, and they too were shot. And when the last group of women had been killed, the house was burned.

Now the soldiers returned to the house by the church, where they smashed the children's heads with the butts of their rifles, slashed them with machetes, and herded many across the street and into the tiny sacristy, into which they then shot their rifles until all of the children were dead. Then they burned the church, the sacristy, and the nearby house and the next morning moved on to the surrounding hamlets, killing a total of 767 individuals.

Why did they do it? One consideration here, as in any case of massacre by a military unit, is that the soldiers were following orders. The brutality of what the men of the Atlacatl Battalion did invites the assumption that the orders were motivated by hate and that the soldiers themselves must have shared that hate, a hatred so genocidal that it could motivate even the individual murder of children.

On closer examination, however, it becomes clear that, like dirty warriors throughout Latin America, those who gave the orders and those who followed them shared identities centered on a combination of patriotic, political, moral, and religious commitments that rationalized a dirty war against subversion, a war in which even the most extraordinary orders could be given and should be obeyed. The Atlacatl Battalion was an elite military unit trained by U.S. Special Forces instructors. The soldiers sang,

> We are warriors!
>   Warriors all!
>   We are going forth to kill
>   A mountain of terrorists! (Danner, 1994, p. 50)

This was a moral mission, in their view; they were saving their country from terrorism. In particular, there is no evidence that Lieutenant Colonel Domingo Monterrosa Barrios, the Battalion's commander, was motivated by hatred. On the contrary, he believed that parts of El Salvador had been infected by communism and that it was his moral duty, as a patriot and military officer, to lead what he called *La Limpieza*—The Cleanup. The cancer had to be removed, even if this entailed the loss of some healthy flesh. According to a reporter well acquainted with him,

> He was not bloodthirsty, but he was so neurotically driven—he wanted at all costs to win the war. The point was to create a turning point, a watershed, to turn the tide, and to do it by scaring the hell out of the enemy. It was a deliberate demonstration of cruelty to show them that the guerrillas couldn't protect them. And he understood that you do this as cruelly, as brutally as possible; you rape, impale, whatever, to show them the cost. (Annunziata, quoted in Danner, 1994, p. 146)

Monterrosa's methods were fully consistent with the policy of the Salvadoran military and government:

> For El Mozote was, above all, a statement. By doing what it did in El Mozote, the Army had proclaimed loudly and unmistakably to the people of Morazán, and to the peasants in surrounding areas as well, a simple message: In the end, the guerrillas can't protect you, and we, the officers and the soldiers, are willing to do absolutely anything to avoid losing this war—we are willing to do whatever it takes. (Danner, 1994, p. 141)

The patron of the dirty wars was the United States. Each dirty war was unique, but the United States supported a network of genocide and terrorism that cut across diverse nationalisms by linking them to a monolithic war against communism. The war on communism included an extensive program to maintain the highly unpopular Salvadoran military government, and this included, among many other things, training and supplying the Atlacatl Battalion. The driving motive for the United States was not genocidal hatred but the containment of communism and the survival of a government favorable to U.S. interests. One of the original U.S. advisers to the Atlacatl Battalion explained this to Danner as follows:

> El Mozote was in a place, in a zone, that was one hundred percent controlled by the guerrillas. You try to dry those areas up. You know you're not going to be able to work with the civilian population up there, you're never going to get a permanent base there. So you just decide to kill everybody. That'll scare everybody else out of the zone. It's done more out of frustration than anything else. (Quoted in Danner, 1994, p. 52)

As it turned out, news of the massacre at El Mozote reached the front pages of both *The New York Times* and *The Washington Post* the day before President Ronald Reagan was legally required to provide Congress with a formal evaluation of El Salvador's human rights record to serve as the basis for a congressional decision on whether to continue military aid. Genocidal massacres at El Mozote and elsewhere, moreover, were just part of the government's multifaceted program of violence against the political left:

> The most visible signs of the "dirty war" were mutilated corpses that each morning littered the streets of El Salvador's cities. Sometimes the bodies were headless, or faceless, their features having been obliterated with a shotgun blast or an application of battery acid; sometimes limbs were missing, or hands or feet chopped off, or eyes gouged out; women's genitals were torn and bloody, bespeaking repeated rape; men's were often found severed and stuffed into their mouths. And cut into the flesh of a corpse's back or chest was likely to be the signature of one or another of the "death squads" that had done the work . . . (Danner, 1994, pp. 25–26)

Acknowledging room for improvement in El Salvador's human rights record, President Reagan sent Congress his formal certification that the government was sufficiently in compliance with legal standards to merit continued military support. There is no reason to think that his continuing support for the government of El Salvador was motivated by a special hatred on Reagan's part for the types of people being killed, however those types might be defined. Nor is there any reason to think that genocidal hatred motivated the Reagan administration more generally or was the basis for the subsequent congressional decisions to continue funding and later to increase it. Certainly there was no public clamor to continue the elimination of the evil Salvadoran villagers, nor was there any effort by politicians to whip up the sort of ethnic hatred that might yield popular support for genocide.

Rather, the Administration was motivated, at least in part, by what it saw as a morally urgent war against communism (Moshman, 2004a), and Congress acquiesced for associated ideological and political reasons. The U.S. public, for the most part, knew too little about the Salvadoran people to hate them—too little, in fact, to care about them at all. Thus, the United States continued to support the genocidal Salvadoran regime for reasons unrelated to genocidal hatred.

THE MASSACRE AT WOUNDED KNEE

The European conquest of the Americas encompassed a set of interrelated genocides and ethnic cleansings on a scale unique in human history. This mega-genocide was deliberately aimed at, and has succeeded in eliminating, hundreds of cultures throughout the Americas. It has for the most part been a consensus policy, moreover, pursued generation after generation by the governments of multiple colonial and emerging nations, regardless of who held political power (Churchill, 1997; Stannard, 1992).

The United States is no exception. On attaining independence it took responsibility for the ongoing elimination of indigenous nations, with the primary locus of ethnic cleansings and genocides moving ever westward, as it had for centuries, generation after generation. Even well into the 19th century, however, the people and cultures of the Great Plains were spared by the fact that the plains were seen primarily as merely a pathway to the West.

As the 19th century progressed, however, with rapidly increasing interest in and settlement of the plains, indigenous nations and cultural groups found themselves pushed step by step into smaller and less hospitable spaces. Some native groups resisted more strenuously than others, and some more violently than others, and some even took on the U.S. Army, but their way of life was doomed regardless (Andrist, 1964/1993).

By 1890, the cultures of the plains had been largely destroyed, leaving remnant populations under U.S. government control in pieces of land so poor no one else wanted them, dependent on the government for minimal sustenance (Coleman, 2000). Under the circumstances, the extermination of all remaining "Indians" was seen by many as necessary and praiseworthy, even as a moral endeavor. L. Frank Baum, who later won lasting fame as the author of *The Wizard of Oz* and its many sequels, wrote in the December 20, 1890, *Aberdeen Saturday Pioneer:*

> The nobility of the Redskin is extinguished . . . The Whites, by law of conquest, by justice of civilization, are masters of the American continent, and the best safety of the frontier settlements will be secured by the

total annihilation of the few remaining Indians. Why not annihilation? Their glory has fled, their spirit broken, their manhood effaced; better that they should die than live the miserable wretches that they are. (Quoted in Churchill, 1997, pp. 244–245)

When I was asked to write a chapter for this book about the psychology of hate, I remembered this quotation from L. Frank Baum and looked it up again, expecting it to be relevant because I recalled it as shockingly hateful. Examining the quote again, however, I think I was guilty in this instance of what I have repeatedly warned against—too quickly reading hatred into genocide. There is indeed in this statement an explicit argument for genocide, but there is no hatred whatsoever. Manifest destiny having worked its course, Baum argues, "Whites" have become "masters of the American continent," and this is both legally and morally fitting, "by law of conquest, by justice of civilization" (Churchill, 1997, p. 244). The remaining Indians are a threat to the White settlers, and this might alone justify killing them, but such "annihilation" is also an act of mercy for the wretched remnants of a vanquished race. The attitude here is contempt and pity, not hatred.

Eight days after Baum's exhortation to genocide, a cold, hungry, and terrified band of 350 Minneconjou, including 230 women and children, were headed from their camp at Cherry Creek, South Dakota, to Pine Ridge, where they thought they would be safer. Their leader, Big Foot, ill with pneumonia, was too sick to ride a horse and so was being dragged on a travois. Near the badlands they encountered four troops of the Seventh Cavalry, about 200 men, under Major S. M. Whitside, to whom Big Foot promptly surrendered.

The Minneconjou were directed to a site near the Wounded Knee Creek to camp for the night. Meanwhile, the commander of the Seventh Cavalry, Colonel George A. Forsyth, arrived with reinforcements, bringing the Army forces to 470. Their armamentation included four Hotchkiss guns, rapid-fire weapons that could hurl two-inch explosive shells more than two miles. The four guns were posted on a rise overlooking the camp, "positioned to rake the length of the Indian lodges" (Brown, 1971, p. 415).

The following morning the Minneconjou were ordered to disarm. Although there was no overt resistance, the number of guns initially surrendered fell far short of expectation. This resulted in a search process that, as it became increasingly intrusive and brutal, led to increasing agitation among the Minneconjou, until one of them apparently fired a hidden rifle and the soldiers immediately responded with a volley at point-blank range:

In the first seconds of violence, the firing of carbines was deafening, filling the air with powder smoke. Among the dying who lay sprawled on the frozen ground was Big Foot. Then there was a brief lull in the rattle of arms, with small groups of Indians and soldiers grappling at close quarters, using knives, clubs, and pistols. As few of the Indians had arms, they soon had to flee, and then the big Hotchkiss guns on the hill opened upon them, firing almost a shell a second, raking the Indian camp, shredding the teepees with flying shrapnel, killing men, women, and children.

"We tried to run," Louise Weasel Bear said, "but they shot us like we were a buffalo." (Brown, 1971, p. 417)

Some 300 of the 350 Minneconjou are estimated to have been killed in the massacre. Witnesses subsequently agreed

that from the moment it opened fire, [the Seventh Cavalry] ceased to be a military unit and became a mass of infuriated men intent only on butchery. Women and children attempted to escape by running up the dry ravine, but were pursued and slaughtered—there is no other word—by hundreds of maddened soldiers, while shells from the Hotchkiss guns, which had been moved to permit them to sweep the ravine, continued to burst among them. The line of bodies afterward was found to extend more than two miles from the camp—and they were all women and children. A few survivors eventually found shelter in brushy gullies here and there, and their pursuers had scouts call out that women and children could come out of their hiding place because they had nothing to fear . . .; some small boys crept out and were surrounded by soldiers who then butchered them. (Andrist, 1964/1993, p. 351)

Was it genocidal hatred that drove the soldiers to destroy the Minneconjou village, including the children? Among the officers were some who had been at the Little Bighorn 14 years earlier, where Seventh Cavalry troops under General Custer had been routed and killed in battle. Some of the soldiers and officers may have hated Indians—at least those, such as the Minneconjou, they classified as Sioux. For some, this hatred may have been sufficiently intense to motivate group extermination, perhaps even via the cold-blooded murder of children (Coleman, 2000).

There is no reason, however, to think genocidal hatred was a primary cause of the genocidal massacre at Wounded Knee, or more generally of the elimination of the plains cultures. There were many reasons to kill Indians and eliminate their cultures, most of them unrelated to hatred. Nationalist, political, and religious ideologies, as well as economic self-interest, converged on the view that the indigenous cultures of the Great Plains were quite properly passing into history and that U.S. soldiers were playing an important and honorable role in this historic transition. "The Regular Army . . . would commit savagely brutal acts against Indians—and not all of them because it was carrying out orders and helpless to do otherwise—but, by and large, it fought as part of a job that had to be done and not from hate" (Andrist, 1964/1993, p. 98).

The massacre at Wounded Knee was the last major massacre of Indians in the United States, but the genocide of indigenous cultures continues around the world (Maybury-Lewis, 2002; Totten, Parsons, & Hitchcock, 2002). Comparative research on such genocides shows that, consistent with the Wounded Knee massacre, they emerge not from hatred but from complex interactions of psychological, economic, political, and ideological factors. The anthropologist David Maybury-Lewis, renowned for his work on cultural survival, provided the following summary:

> Genocide everywhere depends on the perpetrators' dehumanizing their intended victims, establishing them as radically alien creatures who deserve to be eliminated, and having the power to kill them. These conditions normally apply to indigenous peoples who are marginalized and treated as aliens, even in their own countries, and are invariably in a position of political weakness. Moreover, indigenous peoples have in the recent past, and in some places right up to the present day, been considered "savages" who had to be annihilated physically or socially. In recent years indigenous peoples have been threatened in the name of development or for reasons of state.
>
> It is particularly dangerous for them when these two threats come together, as happens when there are valuable resources in indigenous territory that the state wishes to seize in the name of development, and when indigenous wishes to secede from the state (often precisely because the state is trying to take over indigenous resources) are held to constitute a threat to the state.
>
> It is the idea of the threatened state that is particularly insidious and especially likely to lead to genocide. (Maybury-Lewis, 2002, p. 51)

It is not difficult to identify a role for hatred here, but it seems clear that hatred has not been the driving motive in the ongoing genocides of indigenous peoples. As seen throughout this chapter, genocide is advocated, supported, and practiced by people who, far from being creatures of genocidal hatred, act on a variety of nationalist, political, economic, religious, professional, and moral motives not so different from our own.

CONCLUSION

I have presented evidence concerning seven individuals who played important roles in genocide—Rwandan pop star Simon Bikindi, Commandant Franz Stangl of Treblinka, Argentine dirty warriors Adolph Scilingo and Julio Simón, Lt. Colonel Domingo Monterrosa of the Atlacatl Battalion, U.S. President Ronald Reagan, and writer L. Frank Baum. Their involvements in genocide were various: Bikindi wrote songs that were interpreted by many as justifying genocide, whereas Baum explicitly advocated genocide in print. Stangl commanded a death camp, whereas Monterrosa commanded a military force responsible for a program of genocidal massacres. Scilingo and Simón participated in different ways, and perhaps with different degrees of initiative, in a program of disappearances, torture, and murder. Reagan ensured ongoing financial and military support for the extraordinary atrocities of the dirty wars.

Cutting across these differences, however, is an apparent lack of genocidal hatred, at least as a driving force. Bikindi was doing his job and motivated largely by professional advancement. Baum advocated what he saw as justice and mercy for a vanquished foe. Stangl's professional responsibilities evolved step by step, and even as the commander of a death camp he saw himself as a replaceable cog in the Nazi machine. Monterrosa was more enthusiastic about his mission than was Stangl but was motivated by the defense of his country—by patriotism, not hatred. Scilingo and Simón were following what they believed to be morally legitimate orders consistent with their deepest political and religious commitments. Reagan, a former Hollywood actor renowned for his geniality, apparently believed that he was saving the people of Latin America from communism. Probably all of these individuals had other motives as well, and it is likely that some were motivated in part by hatred, but there is no reason to think that any of them was primarily motivated by genocidal hatred.

The absence of genocidal hatred, I should be clear, does not mean the absence of genocide or of moral responsibility. Genocide, as defined earlier, is the extermination, entirely or in part, of an abstractly defined group of people. In Rwanda, Treblinka, and Argentina, and at El Mozote and Wounded Knee, people were killed not because of who they were as individuals but because they were deemed to be affiliated with a group—whether it be Tutsi, Hutu traitors, Jews, subversives, Sioux, or Indians—that was to be eliminated, at least to the extent feasible. Questions about the incidence and role of genocidal hatred do not cast any doubt whatsoever on the genocidal nature of these events.

Similarly, the absence of genocidal hatred does not relieve perpetrators of their moral responsibility. If anything, it makes that responsibility more clear. The relative guilt of these individuals rests on considerations such as whether they were following orders or giving orders, what alternative choices were available to them, and how they perceived their situation.

A comprehensive theory of genocide must address the role of genocidal hatred, which is surely important in many genocides. The cases presented in this chapter, however, suggest that dehumanization may be more important than hatred as a basis for genocide. Hatred is an attitude toward persons—that is, toward those deemed to have sufficient ongoing rational agency to be responsible, in some long-term sense, for what one sees as their evil actions. Dehumanization, in contrast, is a psychological process of placing a person or group outside the realm of personhood, outside the universe of moral obligation. To see Tutsi as cockroaches or Jews as cows makes it more difficult to hate them, not less, but also makes it less difficult to kill them, even in the absence of hatred. To see guerrillas, students, political minorities, and even entire villages as subversive, and to see subversives as weeds to be weeded or as a cancer to be removed, enables genocide without hate. Similarly, the elimination of the indigenous plains cultures of the United States was commonly seen as part of the same process that also included the near-extermination of the bison.

The point, however, is not that dehumanization, rather than genocidal hatred, is the cause of genocide. Genocide is a function of a variety of attitudes, perceptions, ideologies, identities, motives, goals, and social contexts and is rarely or never caused by genocidal hatred or any other single factor (Browning, 1998; Chalk & Jonassohn, 1990; Chirot & Seligman, 2001; Chomsky, 2003; Eidelson & Eidelson, 2003; Fein, 1993; Hinton, 2002; Moshman, 2004a, 2004b; Staub, 2003; Waller, 2002). We overemphasize the role of genocidal hatred because we are motivated to see the perpetrators of genocide as people and governments very different from us and ours. But we can recognize this tendency and consciously resist it. Progress in the psychology of genocide requires us to face the ordinariness of genocidal acts and actors.

In the study of genocide, what we want is different from what we need. What we want is a theory of how perpetrators of genocide differ from us. What we need is a theory that explains how people like us, with motivations like ours, can come to commit genocide.

REFERENCES

Andrist, R. K. (1993). *The long death: The last days of the Plains Indian.* New York: Macmillan. (Original work published 1964)

Arad, Y. (1987). *Belzec, Sobibor, Treblinka: The Operation Reinhard death camps.* Bloomington: Indiana University Press.

Arendt, H. (1994). *Eichmann in Jerusalem: A report on the banality of evil.* New York: Penguin. (Original work published 1963)

Berry, J. A., & Berry, C. P. (Eds.). (1999). *Genocide in Rwanda: A collective memory.* Washington, DC: Howard University Press.

Bouvard, M. G. (1994). *Revolutionizing motherhood: The mothers of the Plaza de Mayo.* Wilmington, DE: SR Books.

Brown, D. (1971). *Bury my heart at Wounded Knee.* New York: Holt, Rinehart & Winston.

Browning, C. R. (1998). *Ordinary men: Reserve Police Battalion 101 and the final solution in Poland.* New York: HarperPerennial.

Chalk, F., & Jonassohn, K. (1990). *The history and sociology of genocide: Analyses and case studies.* New Haven, CT: Yale University Press.

Chirot, D., & Seligman, M. E. P. (Eds.). (2001). *Ethnopolitical warfare: Causes, consequences, and possible solutions.* Washington, DC: American Psychological Association.

Chomsky, N. (2003). *Power and terror*. New York: Seven Stories Press.

Churchill, W. (1997). *A little matter of genocide: Holocaust and denial in the Americas, 1492 to the present*. San Francisco: City Lights.

Coleman, W. S. E. (2000). *Voices of Wounded Knee*. Lincoln: University of Nebraska Press.

Danner, M. (1994). *The massacre at El Mozote*. New York: Vintage.

Des Forges, A. (1999). *Leave none to tell the story: Genocide in Rwanda*. New York: Human Rights Watch.

Donat, A. (Ed.). (1979). *The death camp Treblinka*. New York: Holocaust Library.

Eidelson, R. J., & Eidelson, J. I. (2003). Dangerous ideas: Five beliefs that propel groups toward conflict. *American Psychologist, 58*, 182–192.

Fein, H. (1993). *Genocide: A sociological perspective*. London: Sage.

Feitlowitz, M. (1998). *A lexicon of terror: Argentina and the legacies of torture*. Oxford, England: Oxford University Press.

Fisher, J. (1989). *Mothers of the disappeared*. Boston: South End Press.

Glazar, R. (1995). *Trap with a green fence: Survival in Treblinka*. Evanston, IL: Northwestern University Press.

Gourevitch, P. (1998). *We wish to inform you that tomorrow we will be killed with our families: Stories from Rwanda*. New York: Picador.

Guest, I. (1990). *Behind the disappearances: Argentina's dirty war against human rights and the United Nations*. Philadelphia: University of Pennsylvania Press.

Hinton, A. L. (Ed.). (2002). *Annihilating difference: The anthropology of genocide*. Berkeley: University of California Press.

Mamdani, M. (2001). *When victims become killers: Colonialism, nativism, and the genocide in Rwanda*. Princeton, NJ: Princeton University Press.

Maybury-Lewis, D. (2002). Genocide against indigenous peoples. In A. L. Hinton (Ed.), *Annihilating difference: The anthropology of genocide* (pp. 43–53). Berkeley: University of California Press.

McNeil, D. G., Jr. (2002, March 17). Killer songs: Simon Bikindi stands accused of writing folk music that fed the Rwandan genocide. *The New York Times Magazine*, pp. 58–59.

Mellibovsky, M. (1997). *Circle of love over death: Testimonies of the mothers of the Plaza de Mayo*. Willimantic, CT: Curbstone Press.

Moshman, D. (2001). Conceptual constraints on thinking about genocide. *Journal of Genocide Research, 3*, 431–450.

Moshman, D. (2004a). False moral identity: Self-serving denial in the maintenance of moral self-conceptions. In D. K. Lapsley & D. Narvaez (Eds.), *Moral development, self, and identity* (pp. 83–109). Mahwah, NJ: Erlbaum.

Moshman, D. (2004b). Theories of self and theories as selves: Identity in Rwanda. In C. Lightfoot, C. Lalonde, & M. Chandler (Eds.), *Changing conceptions of psychological life* (pp. 183–206). Mahwah, NJ: Erlbaum.

Moshman, D. (2005). *Adolescent psychological development: Rationality, morality, and identity* (2nd ed.). Mahwah, NJ: Erlbaum.

Moshman, D. (in progress). *The daughters of the Plaza de Mayo.* [A novel of genocide, disappearances, and historical memory.]

Newbury, C., & Newbury, D. (2003). The genocide in Rwanda and the Holocaust in Germany: Parallels and pitfalls. *Journal of Genocide Research, 5,* 135–145.

Osiel, M. J. (2001). *Mass atrocity, ordinary evil, and Hannah Arendt: Criminal consciousness in Argentina's dirty war.* New Haven, CT: Yale University Press.

Sereny, G. (1983). *Into that darkness: An examination of conscience.* New York: Vintage.

Stannard, D. E. (1992). *American holocaust: The conquest of the New World.* Oxford, England: Oxford University Press.

Staub, E. (2003). *The psychology of good and evil.* Cambridge, England: Cambridge University Press.

Totten, S., Parsons, W. S., & Hitchcock, R. K. (2002). Confronting genocide and ethnocide of indigenous peoples. In A. L. Hinton (Ed.), *Annihilating difference: The anthropology of genocide* (pp. 54–91). Berkeley: University of California Press.

Verbitsky, H. (1996). *The flight: Confessions of an Argentine dirty warrior.* New York: New Press.

Waller, J. (2002). *Becoming evil: How ordinary people commit genocide and mass killing.* Oxford, England: Oxford University Press.

Willenberg, S. (1989). *Surviving Treblinka.* Oxford, England: Basil Blackwell.

10

ON THE NATURE OF PREJUDICE: THE PSYCHOLOGICAL FOUNDATIONS OF HATE

JOHN F. DOVIDIO, SAMUEL L. GAERTNER, AND ADAM R. PEARSON

Racial biases are a fundamental form of social control that support the economic, political, and personal goals of the majority group (Liska, 1997). Because of their functionality, racial biases are deeply embedded in cultural values, such as in widely accepted ideologies that justify inequality and exploitation and institutional policies and practices (Jones, 1997). Although the racial climate in the United States has changed because of shifts in social norms over the last several decades, racial biases may still be openly expressed by Whites who strongly adhere to traditional values and conventional beliefs (i.e., Whites high in authoritarianism; Adorno, Frenkel-Brunswik, Levinson, & Sanford, 1950) or who see the superior status of Whites relative to Blacks as legitimate (i.e., Whites high in social dominance orientation; Sidanius & Pratto, 1999). Moreover, racial biases that are less overtly negative but still function to reduce threat and maintain

Preparation of this chapter was supported by National Institute of Mental Health Grant MH 48721 to the first and second authors.

the status quo that provides advantages to Whites are frequently manifested more subtly by many Whites who openly endorse egalitarian values and who believe they are nonprejudiced (Dovidio & Gaertner, 1998, 2004; Gaertner & Dovidio, 1986). The present chapter explores the nature of racial attitudes of White Americans toward Blacks and illustrates the traditional and contemporary role of the psychology of hate—its seeds and its open expression—in race relations.

Racism in the United States has historically manifested itself in a variety of ways, including slavery, segregation, open discrimination, and violent actions such as lynchings. Although adverse economic conditions (Hovland & Sears, 1940; cf. Green, Glaser, & Rich, 1998) and the frustration of basic human needs (Staub, 1996), sparked by specific "trigger" incidents (Torres, 1999), have often instigated such brutal violent actions as lynchings and riots, a foundational, predisposing factor is racial prejudice.

Prejudice is commonly defined as an unfair negative attitude toward a social group or a person perceived to be a member of that group and, like other attitudes, consists of three components: affect, cognition, and behavior. The cognitive component involves specific thoughts or beliefs about the attitude object; the affective component involves feelings and emotions associated with the attitude object; and the behavioral component reflects associations with the person's past or intended action toward the attitude object. The experience and intensity of the negative affect related to prejudice can vary as a function of the specific group and moderating situational conditions. The various emotional reactions involved in prejudice range from mild discomfort, disgust, and fear to anger and, at the extreme, open hatred, with the specific emotions involved corresponding to different patterns of behavioral responses to the other group (Devos, Silver, Mackie, & Smith, 2002).

Hate has long been recognized as an important element of many prejudices, such as racism. Allport (1954) described *hate* as extreme dislike associated with prejudice that produces aggressive impulses. Kovel (1970) characterized the traditional, blatant form of prejudice, which has historically defined the racial attitudes of many White Americans, as *dominative racism*. The dominative racist, according to Kovel, is the type of person "who acts out bigoted beliefs—he represents the open flame of racial hatred" (p. 54).

Prejudice, however, is a collective phenomenon related to one's social identity (Tajfel & Turner, 1979) as well as to one's personal identity and corresponding attitudes. Specifically, when personal identity is salient, a person's individual needs, standards, beliefs, and motives primarily determine his or her behavior. In contrast, when social identity is salient, "people come to perceive themselves as more interchangeable exemplars of a social category than as unique personalities defined by their individual differences from others" (Turner, Hogg, Oakes, Reicher, & Wetherell, 1987, p. 50).

Under these conditions, collective needs, goals, and standards are the critical determinants of responses. Illustrating the dynamics of this distinction, Verkuyten and Hagendoorn (1998) found that when individual identity was primed, individual differences in authoritarianism were the major predictor of prejudice toward immigrants. In contrast, when social identity (i.e., national identity) was made salient, in-group stereotypes and standards primarily predicted prejudiced attitudes toward immigrants.

Sternberg (2003) recently extended conceptions of hate in a way that applies to both individuals and groups. He wrote, "Typically, hate is thought of as a single emotion. But there is reason to believe that it has multiple components that can manifest themselves in different ways on different occasions" (p. 306). The three main components that Sternberg identified are (a) the negation of intimacy, which originates from feelings of disgust; (b) passion, which is expressed in intense anger or fear during periods of threat; and (c) decision–commitment, which involves devaluation of the other group through contempt.

In this chapter, we draw on Sternberg's (2003) conception of hate in our analysis of the psychology of prejudice. We focus on the prejudice of White Americans toward Black Americans because of the central role that this phenomenon has had historically in social relations, policy, and politics in the United States and because it is the most extensively researched prejudice within psychology. We propose that affect plays a key role in racial prejudice and that the seeds of hatred are present in even subtle contemporary forms of prejudice.

We begin by exploring historical changes in the expression of Whites' prejudice toward Blacks from the overt, dominative form to more subtle forms. We then illustrate the dynamics of contemporary prejudice by examining one common form, aversive racism, and its expression in subtle bias. Next, we consider how the interracial anxiety and discomfort that normally characterize aversive racists' feelings toward Blacks can become the seeds of hatred when Whites are provoked or threatened, and how negative stereotypes and justifying ideologies can facilitate the development of hatred and the expression of open discrimination. We conclude by suggesting ways to combat contemporary racial prejudice, focusing on the seeds of hate in normally subtle forms of bias.

THE NATURE OF CONTEMPORARY RACISM

Overt expressions of prejudice and blatant forms of discrimination have declined significantly over the past several decades (Bobo, 2001). These declines have been attributed, at least in part, to the landmark civil rights legislation of the 1960s, which made racial discrimination illegal and helped to facilitate more egalitarian norms and standards in personal behavior (McConahay, 1986). Even after the enactment of such progressive legislation, the potential for racial attitudes to erupt into violence against Blacks still remains. This violence is frequently manifested in *hate crimes*, which are defined as criminal acts motivated in whole or in part by prejudice toward another group (Boeckmann & Turpin-Petrosino, 2002). Because the standards for reporting hate crimes have varied, it is difficult to determine whether incidences of hate crimes have changed systematically over time. Nevertheless, the number of reported hate crimes against Blacks increased from 1,689 (36% of all reported hate crimes) in 1991 to 3,573 (39% of reported hate crimes) in 1998 (Perry, 2002).

Although we recognize that blatant forms of racism still exist and are frequently the basis of violence against Blacks, in this chapter we focus on how the more subtle forms of bias, those that characterize the attitudes of mainstream White Americans, can involve and support a psychology of hate. In particular, we examine how biases in the ways people think, in the nature of their motivations, and in their socialization can predispose people to act in prejudicial and discriminatory ways against members of other groups. Although these processes most typically produce more mild or subtle forms of discrimination, under conditions of competition and threat such biases can lead to explicit conflict and overt expressions of hatred. It is perhaps because of its many sources and manifestations that bias and perceptions of bias play a prominent role in contemporary race relations in the United States (Gallup Organization, 2002).

Research on contemporary racial attitudes, in particular, has hypothesized not only that affect and cognition are distinguishable components of attitudes but also that they may reflect different, and potentially contradictory, types of evaluations and intentions. Whereas the traditional, dominative form of racial prejudice is considered to be direct and generally univalently negative (McConahay, 1986), the contemporary racial attitudes of Whites, particularly White Americans, are hypothesized to be more complex, reflecting both negative and positive reactions.

Approaches such as symbolic racism theory (Sears, Henry, & Kosterman, 2000), modern racism theory (McConahay, 1986), and the aversive racism framework (Gaertner & Dovidio, 1986; see also Dovidio & Gaertner, 1998) converge to emphasize dissociations between the cognitive and affective components of contemporary racial attitudes. A crucial underlying feature that these three different forms of contemporary racial bias share is the fundamental conflict between the denial of personal prejudice and underlying unconscious negative feelings.

What distinguishes the different perspectives on contemporary racism are the conscious beliefs that permit discrimination to be expressed. The *aversive racism framework* has assumed that these positive attitudes are based on political and social liberalism (Gaertner & Dovidio, 1986). *Symbolic racism theory* emphasizes that beliefs about individualism and meritocracy that become racialized motivate opposition to policies designed to benefit racial and ethnic minorities. *Modern racism theory* similarly proposes that beliefs associated with conservative ideologies can justify discriminatory behaviors, but this theory places more emphasis on the moderating effects of contexts that provide a justification for negative responses to minorities. However, one commonality shared by all of these approaches, and that reflects the complexity of contemporary racial attitudes, is the idea that racial bias is expressed in more subtle ways than is "old-fashioned" racism. In the next section, to illustrate the dynamics of contemporary prejudice, we examine one of these approaches, aversive racism theory, in more detail.

AVERSIVE RACISM

According to the aversive racism perspective, many people who consciously, explicitly, and sincerely support egalitarian principles and believe themselves to be nonprejudiced also harbor negative feelings about Blacks and other historically disadvantaged groups. These negative feelings can significantly influence behavior, typically in terms of avoidance or failure to respond positively rather than in terms of direct hostility (Gaertner & Dovidio, 1986). In other words, these feelings, independent of egalitarian beliefs, may produce negative responses toward Blacks ranging from avoidance of direct interracial contact to discrimination and interracial aggression.

A critical aspect of the aversive racism framework (Dovidio & Gaertner, 2004; Gaertner & Dovidio, 1986) is the development of underlying unconscious negative feelings by Whites toward Blacks as a consequence of normal, almost unavoidable, and frequently functional cognitive, motivational, and social-cultural process. In terms of cognitive processes, people inherently categorize others into groups, typically in terms that delineate their own group from other groups. This classification, in turn, creates bias: Once categorized, people begin to value others in their own group more and may often devalue others belonging to different groups (Tajfel & Turner, 1979; Turner et al., 1987). In the United States, Whites automatically categorize people on the basis of race, and this categorization spontaneously elicits racial stereotypes (Blair, 2001).

Motivational processes relate to people's desires to satisfy basic needs of power, status, and control, not only for themselves but also for their group (Sidanius & Pratto, 1999; Tajfel & Turner, 1979). In a world with limited resources, one of the ways that people maintain control or power is by hindering the progress of competing groups. The effects of sociocultural influences can be seen in the tendency for people to internalize the racially biased traditional values and beliefs of American society, beliefs that are often perpetuated by the media. Nevertheless, current cultural values may also be partly responsible for perpetuating the strong convictions concerning fairness, justice, and racial equality held by most White Americans. The existence of both the conscious endorsement of egalitarian values and the unconscious negative feelings toward Blacks makes aversive racists' attitudes complex and produces a distinct pattern of discriminatory behavior. In the next section, we examine the implications of the aversive racism framework and illustrate how bias is expressed in subtle ways but can have profound consequences.

Unmasking Subtle Bias

The aversive racism framework helps to identify when discrimination against Blacks and other minority groups will or will not occur. Whereas old-fashioned racists exhibit a direct and overt pattern of discrimination, aversive racists' actions may appear more variable and inconsistent. At times they discriminate (manifesting their negative feelings), and at other times they do not (reflecting their egalitarian beliefs). Our research has provided a framework for understanding this complex pattern of discrimination.

Because aversive racists consciously recognize and endorse egalitarian values, and because they truly aspire to be nonprejudiced, they will not discriminate in situations with strong social norms when discrimination would be obvious to others and to themselves. Specifically, we propose that when people are presented with a situation in which the normatively appropriate response is clear (when right and wrong are clearly defined), aversive racists will not discriminate against Blacks. In these circumstances, aversive racists will be especially motivated to avoid feelings, beliefs, and behaviors that could be associated with racist intent. Wrongdoing, which could directly threaten their nonprejudiced self-image, would be too costly. However, because they still possess feelings of unease, such feelings will eventually be expressed, but in subtle, indirect, and rationalizable ways. Discrimination will tend to occur in situations in which normative structure is weak, when the guidelines for appropriate behavior are vague, or when the basis for social judgment is ambiguous. In addition, discrimination will occur when an aversive racist can justify or rationalize a negative response on the basis of some factor other than race. Under these circumstances, aversive racists may engage in behaviors that ultimately harm Blacks, but in ways that allow them to maintain their self-image as nonprejudiced.

Aversive racists may be identified by a constellation of characteristic responses to racial issues and interracial situations. First, in contrast to old-fashioned racists, aversive racists endorse fair and just treatment of all groups. Second, despite their conscious good intentions, aversive racists unconsciously harbor feelings of uneasiness toward Blacks and thus try to avoid interracial interaction. This aspect of aversive racism directly relates to the distancing component in Sternberg's (2003) model of hate. Third, when interracial interaction is unavoidable, they experience anxiety and discomfort and consequently try to disengage from such an interaction as quickly as possible. Fourth, because part of the discomfort that they experience is due to a concern about acting inappropriately and appearing prejudiced, they strictly adhere to established rules and codes of behavior in interracial situations they cannot avoid. Finally, their feelings will be expressed, but in subtle, unintentional, and rationalizable ways that disadvantage minorities or unfairly benefit the majority group. Nevertheless, in terms of conscious intent, aversive racists intend not to discriminate against Blacks, and they behave accordingly when it is possible for them to monitor the appropriateness of their behavior.

We have found consistent support across a broad range of situations for the basic proposition that contemporary biases are expressed in subtle rather than blatant ways (see Dovidio & Gaertner, 1998, 2004; Gaertner & Dovidio, 1986; Gaertner et al., 1997). One of our earliest experiments (Gaertner & Dovidio, 1977) demonstrated how aversive racism can operate in dramatic and consequential ways. The scenario for the experiment was inspired by an incident in the mid-1960s in which 38 people witnessed the stabbing of a woman, Kitty Genovese, without a single bystander intervening to help. What might account for this behavior? Research by Darley and Latané (1968) showed that feelings of responsibility play a key role. If a person witnesses an emergency knowing that he or she is the only bystander, that person bears all of the responsibility for helping. Consequently, the likelihood of helping is high. In contrast, if a person witnesses an emergency but believes that there are several other witnesses who might help, then the responsibility for helping is shared. Moreover, if the person believes that someone else will help or has already helped, the likelihood that the bystander will take action is reduced.

To further explore the dynamics of emergency intervention across races, we created a situation in the laboratory in which White participants witnessed a staged emergency involving a Black or White victim. We led some of our participants to believe that they would be the only witness to this emergency and led others to believe there would be other White people who would also witness the emergency. Because aversive racists do not act in overtly bigoted ways, we predicted that Whites would not discriminate when they were the only witness and the responsibility for helping was clearly focused on them. However, we anticipated that Whites would help Black victims much less frequently than White victims when they had a justifiable excuse not to get involved, such as the belief that one of the other witnesses would take responsibility for helping.

The results supported these predictions. When White participants believed that they were the only witness, they helped both White and Black victims very frequently (over 85% of the time) and equivalently. There was no evidence of blatant racism. In contrast, when they thought that others had witnessed the emergency and could therefore rationalize a decision not to help on the basis of a factor other than race, they helped Black victims only half as often as White victims (37.5% vs. 75%). These results illustrate the operation of subtle biases in relatively dramatic, spontaneous, and life-threatening circumstances involving a failure to help, rather than an action intentionally aimed at doing harm. Nevertheless, when the situation permits discrimination while allowing a White person to avoid an attribution of bigotry, aversive racism can have consequences as profound as the effects of dominative racism (racism motivated by overt hatred).

Less dramatic, but potentially equally devastating, is the influence of aversive racism in the workplace. Aversive racism can contribute to the economic stratification of Whites and Blacks under conditions that permit the expression of bias while avoiding the realization of racial motivations. Labor statistics continue to demonstrate fundamental disparities in the economic status of Blacks relative to Whites—a gap that has not only persisted but also widened in recent years for some important indicators, such as family income (see Blank, 2001). Aversive racism may be one contributing factor helping to maintain this economic disparity.

The power and destructive nature of aversive racism can be especially evident at the time of hiring, when it can affect how qualifications are perceived and weighed in a manner that systematically disadvantages Black relative to White applicants. In particular, the aversive racism framework suggests that bias will not be expressed when a person is clearly qualified or unqualified for a position, because the appropriate decision is obvious. However, when the appropriate decision is unclear—for example, when the evidence is ambiguous as to whether a candidate's qualifications meet the criteria for selection or when a candidate's file has conflicting information (e.g., some strong and some weak features)—bias will occur.

In one study of hiring decisions (Dovidio & Gaertner, 2000), college students were presented with excerpts from an interview and were then asked to evaluate candidates for a position in an ostensibly new program for peer counseling at their university. In the study, White participants were asked to evaluate a Black or White candidate who had credentials that were systematically manipulated to represent very strong, moderate, or very weak qualifications for the position. As predicted by the aversive racism framework, when the candidate's credentials clearly qualified him or her for the position (strong qualifications) or when the credentials were clearly inappropriate (weak qualifications), there was no discrimination against the Black candidate. However, when the candidate's qualifications for the position were less obvious and the appropriate decision was more ambiguous (moderate qualifications), White participants recommended the Black candidate significantly less often than a White candidate with the exact same credentials. Moreover, when the responses of participants from 1989 were compared with those of 1999, although overt expressions of prejudice (measured by items on a self-report prejudice scale) declined over this 10-year period, the pattern of subtle discrimination in selection decisions remained essentially unchanged.

Thus, although the discrimination associated with aversive racism may be expressed subtly, its consequences can be comparable to traditional, direct expressions of prejudice resulting in threats to the personal and economic well-being of Blacks. Although our research has focused on race relations in the United States, the processes of aversive racism are not limited by national boundaries and may reflect attitudes toward a number of different groups when overt forms of discrimination are recognized as inappropriate (Esses, Dovidio, Jackson, & Armstrong, 2001; Pettigrew & Meertens, 1995).

Thus far, we have noted the role of Sternberg's (2003) first component of hate, the negation of intimacy, based in negative affective reactions, in contemporary prejudice and have illustrated how subtle forms of bias still function as social control mechanisms that limit the opportunities for Blacks. In the next section, we explore how the racial ambivalence of Whites and the accompanying emotions of discomfort and anxiety can, under conditions of provocation and threat, be transformed into more directed negative emotions, such as fear or anger, that motivate open aggression toward Blacks.

Ambivalence, Amplification, and Response to Provocation and Threat

The existence of nearly unavoidable racial biases, based on normal cognitive, motivational, and sociocultural influences, along with the simultaneous desire to be nonprejudiced represents a basic duality of attitudes for aversive racists. This duality produces racial ambivalence, which often results in response amplification (Katz, Wackenhut, & Hass, 1986). From the aversive racism perspective, because bias is based in Whites' unacknowledged negative feelings toward Blacks, this response amplification often takes the form of more extreme negative responses toward Blacks than Whites.

Stephan and Stephan (1985) posited that a key factor in intergroup ambivalence is the anxiety resulting from intergroup interaction. As suggested by the aversive racism framework, interracial interactions are particularly anxiety provoking. Besides the anxiety aroused within Whites when interacting with a person from a group with which they may have had limited contact, fears of acting in a way that reveals one's racial biases can heighten the anxiety and discomfort that aversive racists experience in interracial interaction. Richeson and Shelton (2003) found that such attempts by aversive racists to avoid wrongdoing appear to involve significant conscious effort. Whites high in implicit prejudice toward Blacks (assessed using a response-time measure) performed more poorly on a cognitively demanding task after interacting with a Black person than did Whites low in implicit prejudice. Richeson and Shelton proposed that for high implicitly prejudiced

Whites, the cognitive effort required to monitor their interracial behavior depleted their cognitive resources, resulting in a decrement in performance on the subsequent task. Members of minority groups may also experience intergroup anxiety, but in part for different reasons. Because of the potential for discrimination, Blacks tend to approach interracial interactions with Whites with anxiety, guardedness, and underlying mistrust (Hyers & Swim, 1998).

As Stephan and Stephan (1985) proposed, because arousal created by one source (e.g., interracial anxiety) can be transferred and attributed to another source (e.g., perceived threat), interracial anxiety can amplify Whites' affective reactions and consequently produces more extreme behavioral responses to Blacks than to Whites. That is, to the extent that arousal, originally interpreted as anxiety, becomes added to the arousal elicited by threat and reinterpreted as the emotional response to threat, the reactions to interracial threat are likely to be more intense than to intraracial threat (Zillman, 1996). This process of transfer and misattribution of arousal is particularly likely to occur when people are not conscious of the original source of arousal, as are aversive racists who do not typically acknowledge their negative reactions to Blacks. Thus, the more diffuse emotions of interracial anxiety and discomfort that are experienced by aversive racists and typically lead to avoidance can (under some circumstances) become the seeds for hate—they can readily be transformed into more intense negative emotions that motivate violent and aggressive actions toward Blacks. In terms of Sternberg's (2003) model of hate, interracial anxiety and discomfort can help amplify the impact of interracial threat, producing anger and fear that are expressed directly in hostility toward Blacks. In this way, aversive racism may have consequences similar to those of blatant dominant racism in response to racial threats.

Research by Rogers and Prentice-Dunn (1981) illustrates how subtle prejudice, which may not be manifested under most normal circumstances, can be a critical factor in interracial aggression and hostility under other conditions. In one study, White male students were led to believe that they were participating in a behavior modification study. They were told that they should administer shocks to another person, actually a Black or White confederate, when a signal indicated that the person's heart rate fell below a predetermined level. In one condition designed to provoke anger, the participant overheard the confederate say to the experimenter (before the task was performed) that the participant looked too "dumb" and "stupid" to operate the apparatus. In a control condition, the confederate simply stated that he was ready to proceed with the experiment and had no objections about participating. In the control condition, where they were not provoked by the insults, White participants administered somewhat lower intensity shocks to Black than to White confederates. From the perspective of aversive racism, White participants were particularly cautious about injuring a Black person without justification. However, after being angered in the insult condition,

White participants administered substantially higher levels of shock to Black than to White confederates. That is, when they were provoked by the confederate, which aroused anger and provided a nonracial explanation for retaliation, Whites were particularly aggressive toward Blacks.

Consistent with the aversive racism framework, Whites' willingness to shock Blacks more than Whites is also moderated by situational factors relating the salience of compliance to nonprejudiced norms. Their interracial aggression is inhibited when Whites anticipate censure from others; it is facilitated when Whites feel freed from prevailing norms through conditions that make them feel anonymous and deindividuated (Donnerstein & Donnerstein, 1973; Donnerstein, Donnerstein, Simon, & Ditrichs, 1972; Rogers & Prentice-Dunn, 1981). Analogously, Mullen's (1986) analysis of newspaper reports of Blacks being lynched by White mobs suggests that the greater anonymity and deindividuation of being in a larger group is a significant contributing factor in such violence against Blacks.

Even without direct provocation, general feelings of intergroup threat can be a catalyst for the transformation of aversive racism into the open, dominative form characterized by racial antipathy and hatred. Theories based on functional relations often point to competition and consequent perceived threat as a fundamental cause of intergroup conflict. *Realistic group conflict theory* (Campbell, 1965), for example, posits that perceived group competition for resources produces efforts to reduce the access of other groups to the resources. From a sociological perspective (see also Bobo, 1999), Blumer (1958) wrote, "Race prejudice is a defensive reaction to such challenging of the sense of group position . . . As such, race prejudice is a protective device. It functions, however shortsightedly, to preserve the integrity and position of the dominant group" (p. 5). From a psychological orientation, the classic Robbers Cave study by Sherif, Harvey, White, Hood, and Sherif (1961) similarly proposed that the functional relations between groups are critical in determining intergroup attitudes. According to this position, competition between groups produces prejudice and discrimination, which become instruments for protecting the resources and opportunities for one's group (Esses et al., 2001). In contrast, intergroup interdependence and cooperative interactions that result in successful outcomes tend to reduce intergroup bias.

Although the effect of economic threat has traditionally received the primary empirical attention (Hovland & Sears, 1940) as a cause of hate and violence against Blacks (e.g., lynchings), other forms of threat, such as symbolic threats to a group's sense of identity or to a group's cultural values and ideals (Stephan et al., 2002), can arouse intense affective reactions and facilitate open discrimination. Glaser, Dixit, and Green (2002) theorized that "hate crimes against African Americans typically result not so much from economic concerns or frustrations, or competition for material resources, but more often from the perceived threat to the integrity, separateness, and hegemony of the ingroup" (p. 180). They found that White racists were more threatened by, and advocated violence more strongly in response to, interracial marriage and Blacks moving into the neighborhood than job competition. McDevitt, Levin, and Bennett's (2002) analysis revealed that a substantial portion of hate crimes, 33% in their sample, were based on defensive or retaliatory motivations related to perceived threat. Thus, the roots of the many violent actions against Blacks may reside in collective identity and the forces of in-group favoritism—the fundamental elements of aversive racism (Gaertner et al., 1997).

Although the Robbers Cave study described in detail by Sherif et al. (1961) is widely considered a classic example of the role of competition and threat in intergroup conflict, in the course of the study, intergroup hate began to emerge even before explicit competition was introduced. In the study, twenty-two 12-year-old boys attending summer camp were randomly assigned to two groups (who subsequently named themselves the Eagles and the Rattlers). The groups first interacted in isolation from each other, unaware of the other group's existence, and later were brought together in physical proximity, but without direct contact. Over the ensuing several weeks, the groups engaged in several competitive activities that generated overt intergroup conflict. Finally, toward the end of the experience, the groups participated in a series of cooperative activities designed to ameliorate conflict and bias.

Sherif et al.'s (1961) detailed account of the first few days at Robbers Cave reveals that intergroup bias actually preceded the introduction of functionally competitive relations between the groups. Even before the groups met face-to-face or engaged one another in competitive activities, knowledge of the mere existence of the other group appeared to initiate bias and create new stereotypes. Sherif et al. observed,

> When the in-group began to be clearly delineated, there was a tendency to consider all others as out-group . . . The Rattlers didn't know another group existed in camp until they heard the Eagles on the ball diamond; but from that time on the out-group figured prominently in their lives . . . Simpson was convinced that "those guys" were down at our diamond again . . . When the Eagles were playing on the ball diamond and heard the Rattlers, Wilson referred to those "nigger campers." (pp. 94–95)

Consistent with the hypothesized catalytic role of threat, however, the introduction of competitive relations between the groups (in the form of repeated competitive athletic activities centering around tug-of-war, baseball, and touch football) during the second week further generated derogatory stereotypes and escalated conflict between the groups. The groups conducted raids on the other group's cabins that resulted in the destruction and theft of property; the boys carried sticks, baseball bats, and socks filled with rocks as potential weapons; fistfights broke out between members of the groups; and food and garbage fights erupted in the dining hall. In addition, group members regularly exchanged verbal insults (e.g., "ladies first") and name-calling (e.g., "sissies," "stinkers," "pigs," "bums," "cheaters," and "communists").

Although stereotypes are often assumed to be a causal factor in discrimination, Sherif et al.'s (1961) observation of the emergence of stereotypes following conflict further implicates the role of normative justifications (which is central to the aversive racism framework) on the expressions of discrimination toward Blacks. As Allport (1954) noted, stereotypes can be a consequence as well as a cause of discrimination because they serve to both justify past episodes of discrimination and perpetuate new forms. In the next section, we review the effects of stereotypes and norms that devalue Blacks as a key factor in the expression of racism.

Social Devaluation: From Subtle to Overt Bias

The third component Sternberg (2003) identified in his model of hate is decision/commitment, "characterized by cognitions of devaluation and diminution through contempt for the target group" (p. 308). Staub (1996) also identified the systematic devaluation and dehumanization of members of another group as a key element in the "psychology of evil" leading to open, and often mass, violence against the group. This aspect of the psychology of hate also has roots in prejudice, including contemporary forms such as aversive racism as well as the traditional blatant form.

As we noted earlier, social categorization forms a foundation for the development of intergroup biases, both blatant and subtle. In the United States, people tend to automatically categorize others on the basis of race (Dovidio & Gaertner, 1993), although other ways of categorizing them are possible (Gaertner & Dovidio, 2000). When people (or objects) are categorized into groups, actual differences between members of the same category tend to be minimized and often ignored in making decisions or forming impressions. At the same time, between-group differences tend to become exaggerated (Turner et al., 1987). Once social categorization occurs, people tend to respond more favorably to in-group than to out-group members in a wide range of ways.

Perceiving others in terms of their group membership initiates, typically spontaneously, an overall bias in which people categorized as in-group members are evaluated more favorably than out-group members (see Gaertner & Dovidio, 2000). In general, people tend to ascribe more positive traits to in-group members, are more attracted to in-group members, recall more positive and fewer negative incidences of the behaviors of in-group relative to out-group members, and are more likely to make situational attributions for their negative actions and dispositional attributions for their positive behaviors (see Gaertner & Dovidio, 2000). Furthermore, different standards of justice and morality are applied to in-group and out-group members: More emphasis is placed on processes of procedural fairness and justice in interactions with in-group members than with out-group members (Tyler & Blader, 2000), often leading to the "moral exclusion" of members of the out-group. These biases occur even when assignment to groups is random or based on socially irrelevant criteria, such as whether one is an "overestimator" or "underestimator," and become more pronounced for more enduring and important group memberships (Mullen, Brown, & Smith, 1992).

Beyond its cognitive and general evaluative effects, the social categorization of people as in-group and out-group members can also have immediate affective consequences (Dovidio & Gaertner, 1993). At the most basic level, there is a tendency for more positive emotional responses to in-group members. However, unique emotional reactions (e.g., fear, disgust; see Mackie & Smith, 2002) may also be elicited through social categorization of people as members of meaningful out-groups. Also, people perceive that in-group and out-group members have different capacities for human emotions. Paladino et al. (2002) proposed that out-group members are perceived as less fully "human" compared with in-group members and thus have a more basic and limited range of emotional reactions. In-group members are attributed higher order, uniquely human emotions (or "sentiments"), such as love, hope, contempt, and resentment, whereas out-group members are attributed more basic, non–uniquely human emotions, such as joy, surprise, fear, and anger.

The cognitive and affective responses to classifying others as out-group members also combine to predispose people to devalue members of some groups and elicit distinctly negative emotions. In general, people tend to view an out-group as more homogeneous (i.e., the members are more alike) than the in-group (Mullen & Hu, 1989), and this effect, coupled with the tendency to ascribe more negative traits to out-group members, predisposes people to negative stereotyping of the out-group. This process was illustrated in the excerpt from Sherif et al.'s (1961) notes on the Robbers Cave study, presented earlier. Thus, even though many Whites do not admit to consciously holding negative racial stereotypes, there is evidence that even Whites who say they are not prejudiced (such as aversive racists) and who may not consciously endorse negative stereotypes typically associate negative stereotypic characteristics with Blacks, implicitly and unconsciously (Blair, 2001).

Affective reactions to different groups are then shaped by the content of a group's stereotypic qualities, primarily on the basis of the dimensions of perceived competence and warmth. Fiske, Cuddy, Glick, and Xu (2002) found that whereas groups high in competence and high in warmth (such as Black professionals) produce admiration, groups viewed as low in competence and low in warmth (such as poor Blacks) generate contempt. In general, the more the lower status of another group is attributed to controllable factors (such as incompetence from a lack of effort), the more negative is the affect aroused by the group (Weiner, 1995). Because the types of perceptions that generate feelings of contempt are similar to those that aversive racists might adopt to justify a negative response, even aversive racists may be predisposed to exhibit overt discrimination under these conditions.

Cultures also tend to develop system-justifying ideologies that provide an acceptable explanation for the different contemporary statuses of various groups within a society that might have historical roots in injustice and discrimination. Jost and Major (2001) explained that

> if a system that distributes outcomes unequally among its members is to survive, then its members must view the inequalities as justified and legitimate. Thus, perceived legitimacy must come not only from those who benefit, but also from those who are disadvantaged by the system. (p. 14)

Glick (2002) identified this type of ideological commitment by majority group members as a determining factor in scapegoating, in which innocent groups become the target of displaced aggression. Staub (1989), who refined the traditional frustration–aggression perspective on scapegoating in his social psychological explanation of genocide, proposed that difficult social, economic, or political conditions can frustrate people's basic needs relating to esteem, well-being, and belonging. According to Glick, this frustration, when experienced collectively, can often lead to scapegoating movements that focus social blame on another group. These movements are successful to the extent that people believe that action against the group, even if it is objectively innocent, will address their problems directly or meet their needs indirectly (e.g., for esteem, control, or belonging). Collective hostile action against the group initiates a destructive and escalating cycle that becomes justified through further devaluation of the group. Under these circumstances, hate becomes rationalized with evolving stereotypes that warrant contempt, and aggression is seen as instrumental, rational, and appropriate.

Traditionally disadvantaged groups, such as Blacks in the United States, are often trapped by cultural legitimizing ideologies. Collective action by minority group members requires a rejection of these ideologies, but rejecting such fundamental codes can arouse threat and contempt among Whites (Rozin, Lowery, Imada, & Haidt, 1999). Furthermore, contexts that arouse perceptions of group competition increase the salience of ideologies that justify discrimination (Jost & Major, 2001) and elicit the types of negative emotions, such as contempt or hatred, that can produce aggressive reactions.

Cultural values expressed in social norms have a particularly important function moderating the expression of racial prejudice. Social norms in the United States typically function to inhibit prejudice and discrimination. As we illustrated earlier, aversive racists do not discriminate when the acts will violate dominant egalitarian norms. However, deviant behavior can occur in direct opposition to these norms. McDevitt et al. (2002) found that the majority of hate crimes that they studied were motivated by the "thrill" of the crime, which is related to the violation of conventional norms and standards.

Nevertheless, despite general norms against prejudice and discrimination, more local and immediate norms can frequently support racial bias. Blanchard, Crandall, Brigham, and Vaughn (1994), for instance, found that participants who heard another student support prejudicial views (which signaled prejudiced contextual norms) subsequently adopted more racist positions than did those in a control condition. In contrast, those who heard another student condemn racial prejudice later advocated less racist positions. More important, these effects occurred equivalently for participants' private and public responses, indicating that the communication of these immediate norms relating to prejudice influenced participants' internal standards.

Because aversive racism represents a latent form of bias that is strongly moderated by social circumstances and norms, a change in perceived norms can allow this bias to operate more directly and openly. For example, Gaertner, Dovidio, and Johnson (1982) demonstrated, consistent with the findings of Gaertner and Dovidio (1977) discussed earlier, that although White bystanders who were the only witness to an emergency helped Black and White victims equally, those in a group of White nonresponsive bystanders conformed to the immediate norm of nonintervention more when the victim was Black than when the victim was White. Participants' physiological responses and postexperimental explanations indicated that they felt normative pressure from the group not to intervene in this situation; however, they succumbed to this pressure more when the victim was Black than when the victim was White.

This latent form of racism also has important organizational implications. In corporate settings, racial discrimination in personnel selection decisions emerges when norms, which typically condemn discrimination, change. For example, Whites are more likely to discriminate against Black job applicants when they learn that an organizational authority condones discrimination (Brief, Buttram, Elliott, Reizenstein, & McCline, 1995). People who harbor contemporary forms of racism may be especially sensitive to this change in norms. Brief, Dietz, Cohen, Pugh, and Vaslow (2000) demonstrated that when an organizational superior provided a business justification that permitted discrimination on an ostensibly nonracial basis, White participants, particularly those high in modern racism (McConahay, 1986), discriminated against Black candidates in their recommendations. Thus, besides its subtle contemporary influence, if left unaddressed, aversive racism provides the seed for bias to emerge when conditions allow or encourage a more open expression of discrimination.

CONCLUSION

In this chapter, we have explored the role of hate, both individually and collectively, in racial prejudice and discrimination. We have argued that although dominative racism, or racism motivated by racial hatred (Kovel, 1970), is now relatively rare, contemporary forms of racism still have a negative impact on Blacks. In addition, the biases associated with contemporary forms of racism tend to be subtle. With respect to aversive racism, discrimination typically occurs when the behavior can be justified on the basis of some factor other than race, insulating the aversive racist from attributions of bigotry.

Although the expression bias from aversive racism is typically subtle, its effects can be as pernicious as the impact of traditional, overt racism, as seen for instance in the restriction of economic opportunities for Blacks. Moreover, aversive racism contains the seeds of more blatant racism, rooted in the three main components of Sternberg's (2003) duplex model of hate: the negation of intimacy, intense anger or fear during periods of threat, and devaluation of the other group through contempt. First, aversive racists experience anxiety and discomfort in interracial situations, which motivates avoidance of contact and limits intimacy (Gaertner & Dovidio, 1986). Second, when confronted with interracial situations, anxiety and discomfort can intensify affective responses to provocation and threat, leading to more negative emotional reactions and more extreme actions toward Blacks than might otherwise occur toward Whites (Stephan & Stephan, 1985). Third, the forces of in-group favoritism, which represent a critical underpinning of aversive racism (Gaertner et al., 1997), provide a foundation from which negative stereotypes evolve, different standards for fairness and justice develop, and members of other groups become devalued through justifying ideologies. As a consequence, when prevailing norms against prejudice become weakened or superseded by local norms that support discrimination, aversive racists may be predisposed to engage in blatant and aggressive forms of discrimination.

Although hate crimes are currently rare, with deviant acts comprising only a small portion of all crimes (Perry, 2002), even subtle forms of contemporary prejudice reflect a potential for extreme responses motivated by racial hatred that may be realized under conditions of threat and supportive norms or cultural values. Some scholars have argued that these norms and values have already begun to change. Torres (1999) wrote the following:

> The attitude in the United States today gives rise to a belief that bigotry is no longer politically incorrect, and is once again finding a degree of respectability. The prejudicial attitudes that have always been present in some people have not been manifested because the social and political climate was not conducive to such expressions of bigotry. However, what used to be kept below the surface or whispered behind closed doors

about African Americans is now openly flaunted because of a social and political climate now conducive to such expression. (p. 57)

Although we do not necessarily agree with Torres's assessment of how dramatically the social and political climate has changed, we do agree, on the basis of the psychological research and theory about prejudice, that the capacity for bigotry and racial hatred does reside just "below the surface."

We have proposed a variety of techniques for limiting the effects of aversive racism and combating aversive racism at its roots (Dovidio & Gaertner, 2004; Gaertner & Dovidio, 2000). These techniques include strengthening policies and norms against discrimination, making aversive racists aware of their prejudice and how their biases are expressed, providing aversive racists opportunities to develop and practice nonprejudiced responses, and altering the primary basis of social categorization from different racial groups (i.e., Blacks and Whites) to members of a common superordinate group (e.g., on the basis of university or national identity).

To control for the adverse impact of aversive racism on Blacks, policymakers need to design policies and laws to address subtle forms of discrimination. As Krieger (1995, 1998) has observed, for successful prosecution, current antidiscrimination laws require that racial bias be identified as the sole cause for disparate treatment, that intention to discriminate be demonstrated, and that the action directly harm the complainant. Research on aversive racism has shown that disparate treatment is most likely to occur in combination with other factors that provide nonracial rationales for negative treatment; that racial bias is typically unconscious and often unintentional; and that disparate treatment, because of in-group biases, often represents in-group favoritism (pro-White responses) rather than outright rejection of out-group members (anti-Black responses). Thus, as Krieger explained, the consequences of contemporary forms of bias are difficult to address with existing legislation. Revising laws to combat subtle forms of discrimination can convey an important message to society—one that would enhance the salience of egalitarian standards and promote more inclusive social norms (McConahay, 1986).

Whereas legal interventions offer more immediate control of the effects of subtle bias rather than a "cure" for contemporary racism, other strategies can combat it directly by focusing on its roots—unacknowledged negative feelings that can evolve into more openly negative emotions such as contempt and hate. In general, traditional approaches that focus on the evils of prejudice and discrimination tend to be ineffective in addressing aversive racists. Aversive racists already endorse egalitarian values, recognize norms against prejudice, and possess quite positive conscious cognitions about Blacks. In addition, because they believe that they are not prejudiced, they may not see the relevance of such appeals to them. However, because they experience negative affect with regard to Blacks, strategies aimed at this component may be more effective than more traditional approaches to combating prejudice (Dovidio, Esses, Beach, & Gaertner, 2002).

Esses and Dovidio (2002), for example, found that Whites who were asked to focus on their feelings, rather than their cognitions, while viewing incidents of discrimination against Blacks subsequently showed less avoidance and an interest in more intimate contact with Blacks. Considerable research further demonstrates that intergroup contact under appropriate conditions specified by the *contact hypothesis* (Allport, 1954; Pettigrew, 1998) is one of the most effective and robust strategies for improving intergroup relations, largely because it helps to alleviate intergroup anxiety (Pettigrew & Tropp, 2000). Interventions that help to promote an inclusive, one-group categorization for groups (such as Blacks and Whites) that were previously seen as different groups can enhance the effectiveness of intergroup contact by redirecting the forces of in-group favoritism to produce more positive affective reactions and improving attitudes towards others formerly perceived as only out-group members. Emphasizing common group identity (e.g., by wearing clothing demonstrating common university membership) has been shown to eliminate Whites' racial biases in helping Blacks (Nier, Gaertner, Dovidio, Banker, & Ward, 2001).

In conclusion, although blatant prejudice still exists and crimes against Blacks represent a large proportion of hate crimes (Perry, 2002), contemporary racism is generally more subtle than the traditional form, and a large proportion of Whites who consciously endorse egalitarian principles are unaware of their prejudices. Thus, the simple characterization of hate as intense dislike (Allport, 1954) rarely characterizes the racial attitudes of White Americans today. Instead, more sophisticated conceptualizations of hate, such as Sternberg's (2003) multidimensional duplex model, are needed to capture the complexity and potentially destructive nature of contemporary prejudice more accurately.

Old-fashioned, dominative racism and contemporary racism are frequently considered qualitatively different types, but the seeds of hate, as identified by Sternberg, are present even in Whites who possess a subtle form of prejudice, such as aversive racism. As Torres (1999) argued, this prejudice represents latent racism that can be transformed into open hatred, discrimination, and violence by threat, provocation, negative stereotypes, and cultural ideologies that justify disadvantage. Greater prejudice toward people with ethnic backgrounds from the Middle East, support for more exclusionary immigration policies, and the increased incidence of hate crimes toward Arabs illustrate the dramatic impact of a single catastrophic event, the terrorist attacks of September 11, 2001, on the United States, on basic orientations toward minority groups (Esses, Dovidio, & Hodson, 2002). Nevertheless, a better understanding of the relation between a psychology of hate and racial bias can guide interventions that effectively address the potential for hate, hostility, and group-based violence at the foundations of prejudice, which too often lies just below the surface.

REFERENCES

Adorno, T. W., Frenkel-Brunswik, E., Levinson, D. J., & Sanford, R. N. (1950). *The authoritarian personality.* New York: Harper.

Allport, G. W. (1954). *The nature of prejudice.* New York: Addison-Wesley.

Blair, I. V. (2001). Implicit stereotypes and prejudice. In G. B. Moskowitz (Ed.), *Cognitive social psychology: The Princeton Symposium on the Legacy and Future of Social Cognition* (pp. 359–374). Mahwah, NJ: Erlbaum.

Blanchard, F. A., Crandall, C. S., Brigham, J. C., & Vaughn, L. A. (1994). Condemning and condoning racism: A social context approach to interracial settings. *Journal of Applied Psychology, 79,* 993–997.

Blank, R. M. (2001). An overview of trends in social and economic well-being, by race. In N. J. Smelser, W. J. Wilson, & F. Mitchell (Eds.), *Racial trends and their consequences* (Vol. 1, pp. 21–39). Washington, DC: National Academy Press.

Blumer, H. (1958). Race prejudice as a sense of group position. *Pacific Sociological Review, 1,* 3–7.

Bobo, L. (1999). Prejudice as group position: Micro-foundations of a sociological approach to racism and race relations. *Journal of Social Issues, 55,* 445–472.

Bobo, L. (2001). Racial attitudes and relations at the close of the twentieth century. In N. J. Smelser, W. J. Wilson, & F. Mitchell (Eds.), *Racial trends and their consequences* (Vol. 1, pp. 264–301). Washington, DC: National Academy Press.

Boeckmann, R. J., & Turpin-Petrosino, C. (Eds.). (2002). Understanding the harm of hate crimes. *Journal of Social Issues, 58,* 207–225.

Brief, A. P., Buttram, R. T., Elliott, J. D., Reizenstein, R. M., & McCline, R. L. (1995). Releasing the beast: A study of compliance with orders to use race as a selection criterion. *Journal of Social Issues, 51,* 177–193.

Brief, A. P., Dietz, J., Cohen, R. R., Pugh, S. D., & Vaslow, J. B. (2000). Just doing business: Modern racism and obedience to authority as explanations for employment discrimination. *Organizational Behavior and Human Decision Processes, 81,* 72–97.

Campbell, D. T. (1965). Ethnocentric and other altruistic motives. In D. Levine (Ed.), *Nebraska Symposium on Motivation: Vol. 13.* (pp. 283–311). Lincoln: University of Nebraska Press.

Darley, J. M., & Latané, B. (1968). Bystander intervention in emergencies: Diffusion of responsibility. *Journal of Personality and Social Psychology, 8,* 377–383.

Devos, T., Silver, L. A., Mackie, D. M., & Smith, E. R. (2002). Experiencing intergroup emotions. In D. M. Mackie & E. R. Smith (Eds.), *From prejudice to intergroup emotions: Differentiated reactions to social groups* (pp. 111–134). New York: Psychology Press.

Donnerstein, E., & Donnerstein, M. (1973). Variables in interracial aggression: Potential ingroup censure. *Journal of Personality and Social Psychology, 27,* 143–150.

Donnerstein, E., Donnerstein, M., Simon, S., & Ditrichs, R. (1972). Variables in interracial aggression: Anonymity, expected retaliation, and a riot. *Journal of Personality and Social Psychology, 22,* 236–245.

Dovidio, J. F., Esses, V. M., Beach, K. R., & Gaertner, S. L. (2002). The role of affect in determining intergroup behavior: The case of willingness to engage in intergroup contact. In D. M. Mackie & E. R. Smith (Eds.), *From prejudice to intergroup emotions: Differentiated reactions to social groups* (pp. 153–171). New York: Psychology Press.

Dovidio, J. F., & Gaertner, S. L. (1993). Stereotypes and evaluative intergroup bias. In D. M. Mackie & D. L. Hamilton (Eds.), *Affect, cognition, and stereotyping: Interactive processes in intergroup perception* (pp. 167–193). Orlando, FL: Academic Press.

Dovidio, J. F., & Gaertner, S. L. (1998). On the nature of contemporary prejudice: The causes, consequences, and challenges of aversive racism. In J. Eberhardt & S. T. Fiske (Eds.), *Confronting racism: The problem and the response* (pp. 3–32). Newbury Park, CA: Sage.

Dovidio, J. F., & Gaertner, S. L. (2000). Aversive racism and selection decisions: 1989 and 1999. *Psychological Science, 11,* 319–323.

Dovidio, J. F., & Gaertner, S. L. (2004). Aversive racism. In M. P. Zanna (Ed.), *Advances in experimental social psychology* (Vol. 36, pp. 1–52). San Diego, CA: Academic Press.

Esses, V. M., & Dovidio, J. F. (2002). The role of emotions in determining willingness to engage in intergroup contact. *Personality and Social Psychology Bulletin, 28,* 1202–1214.

Esses, V. M., Dovidio, J. F., & Hodson, G. (2002). Public attitudes toward immigration in the United States and Canada in response to the September 2001 "Attack on America." *Analysis of Social Issues and Public Policy, 2,* 69–85.

Esses, V. M., Dovidio, J. F., Jackson, L. M., & Armstrong, T. M. (2001). The immigration dilemma: The role of perceived group competition, ethnic prejudice, and national identity. *Journal of Social Issues, 57,* 389–412.

Fiske, S. T., Cuddy, A. J. C., Glick, P., & Xu, J. (2002). A model of (often mixed) stereotype content: Competence and warmth respectively follow from perceived status and competition. *Journal of Personality and Social Psychology, 82,* 878–902.

Gaertner, S. L., & Dovidio, J. F. (1977). The subtlety of White racism, arousal, and helping behavior. *Journal of Personality and Social Psychology, 35,* 691–707.

Gaertner, S. L., & Dovidio, J. F. (1986). The aversive form of racism. In J. F. Dovidio & S. L. Gaertner (Eds.), *Prejudice, discrimination, and racism* (pp. 61–89). Orlando, FL: Academic Press.

Gaertner, S. L., & Dovidio, J. F. (2000). *Reducing intergroup bias: The Common Ingroup Identity Model.* Philadelphia: Psychology Press.

Gaertner, S. L., Dovidio, J. F., Banker, B., Rust, M., Nier, J., Mottola, G., & Ward, C. (1997). Does racism necessarily mean anti-Blackness? Aversive racism and pro-Whiteness. In M. Fine, L. Powell, L. Weis, & M. Wong (Eds.), *Off white* (pp. 167–178). London: Routledge.

Gaertner, S. L., Dovidio, J. F., & Johnson, G. (1982). Race of victim, nonresponsive bystanders, and helping behavior. *Journal of Social Psychology, 117*, 69–77.

Gallup Organization. (2002). *Poll topics & trends: Race relations*. Washington, DC: Author. Retrieved October 3, 2003, from http://www.gallup.com/poll/topics/race.asp

Glaser, J., Dixit, J., & Green, D. P. (2002). Studying hate crimes with the Internet: What makes racists advocate racial violence? *Journal of Social Issues, 58*, 177–193.

Glick, P. (2002). Sacrificial lambs dressed in wolves' clothing: Envious prejudice, ideology, and the scapegoating of Jews. In L. S. Newman & R. Erber (Eds.), *Understanding genocide: The social psychology of the Holocaust* (pp. 113–142). London: Oxford University Press.

Green, D. P., Glaser, J., & Rich, A. (1998). From lynching to gay bashing: The elusive connection between economic conditions and hate crime. *Journal of Personality and Social Psychology, 75*, 82–92.

Hovland, C. I., & Sears, R. R. (1940). Minor studies of aggression: VI. Correlation of lynchings with economic indices. *Journal of Psychology, 9*, 301–310.

Hyers, L. L., & Swim, J. K. (1998). A comparison of the experiences of dominant and minority group members during an intergroup encounter. *Group Processes and Intergroup Relations, 1*, 143–163.

Jones, J. M. (1997). *Prejudice and racism* (2nd ed.). New York: McGraw-Hill.

Jost, J. T., & Major, B. (2001). Emerging perspectives on the psychology of legitimacy. In J. T. Jost & B. Major (Eds.), *The psychology of legitimacy: Emerging perspectives of ideology, justice, and intergroup relations* (pp. 3–30). New York: Cambridge University Press.

Katz, I., Wackenhut, J., & Hass, R. G. (1986). Racial ambivalence, value duality, and behavior. In J. F. Dovidio & S. L. Gaertner (Eds.), *Prejudice, discrimination, and racism* (pp. 35–59). Orlando, FL: Academic Press.

Kovel, J. (1970). *White racism: A psychohistory*. New York: Pantheon Books.

Krieger, L. H. (1995). The content of our categories: A cognitive bias approach to discrimination and equal employment opportunity. *Stanford Law Review, 47*, 1161–1248.

Krieger, L. H. (1998). Civil rights perestroika: Intergroup relations after affirmative action. *California Law Review, 86*, 1251–1333.

Liska, A. E. (1997). Modeling the relationships between macro forms of social control. *Annual Review of Sociology, 23*, 39–61.

Mackie, D. M., & Smith, E. R. (Eds.). (2002). *From prejudice to intergroup emotions: Differentiated reactions to social groups*. New York: Psychology Press.

McConahay, J. B. (1986). Modern racism, ambivalence, and the modern racism scale. In J. F. Dovidio & S. L. Gaertner (Eds.), *Prejudice, discrimination, and racism* (pp. 91–125). Orlando, FL: Academic Press.

McDevitt, J., Levin, J., & Bennett, S. (2002). Hate crime offenders: An expanded typology. *Journal of Social Issues, 58,* 303–317.

Mullen, B. (1986). Atrocity as a function of lynch mob composition: A self-attention perspective. *Personality and Social Psychology Bulletin, 12,* 187–197.

Mullen, B., Brown, R. J., & Smith, C. (1992). Ingroup bias as a function of salience, relevance, and status: An integration. *European Journal of Social Psychology, 22,* 103–122.

Mullen, B., & Hu, L. (1989). Perceptions of ingroup and outgroup variability: A meta-analytic integration. *Basic and Applied Social Psychology, 10,* 233–252.

Nier, J. A., Gaertner, S. L., Dovidio, J. F., Banker, B. S., & Ward, C. M. (2001). Changing interracial evaluations and behavior: The effects of a common group identity. *Group Processes and Intergroup Relations, 4,* 299–316.

Paladino, P. M., Leyens, J. P., Rodriguez, R. T., Rodriguez, A. P., Gaunt, R., & Demoulin, S. (2002). Differential association of uniquely and non uniquely human emotions to the ingroup and the outgroups. *Group Processes and Intergroup Relations, 5,* 105–117.

Perry, B. (2002). Defending the color line: Racially and ethnically motivated hate crime. *American Behavioral Scientist, 46,* 72–92.

Pettigrew, T. F. (1998). Intergroup contact theory. *Annual Review of Psychology, 49,* 65–85.

Pettigrew, T. F., & Meertens, R. W. (1995). Subtle and blatant prejudice in Western Europe. *European Journal of Social Psychology, 25,* 57–76.

Pettigrew, T. F., & Tropp, L. R. (2000). Does intergroup contact reduce prejudice? Recent meta-analytic findings. In S. Oskamp (Ed.), *Reducing prejudice and discrimination* (pp. 93–114). Mahwah, NJ: Erlbaum.

Richeson, J., & Shelton, J. N. (2003). When prejudice does not pay: Effects of interracial contact on executive function. *Psychological Science, 14,* 287–290.

Rogers, R. W., & Prentice-Dunn, S. (1981). Deindividuation and anger-mediated interracial aggression: Unmasking regressive racism. *Journal of Personality and Social Psychology, 41,* 63–73.

Rozin, P., Lowery, L., Imada, S., & Haidt, J. (1999). The CAD triad hypothesis: A mapping between three moral emotions (contempt, anger, disgust) and three moral codes (community, autonomy, divinity). *Journal of Personality and Social Psychology, 76,* 574–586.

Sears, D. O., Henry, P. J., & Kosterman, R. (2000). Egalitarian values and contemporary racial politics. In D. O. Sears, J. Sidanius, & L. Bobo (Eds.), *Racialized politics: The debate about racism in America* (pp. 75–117). Chicago: University of Chicago Press.

Sherif, M., Harvey, O. J., White, B. J., Hood, W. R., & Sherif, C. W. (1961). *Intergroup conflict and cooperation: The Robbers Cave experiment.* Norman: University of Oklahoma Book Exchange.

Sidanius, J., & Pratto, F. (1999). *Social dominance: An intergroup theory of social hierarchy and oppression*. New York: Cambridge University Press.

Staub, E. (1989). *The roots of evil: The origins of genocide and other group violence*. New York: Cambridge University Press.

Staub, E. (1996). Cultural-societal roots of violence: The examples of genocidal violence and of contemporary youth violence in the United States. *American Psychologist, 51*, 117–132.

Stephan, W. G., Boniecki, K. A., Ybarra, O., Bettencourt, A., Ervin, K., Jackson, L. A., et al. (2002). The role of threats in the racial attitudes of Blacks and Whites. *Personality and Social Psychology Bulletin, 28*, 1242–1254.

Stephan, W. G., & Stephan, C. W. (1985). Intergroup anxiety. *Journal of Social Issues, 41*, 157–175.

Sternberg, R. J. (2003). A duplex theory of hate: Development and application to terrorism, massacres, and genocide. *Review of General Psychology, 7*, 299–328.

Tajfel, H., & Turner, J. C. (1979). An integrative theory of intergroup conflict. In W. G. Austin & S. Worchel (Eds.), *The social psychology of intergroup relations* (pp. 33–48). Monterey, CA: Brooks/Cole.

Torres, S. (1999). Hate crimes against African Americans: The extent of the problem. *Journal of Contemporary Criminal Justice, 15*, 48–63.

Turner, J. C., Hogg, M. A., Oakes, P. J., Reicher, S. D., & Wetherell, M. S. (1987). *Rediscovering the social group: A self-categorization theory*. Oxford, England: Basil Blackwell.

Tyler, T. R., & Blader, S. L. (2000). *Cooperation in groups: Procedural justice, social identity, and behavioral engagement*. Philadelphia: Psychology Press.

Verkuyten, M., & Hagendoorn, L. (1998). Prejudice and self-categorization: The variable role of authoritarianism and in-group stereotypes. *Personality and Social Psychology Bulletin, 24*, 99–110.

Weiner, B. (1995). *Judgments of responsibility: A foundation for a theory of social conduct*. New York: Guilford Press.

Zillman, D. (1996). Sequential dependencies in emotional experience and behavior. In R. D. Kananaugh & B. Zimmerberg (Eds.), *Emotion: Interdisciplinary perspectives* (pp. 243–272). Hillsdale, NJ: Erlbaum.

11

HATE IS
THE IMITATION OF LOVE

C. FRED ALFORD

On the morning of May 28, 1995, Sinedu Tadesse, a junior at Harvard, stabbed her roommate, Trang-Ho, 45 times while Trang lay sleeping in her bed in their Harvard dormitory. By the time police arrived, Sinedu had hanged herself in the bathroom. Unlike most killers, the Ethiopian student left a detailed diary of her emotional state in the years leading up to the killing.

Unlike her roommate, Sinedu was not a popular student. She had difficulty finding a roommate and was elated when Trang-Ho agreed to share a suite with her. But they did not get along, in part because Trang's boyfriend frequently slept over, and Trang was looking for another roommate. Sinedu found the humiliation intolerable.

> You know what I fear? I fear that shitty cringing feeling that accompanies me . . . . Should my rooming thing does [sic] not work out in a way that makes me hold my head high & speak of it proudly. (Thernstrom, 1996, p. 65)

If she could have, Sinedu would have inflicted this terrible cringing feeling on her roommate. Only that, it seems, would have made her feel better, and she knew that it was impossible. "Our situations would never reverse, for me to be the strong & her to be the weak. She'll live on tucked in the warmth & support of her family while I cry alone in the cold" (Thernstrom, 1996, p. 65).

The situation was made worse, or at least more pathetic, by the way so many seemed to confuse them, regarding the roommates as virtually identical, non-Western exotics. Even at the memorial service, Harvard's minister could not seem to keep victim and executioner straight, referring to both as victims, asking the Lord to forgive them both. "Media accounts made them sound like twins, petite, hardworking foreign-born premed junior biology majors" (Thernstrom, 1996, p. 62).

Unable to become Trang-Ho, unable to trade places with her, Sinedu decided to kill herself and to take Trang-Ho with her. Only that would feed her hatred. "The bad way out I see is suicide & the good way out killing, savoring their fear and [then] suicide. But you know what annoys me the most, I do nothing" (Thernstrom, 1996, p. 65).

In the novel *Immortality* by Czech author Milan Kundera (1990) one character says that "hate traps us by binding us too tightly to our adversary" (p. 24). What Kundera (or perhaps just this character) fails to understand is that this is the state that haters desire; hatred allows them to pretend that what they want is to be free but never gives them the chance. In hatred one transforms interpersonal bonds into bondage and relationships into prisons. For a little while, hate allowed Sinedu to come in out of the cold, as she cocooned herself in the warmth of her hate.

Sinedu's strategy did not work for very long; it usually does not. Hatred culminates in violence when the one who hates comes suddenly and late to reality, recognizing that the intensely desired fusion is impossible. By then, however, the one who hates has given up so much of him- or herself to the desire to be the other that there is no going back. The self of the hater has been depleted, and no return is possible, only the perverse satisfaction that the one who is hated will share the annihilation, fusion in the realm of entropy.

To understand the hatred that binds communities and nations, the hatred that is the imitation of love, one needs to investigate further the hatred that binds those who hate to their victims, not because group psychology is individual psychology writ large, but because hatred is a relationship on whatever scale it is conducted. Although the importance of hatred is widely appreciated, far too little has been written about it from a perspective that seeks to join psychological insight with social theory.

Hatred is a relationship with others, and it is a relationship with oneself, which is another way of saying that in structuring their relationships with others, people are at the same time structuring their psyches, themselves. I believe that this is a noncontroversial assumption (at least

236   C. FRED ALFORD

when stated so generally); it is the foundation of object relations theory in psychoanalysis. It is not the case that people's relationships with others are mirrored, or reflected, in psychic structure; the relationship is more subtle than that. But the principle remains because intrapsychic relationships resonate with extrapsychic ones.

The examples that follow are taken from my research with prisoners, most of whom have committed *affective violence*, or a murderous assault on a relative or loved one. I spent over a year talking with these prisoners, whom I contacted following a strange self-selection process. I began my prison research advertising that I wanted to talk with those who had committed serious crimes of violence; the ones who remained in my discussion group after a year were those who had committed that most terrible crime of attachment—murder.

Much violence among humans takes place outside the bonds of attachment, or so it seems. Sometimes modern warfare seems more about the conflict of economic and political systems, aided by machines, than humans killing humans. In fact, through the power of projective identification (i.e., the power to identify with one's victim), most violence has the quality of attachment. The way the mass media cover warfare, bringing scenes of death and destruction into viewers' living rooms, only intensifies this identification. Most of my examples concern violence among intimates. This form of violence is not rare; in most respects it is the norm, even if the intimacy is only in the aggressor's mind, the product of fantasy, where all intimacy is created and preserved. Those who inflict violence are almost always attached to their victims.

Today much writing about hatred assumes that what one really hates is the "other." Unassimilated otherness and difference is almost unbearable to the benighted human psyche, or so it is often argued. Some, such as Pagels (1995) in *The Origin of Satan*, wrote as if otherness itself were the demon: "Concluding this book, I hope that this research may illuminate for others, as it has for me, the struggle within Christian tradition between the profoundly human view that 'otherness' is evil and the words of Jesus that reconciliation is divine" (p. 184). Other more psychoanalytically astute writers, such as Gay (1993, pp. 68–71) in *The Cultivation of Hatred*, wrote of hatred of the other in terms of denied sameness. People project onto the other what they cannot abide in themselves.

Hatred, I argue, is about more than the intolerance of otherness. Hate reflects a perverted desire to know otherness, fusing with it to become what otherness knows—or is. In this regard, hatred comes frighteningly close to love, and love intriguingly close to the pursuit of knowledge, an affinity with which the West is long familiar (Plato, *Symposium*). This chapter explores the implications of this transitivity. If hatred comes close to love, and love comes close to knowledge, then does hatred come close to knowledge? Yes, hatred wants to know, but only on its own terms, whose ground rules are utter control. Although hatred wants to know much, there is one knowledge it cannot abide—that of its own dread.

PSYCHOANALYSIS OF HATE

Before turning to some stories about hatred, most drawn from my research with prisoners, I explore the nature of hatred further. Freud (1915/ 1957, p. 138) defined *hatred* as an ego state that wishes to destroy the source of its unhappiness. What Freud calls the death drive, what has come to be called *Thanatos*, is not hatred, but something more and less: more destructive perhaps, but less intensely involved with the object, the source of unhappiness. Nevertheless, it may be useful to think of Thanatos, or death drive, as the origin of hatred, particularly the hatred that leads to violence.

Thanatos is not merely the instinct to destruction. It is the more general impulse to death, which Freud understood as having the quality of nirvana, or total cessation of stimulation. Darkness, night, stillness, and death—all are related in their absence of tension and conflict. "All instincts tend toward the restoration of an earlier state of things," says Freud, (1920/ 1961, pp. 30–31), and the earliest state of things is a state of tensionless nonexistence: the inertia of nonbeing.

It is not necessary, by the way, to see Thanatos as a death drive, that is, as an instinct. Thanatos may have more the quality of a raging protest against pain, a protest that makes no distinction between subject and object, cause and effect. As Marcuse (1962, pp. 119–126) argued in *Eros and Civilization*, his philosophical reinterpretation of Freud, Thanatos is a protest against the agony of existence. The more painful the existence, the more attractive the annihilation of death. The mark of Thanatos is that it hardly cares whose death: yours, mine, ours—to Thanatos they are all the same.

To see hatred as rooted in Thanatos, and Thanatos in pain, is not to minimize its destructiveness, but only to point out that it is a destructiveness of a certain type, one that would end all tension with the other by obliterating the other along with the self, fusing in the nothingness of the All (Freud, 1920/1961, pp. 32–37). Thanatos is the rage to obliteration: of self, of other, of tension with the other, of tension in the self—among these Thanatos makes no distinction. Thanatos is obliteration as fusion, coming close to what Germans calls *Liebestod* (e.g., Romeo and Juliet united for all eternity in death). This is not so far from what Sinedu wanted.

Klein was one of the few psychoanalysts to take Thanatos seriously, although in Klein's account Thanatos loses its quest for nirvana, becoming tantamount to primal hatred at the source of one's pain. For Freud's Eros contra Thanatos, Klein substituted love contra hate, the eternal conflict that makes the world go around. Klein rarely, if ever, wrote about hate except as being at war with love. For Klein, hate is most frequently encountered as a paranoid fear of aggression, one's own hatred projected into the world. The key problem of mental life for Klein is to separate one's love and hate sufficiently in early life to be able to integrate them later. Otherwise, one would be eternally confused as to what is good and what is bad, and so likely to confuse love and hate.

Although envy was not the root of hatred for Klein, it was hatred's most pernicious expression. Envy hates the good because it is good, because it is separate, whole, and beyond the ability of the hateful one to possess. Envy is hatred of the good because it is good, filled with itself and life, something the envious one cannot bear because it makes him or her feel so empty and cold. Envy hates the good because good alone is truly self-sufficient, needing and wanting nothing from the envious one (Klein, 1957/1975b). Envy is precisely what Sinedu expressed in her diary, destroying Trang-Ho because she was cocooned in a goodness Sinedu could never enter, let alone possess.

Although Klein's account is enormously fruitful in placing envy and hatred at the center of psychic life, she paid less attention (particularly in her earlier works) to the relationships in which these passions are embodied, relationships that structure and defend psyches and give life meaning. Weininger (1996, pp. 12–21) was helpful in this regard, pointing out that people frequently turn the death instinct against themselves, destroying their vitality, separateness, and creativity to maintain a relationship with a loved one, especially a parent. Most people murder a part of themselves, rather than another. It is a supreme ethical difference, but perhaps not such a momentous psychological distinction.

Seen from this perspective, hatred is self-chosen bondage to another, bondage serving to structure the psyche, as though slavery were the only alternative to psychic fragmentation. Hatred is self-structure on the cheap. In this regard hatred is a more complex relationship than is often appreciated. Hatred is not the opposite of love, love's eternal enemy. Hatred is the imitation of love, creating and preserving imitations of those love relationships on which psychic structure depends. Kernberg (1995) put it this way: "The underlying mechanism [of hatred], I am suggesting, is the establishment of an internalized object relationship under the control of structured rage, that is hatred . . . Hatred consolidates the unconscious identification with victim and victimizer" (p. 69).

Some may object to the term *psychic structure*, as though the term must reify an entity that does not exist. With the term *structure* I mean nothing more, or less, than history, the stories people tell themselves to make sense of their lives and so give them continuity and purpose. The structure created by hatred is history, the history of people's hatreds, narratives of their malevolent attachments that help hold self and world together.

Frequently these narratives are expressed in an almost loving recitation of harms suffered and revenge inflicted. One hears this from many prisoners, but one learns much the same thing from reading the stories that groups and nations tell about their origins. The history of one's hatreds constitutes the single most important, most comprehensible, and most stable sense of identity for many people, and more than one nation.

Lewin (1996) wrote about a man in his 30s who had

> as his defining passion in life a hatred for his father . . . His world was utterly patricentric . . . Intense hatred against his father represented the conflict over how and whether to break free not only of his father but also of an identification with his mother that was so global, so extensive, so infiltrative as to amount to a virtual merger. The intensity of the hatred was in proportion to the internal feeling of helplessness and hopelessness over achieving a new status of increased autonomy and personal scope not only in the external world but also in the internal world. (pp. 298–299)

Consider the functions served by hatred in this one case. It energizes the self, keeping feelings of helplessness and hopelessness at bay, while imprisoning the self in its hatred in a way that is experienced as preferable to the terror of freedom, preventing a complete fusion with mother by means of a partial fusion in hatred with father.

Nor do these functions exhaust the meaning of hatred. Hatred is itself a comfort, a nursemaid: "As he nursed this monumental grudge against his father, it nursed him, too, reducing him to the status of a suckling without any greater range of initiative than an infant" (Lewin, 1996, p. 299). One inmate I interviewed had nursed his hatred for years, doing nasty things to the family members he despised, such as swishing their toothbrushes in the toilet bowl without saying a word. His only comfort, it seems, was imagining all the terrible things he was going to do to them when he got out. It's a fascinating idea, "nursing one's hatred," harboring it, taking care of it, so that it will take care of you. It can even make life seem worth living, a mighty hatred, something worth existing for.

"We are born to hate, and learn to perfect it," was how another inmate, Mr. Prior, put it. Murderer of his mother's sister, the 33-year-old Mr. Prior understood something important about hatred. It is the same thing that the authors of one of the few psychoanalytic books devoted to the topic, *Birth of Hatred,* understood (Akhtar, Kramer, & Parens, 1995). Hatred has an emergent quality, taking on a life of its own, almost as if it were the child of one who hated, although perhaps the term *nursling* puts it better. People can nurse their hatred until it takes on a life of its own. Like the authors of *Birth of Hatred,* Mr. Prior was impressed by all the time and energy people put into their hatreds, how creative they can be, or seem to be: "Man, I could spend a lifetime thinking about how to get back at all the people who done me wrong."

Although the connection of hatred appears vitalizing, in the end hatred corrodes the ego, wearing away the self. It corrodes because hatred is built on a lie. The lie of hatred is that it can connect a person with others as love does, without risking love's vulnerability and heartache. Hatred is not the opposite of love. Hatred is the imitation of love, love in the realm of malevolence. "Evil be thou my Good," says Milton's Satan in *Paradise Lost* (4:110), capturing something of this reversal, the way in which evil, defined by Klein as hatred of the good, itself becomes a kind of good.

Hatred has many qualities analogous to love; it establishes a connection between the hater and his or her world, giving meaning and purpose to life, and so providing an experience of transport and transcendence in being lifted up by hate to a higher and purer realm. Another inmate put it this way: "Hatred is good for you. It cleans you out, puts you on a higher plane, where you don't care about all the crap the guards give you." In the end, however, hatred empties the self, unlike most expressions of love (e.g., romantic, parental), which enlarge the ego to incorporate the beloved. Hatred chains the individual to those he or she hates, so that even when the hated one dies, the fetters remain. The result resembles those prisoners in "administrative segregation" (what used to be called *solitary confinement,* or *stir*), who wear shackles everywhere they go and develop a strange, shuffling gait even when they are no longer chained.

HATE AS METAPHYSICS AND EPISTEMOLOGY

Hatred, it seems, is a way of being in the world. Like all ways of being, it contains within itself an implicit metaphysics and epistemology: that is, a theory of ultimate reality (metaphysics), as well as a theory of how that ultimate reality may be known (epistemology). Klein (1930/1975c) argued that this ultimate reality is mother's body and that it may be known only through intrusion and destruction:

> The sadistic phantasies directed against the inside of [mother's] body constitute the first and basic relation to the outside world and to reality. Upon the degree of success with which the subject passes through this phase will depend the extent to which he can subsequently acquire an external world corresponding to reality. (p. 221)

What is the relationship of sadism and hatred? One might argue that sadism is the vehicle of hatred, its medium, but that would not be giving hatred its due. Hatred is the persistence of sadism over time. Hatred is the structuralization of sadism, sadism with a history and a story. This is the attraction of hatred, why so many cling to it, like Lewin's patient who clung to his hatred of his father and could not let go. Hatred links past and present with the future and so offers one tomorrow. It is a tomorrow exactly like today, but perhaps that is hatred's attraction. Hatred makes hopelessness meaningful, and thus bearable.

Although Klein stated that the sadistic epistemological goal is to know the inside of mother's body, this is not the whole story, not even for Klein. Klein (1928/1975a, p. 188) also wrote about another epistemological goal: to know the answer to the question that cannot be uttered. Although much of their violence could be interpreted as sadistic penetration and destruction, it was my sense that many of the prisoners sought something more abstruse and ineffable through their violence. One might argue that the prisoners were hardly average; they were not even average prisoners. Average prisoners do not kill relatives or loved ones. The prisoners I worked with were, as Freud (1913/1955, p. 161) said about "neurotics," like the rest of us, only more so.

> "I read about this Nazi soldier," said Mr. Leotine, one of the prisoners with whom I talked with every week for over a year. "He didn't just kill his enemies, he spent hours lovingly stomping them to death."
>
> "Why?" I asked.
>
> "He wanted to get to know his victim. He wanted a close personal relationship. He wanted to know the other man's secret."
>
> "What secret?"
>
> Mr. Leotine had not a clue. Another inmate chimed in. (Most of my work with the prisoners was conducted in a small group.) "You know why Jeffrey Dahmer ate all those guys?" (Dahmer was a mass murderer who kept body parts from some of his victims in his refrigerator; he seems to have practiced cannibalism.) "Because he wanted to get to know them better, so he could have them inside him. I'm not saying it's good. I think it's crazy. But that's what he said."
>
> "Do you think it's true?" I asked.
>
> "Only for faggots," said another inmate. He wasn't being cruel, just literal, concrete.

What if the secret isn't a secret at all? What if the secret is simple? That we are all, each one of us, so terribly alone in the world? So alone that sometimes the only way we can make contact is through our hate and rage at being so alone? Could this be the root of hatred: the desire to eat rather than to see, to possess rather than to relate? Because we are so scared that if we let go, we shall have nothing? Because we fear that we are so evil and destructive, we deserve nothing?

Inmates drew a sharp distinction between what they called "skin crimes" and other forms of violence. In the inmate lexicon, skin crimes include not only sexual assault but also any violence in which there is close physical contact with the victim. Yet "skin crime" is not really a physical category. A man who stabs another in a fight would not ordinarily be regarded as having committed a skin crime. Skin crime is a physical-cum-emotional category, in which the attacker's psychological need for violent intimacy with his victim is key. One inmate put it this way:

> "Some guys, they use a knife because it's cheap and easy to carry. But others, they don't just cut people. They like to feel their insides on their blade."
> "Why?" I asked.
> "I don't know, man. It's like they want to get inside them or something. They should try sex instead."

I laughed, but none of the other inmates thought it was funny. Skin criminals, it should be noted, rank low in the status hierarchy among prisoners. Those who use a gun for apparently instrumental purposes, such as theft, rank highest. In prison (as in most threatening environments, including many workplaces, and more than a few families), it does not help to show one's need.

In "Über die Würzel der Wissbegierde" [The Origin of the Desire to Know], Chadwick (1925) wrote that originally the desire to know and the desire to possess are one: "It is for that very reason that frustration in matters of knowledge is so serious. It is as if the object satisfaction were taken from the child's hand or mouth" (p. 58). Chadwick's view informed Klein's (1928/1975a) account of *epistemophilia*, or the desire to know (Petot, 1990, p. 189). Where do babies come from? What do Mommy and Daddy do together? What's inside Mommy? Certainly these are things children want to know. But they are not the whole story.

What people really want to know is what they really want to know. Humans' inability to even formulate the question of their suffering, their desire, and perhaps their wonder gives rise to the frustration and tension that transform epistemophilia into sadism, or rather binds them together. Because it lacks language, the infantile ego cannot even begin to formulate its desire, its lack, or its need. "One of the most bitter grievances which we come upon in the unconscious is that these many overwhelming questions, which are apparently only partly conscious and even when conscious cannot be expressed in words, remained unanswered" (Klein, 1928/1975a, p. 188).

It is this ineffable desire to know what one wants to know that evidently lies behind Mr. Leotine's fascination with stomping for knowledge, as though the question as well as the answer reside in the blood of the victim. Or as Klein (1928/1975a) put it in accounting for the sadism of epistemophilia, "these grievances give rise to an extraordinary amount of hate" (p. 188). Originally an expression of the possessive love associated with the early Oedipus conflict, epistemophilia is quickly suffused with sadism. The question, as far as future development is concerned, is whether the sadistic desire to know the other by possessing him or her utterly can be sublimated.

Mr. Leotine was not in prison for stomping anyone. He was in prison for murdering his parents. "I stood over them and watched them die," he said. "I shared their last moments, their pain, their sorrow. For once my family was close." He was talking as if his parents had died in a car wreck, as if he had rushed to the hospital to share their beautiful deaths, as if he hadn't shot and killed them as they slept. Mr. Leotine's eyes closed for a moment. I thought he was experiencing bliss, an oceanic merger with the idea of his parents separated from their awful reality.

He wanted to be close to his parents and free of them at the same time. Only he could not do the abstraction, the distinction between his real parents and their mental representation, internalizing their image while leaving their bodies behind. Or rather, the intensity of his hatred bound him to them so that the only way he could have their image was to destroy their bodies. Mr. Leotine killed to possess the souls of his soul-murdering parents (even the state prosecutor admitted how awful they were) without the bother of their bodies: the terrible, and terribly complex, reality of their sickness, their power, and perhaps even their love, totally under his control for the first time in his life.

Since he killed his parents, Mr. Leotine had dreamt about them almost nightly. He liked it that way. "While they were still alive, I never dreamed about them. I was too angry. It's better this way. Now I can have them in my dreams."

Mr. Leotine did not just want to kill his parents. He wanted to know them. More important, he just wanted to know. Why was he born to them, and not other parents? Why was he himself, and not someone else? Why was he even born? He could not, evidently, even begin to formulate these questions, much less the answers, until after he had killed his parents, until after he could separate their bodies from his thoughts about them. "I never thought about these things before," he said. His were, I believe, the adult philosophical version of questions infants would ask if they could. Or perhaps I should put it the other way around: Philosophy is the adult version of the infant's ineffable desire to know.

Segal (cited in Spillius, 1988) called it the symbolic equation, the symbol confused with the object to the point of becoming the object. Her example was of a psychotic man who could not play the violin because it meant masturbating in public. "In such a state of mind the ego is confused with the object through projective identification; it is the ego which creates the symbol; therefore the symbol is also confused with the object" (pp. 153–154). Mr. Leotine was not psychotic, but one wonders. If he had to kill his parents to have his own thoughts about them, then was he not operating from some deep psychotic experience of confusion, in which he could not separate his thoughts about his parents from their reality to him? Not, that is, until he eliminated their reality.

Not just emotional, but also intellectual, development requires that the object be given up. We must mourn to know—that is, to be able to use symbols to represent others. We must be able to give up the object to think about it, as opposed to projectively identify with it.

> In the depressive position, where there is greater awareness of differentiation and separateness between ego and object and recognition of ambivalence towards the object, the symbol, a creation of the ego, is recognized as separate from the object. It represents the object instead of being equated with it, and it becomes available for use to displace aggression and libido away from the original objects to others, as Klein described in her symbolism paper. (Spillius, 1988, p. 154)

One reason we create symbols, representations of others, is to protect them from our intrusive, sadistic wrath, manipulating, creating, and destroying the symbol in lieu of those we love and hate.

In killing his parents, did Mr. Leotine free himself to mourn them? Or had he forever prevented himself from mourning their loss? Both, one suspects, and this is the point of hatred: to be free of the binding, separation-denying power of love by substituting the binding, separation-denying power of hate, which at least appears to be more subject to one's control. People can't make others love them, but sometimes they can make them hate them—just act hateful. "Love is not the opposite of hate. Indifference is." Half a dozen inmates said this. For many it was their mantra, the meaning of their lives. Only it is not just inmates who think this, or act as if they do.

Ms. Gans had been thinking about killing herself for months. What stopped her was how terribly loud it would sound when she put the gun to her head and pulled the trigger. Experimenting with different hairstyles, she was trying to find the one that would let her put a bullet in her brain without messing up her "do." "I had a date with the mortician," she said with the ironic detachment that is more than just her style, but her way of being.

Instead of killing herself, she shot and killed her lover. It was Christmas Eve. Holding a beloved stuffed animal in her left hand and a gun in the right, she shot him dead. Carefully placing his body under the Christmas tree, she placed a stuffed bunny in his folded arms. Then she wrapped him in a crazy quilt, "you know, the kind where the pieces don't fit together right, like there's no pattern." Then she lay down beside him for a while, sharing the endless quiet. After years of struggle she had finally achieved nirvana. Eventually she called the police. When they arrived they found a note on her lover's body that read, "In killing Jim, I killed myself."

Apparently Ms. Gans wanted to leave Jim and return to her parents, the parents of her childhood, whom she remembered fondly, especially at Christmas. It was why stuffed animals and Christmas were such central themes in her murderous tableau, images of cuteness and family closeness juxtaposed with murder. Irony is the logic of the borderline, playing both sides at once while pretending to be elsewhere. It is why borderline characters, such as the protagonists of many of the stories of novelists Philip Roth and Frederick Barthelme, are frequently defined by their ironic detachment toward life.

Because irony accepts and rejects reality, much as creativity does, it is important to know the difference, not between irony and creativity, for much irony is creative, but between Ms. Gans's irony-filled murder of her lover and genuine creativity. The difference is the way in which Ms. Gans's murder was so bound to the body that it could not escape it. Ms. Gans knew that her crime told a story, but she could not decipher it: "I know it means something. It's even kind of funny. But it's been two years, and I just can't crack the code." When she does, she will have done more than figure out the meaning of her murder. She will have entered another conceptual world, in which symbols are more abstract, less embodied and thinglike. She will have left the symbolic equation.

When the rumor went around the prison that Ms. Gans had chopped her lover into pieces, sending parts of his body wrapped as Christmas presents to his parents, Ms. Gans was horrified. "Jim was a beautiful and graceful man; I would never have disfigured him in any way. I cherished his body, even in death." Especially in death, one might say.

Hatred traps people in a world of bodies—not bodies that point beyond themselves to the richness of the world, the world suffused with erotic energy and promise, which is how romantic love experiences bodies. This was how Plato wrote about the bodies of lovers in *The Symposium*. Just bodies. Rather than nonbody symbolizing body, the direction artistic creativity flows (think of a voluptuous vase), body comes to symbolize a world reduced to its bare essentials, pain and power. *Symbolize* is a misleading term, however, suggesting a degree of abstraction absent in intense hatred.

Hatred does not, it seems, trap us inside bodies, the world with which Klein was most concerned. The surface of bodies, the body per se, is more important than Klein evidently imagined. In *The Primitive Edge of Experience,* Ogden (1989, pp. 4–5) wrote of the autistic–contiguous position, which precedes (or rather, is the earliest version of) Klein's paranoid–schizoid position. In the autistic–contiguous position, experience is generated from the contact between two bodies, two skin surfaces that feel like one. Imagine, said Ogden, that while sitting in your chair you felt neither your buttocks nor the chair, but simply "impression." That would be something like autistic–contiguous experience, one that can hardly be symbolized but only wordlessly experienced as either the joy of fusion or the dread of dissolution. It must be the autistic–contiguous experience that the *Tao Te Ching* referred to when it characterized the ultimate reality as more than one, less than two.

It was the surface of bodies, not their insides, to which many of the inmates seemed so hatefully attached (Mr. Leotine was not attached to the beautiful surface of his parents' bodies, but he was certainly attached to their bodies, even more in death than in life), because these bodies substitute for the ineffable questions the inmates, and perhaps all humans, cannot utter. Bodies take the place of words, and it is no accident that they sometimes end up as dead bodies. Used by enraged adults in place of words, bodies are parsed as though they were sentences, with no respect for their integrity, their living form—not because the inmates were so interested in the insides of bodies, but because bodies functioned as words of dread, which on being uttered can be annihilated. Or so the fantasy of evacuative attachment, as it might be called, goes—the murderer inserts his or her dread into the victim's body and seals it up there forever and the victim's dead body functions as the coffin of the murderer's dread. In fact, the use of bodies in this way only bound them to the bodies more tightly than ever, as the stories of Mr. Leotine and Ms. Gans reveal.

Seen from this perspective, the epistemological problem is not that people lack confidence in their answers. The problem is the inability to formulate the questions. The question is so important because the question is itself the form within which people frame and contain their ineffable angst. To be able to formulate the question, such as "Why do I hurt so much?" or "Why am I not you?" or "Why was I born if it was not forever?" is already the answer. But it is the answer only if the person understands that the question is not so much a search for an answer as it is a search for a form and frame to express the anxiety in the first place, and so make it less dreadful by containing it. The question is the answer, a far better one than dead bodies.

Since Plato's *Symposium*, the West has known the connection between the pursuit of beautiful bodies and the pursuit of knowledge. Plato calls it the "ladder of love"—from the love of beautiful bodies to the love of beautiful Ideas (*Symposium*, 211c). The term Plato uses to characterizes intellectual intercourse with the Ideas, *suneinai*, may be used to refer to sexual intercourse as well (211d6).

My considerations support this connection between bodies and ideas, but with a caveat. For Plato the goal was to leave bodies behind, as though one could kick away the ladder once one had climbed it to the stars. This, though, seems to be the wrong way to look at it, at least from the perspective of hate, or love turned upside down. The knowledge that words are substitutes for bodies should not lead one to devalue bodies, but only to revalue them. Without words, bodies must become the objects of all one's hatred and all one's desire, too great a burden for any body to bear.

Or as Chasseguet-Smirgel (1994) put it, "symbol formation derives from the need of the child to protect his object, or parts of the object, from the effects of his attacks" (p. 235). People speak and write and do philosophy in order to protect those they love from their unutterable wrath.

FROM INMATES AND INTIMATES TO NATIONS

If the hatred present in affect violence traps intimates within a world of bodies that point only to themselves, in what way does the hatred present in politics trap its participants? It traps them in relationships that are the imitation of community, as the bonds of common affection are transformed into bondage: to those who hate with one, as well as those one hates.

Humans are creatures of attachment. Love is not universal, but attachment, or connection with others, is. That humans are creatures of attachment is the foundation of object relations theory, but that really puts it too narrowly. It is an insight that begins with Aristotle's (*Politics*, 1253a1-3) definition of humanity as *zoon politikon*, a political animal, realizing him or herself only in a community of others.

Hatred, too, creates communities: the community of those who hate the same other, and the community between those who hate each other. Or, as the Furies in Aeschylus' *Oresteia*, the playwright's paean to the Athenian polis, put it when encouraging the Athenians to unite, "Let them hate with a single heart. Much wrong in the world thereby is healed" (*Eumenides* lines 986–987). Much wrong is healed, and as much or more will be done to others. The *Oresteia* was Klein's (1963/1975d) favorite Greek tragedy, the subject of a late essay of hers (Alford, 1990).

Kevin Phillips (1969), political advisor to President Richard Nixon, who knew something about hatred, constructed a winning political coalition for Nixon in the 1968 election on the basis of who hated whom. Phillips knew that the strongest coalitions are built not on mutual interest or affection, but shared hatreds. In his office Phillips had a map of who hated whom: Polish Catholics hate the Jews, who are hated by the Blacks, who are hated by just about everybody but the Jews, who really hate the Catholics, who hate northern liberals, except in Massachusetts, where they are the liberals, except when it comes to homosexuals, which makes it hard to be liberal, except that the Massachusetts Catholics hate southern rednecks more, and they all hate the hairy young people, especially the suburbanites, many of whose children are young and hairy (remember, this is the 1960s), which just means that they hate them all the more, only they can't show it politically, so they hate someone else. And so it goes.

Hatred is a political phenomenon far better understood and appreciated by *politicos*, men and women involved in the practical politics of securing and maintaining power, than by social theorists. Not even Hobbes (1968, p. 119 [I, 6]) understood hatred, making fear of violent death too important and hatred too impuissant, a mere expression of aversion. Machiavelli (trans. 1979, pp. 127–128) came closer to the mark in *The Prince*, understanding how dangerous it is to be hated. Those who wish to retain power, he counseled, must cultivate fear while avoiding hatred. Unlike fear, hatred will not stop at self-interest, risking the destruction of self and society in its pursuit of annihilation. For these reasons, those who hate cannot be readily deterred.

Hatred as a political force has received far less attention than love and fear, its emotional complements. Love, one learns early, may be translated into patriotism and loyalty, fear into obedience and the corruption of national spirit in diverse ways, from militarism to appeasement. But what of hatred? What is needed is not a new subdiscipline, the political theory of hatred; what is needed is a better understanding of how hatred infiltrates and corrupts all the political virtues, such as patriotism, community, loyalty, tolerance, and citizenship. What is needed is the analysis of the way in which each of these virtues has its dark side, its correlate rooted in hatred, as when loyalty to one's own nation depends on hatred of others.

Hatred is capable of simulating not just love, but almost all the virtues. Sometimes hatred takes the place of these virtues, as when patriotism is defined as hatred of the enemy. More often, hatred infiltrates these virtues, so that hatred of the enemy becomes so confused with love of country that it becomes almost impossible to sort them out. A better understanding of hatred is not enough, but it's a good place to start.

I do not wish to offer yet another psychological explanation of the Holocaust. One should not reduce the Holocaust to the psychology of its perpetrators. Still, it would be naïve to ignore the hatred of those who perpetrated the Holocaust. Indeed, this is the (not always explicit) attraction of Goldhagen's (1996) surprise bestseller of several years ago, *Hitler's Willing Executioners: Ordinary Germans and the Holocaust*. For many years, structuralists, functionalists, and others have explained the Holocaust in terms of bureaucratic imperatives, the "banality of evil," and so forth. No, said Goldhagen, Germans killed Jews because they wanted to, because it gave many Germans pleasure. What kind of pleasure? The pleasure of hatred and destruction. As Miller (1983) put it in the following:

> I know a woman who never happened to have any contact with a Jew up to the time she joined the Bund Deutscher Mädel, the female equivalent of the Hitler Youth. She had been brought up very strictly. Her parents needed her to help out in the household after her siblings (two brothers and a sister) had left home . . . Much later she told me with what enthusiasm she had read about "the crimes of the Jews" in *Mein Kampf* and what a sense of relief it had given her to find out that it was permissible to hate someone so unequivocally. She had never been allowed to envy her siblings openly for being able to pursue their careers . . . And now, quite unexpectedly, there was such a simple solution: it was alright to hate as much as she wanted; she still remained (and perhaps for this reason was) her parents' good girl and a useful daughter of the fatherland. (p. 64)

Pleasure in hatred and destruction is not the answer to "why genocide?"[1] There is no answer, only answers. I emphasize the pleasure in hatred because it has received relatively little attention.

Seeing the world in this dark way has its advantages, for it indicates something that can be done. Focusing on the generally secret and denied pleasures of hatred and destruction makes bystanders more important, especially early on. *Bystander* is an inclusive category; it includes native populations who are not targets, and it includes other nations. The attitude of bystanders can make a difference by confronting those who have embarked on a policy of organized hatred and destruction with severe doubts. Silence, on the contrary, only encourages murder, as do weak words.

Those who practice annihilation share a guilty secret: the pleasure of destruction. They likely feel a satisfying closeness with those who share their guilty secret. Guilty secrets bind people more tightly than any passion but romantic love. In what is otherwise a severely academic work, even Goldhagen (1996) allowed himself to fantasize about this closeness, imagining the intimacy between the men and women who worked as concentration camp guards.

> What did they talk about when their heads rested quietly on their pillows, when they were smoking their cigarettes in those relaxing moments after their physical needs had been met? Did one relate to another . . . the rush of power that engulfed her when the righteous adrenaline of Jew-beating caused her body to pulse with energy? (p. 339)

In these circumstances, the most important—and most difficult—thing is to break into this secret world. Bystanders offer the best hope, but they must act.

Faced with overwhelming force, Danes, Italians, and Bulgarians all successfully resisted the Nazis, saving tens of thousands of Jews:

- Danes resisted openly, sending the vast majority of Danish Jews to safety in Sweden.

---

[1]A definition of *genocide* might be helpful. A recent term, which was coined in 1933, genocide means literally the killing of a *genos*, a race or tribe. How the term is used varies. Some include political groups, as well as religious, racial, and national groups under the category *genos*. Others argue that it is too difficult to identify political groups.

In *Roots of Evil*, Staub (1989) went further, joining genocide with mass killing, or the murder of larger numbers of a group, including political groups, without the express intention of eliminating the entire group. Thus, he included Cambodia (*autogenocide*, it is sometimes called) and the disappearances in Argentina, which resulted in the torture and death of about 30,000 "leftists." Staub's argument for the extensive definition is that the psychology, ideology, and practice are roughly the same for genocide and mass killing.

In *Crimes of Obedience*, Kelman and Hamilton (1989) included what they called "state sanctioned massacres," among which must have been included the Serbs in Kosovo. The goal, evidently, was not to eliminate every Albanian Kosovar, but to demoralize and terrify them so they would leave. Toward this goal state-sanctioned murder played a role.

- Italians resisted tacitly, sabotaging orders, saying "yes" and doing "no." The result was that less than 10% of Jews living in Italy (about 100,000) were deported to the death camps.
- Bulgarians fell somewhere in the middle, both in their strategy and in its outcome. Eighty-two percent of the Jews living in Bulgaria survived the war.

Why was local resistance so effective in these cases? Not only did the Nazis have the power; they had shown over and over again that they were willing to divert resources from winning the war to killing Jews.

The reason resistance worked, said Arendt (1964) was that "local German officials became unsure of themselves" (p. 175). They came to doubt their own cause; they became unreliable. The goal of the bystander is to increase doubt by speaking to the secret, the shared pleasure in hatred and destruction. One speaks to this secret in a simple and straightforward manner:

- We see what is going on.
- We know what is happening.
- We are taking names and keeping records.
- There will be consequences.

It is neither necessary nor desirable that bystanders interpret the acts they observe as ones of sadism and pleasure in destruction. Mass murder is not a "teachable moment." It is necessary only that the bystanders make their presence known, a presence that remembers.

The practitioners of violence and destruction expect verbal resistance. Frequently they fantasize that the outside world not only does not care but also secretly agrees, as Joseph Goebbels put it in his diary entry of December 13, 1942: "I believe that the English and the Americans are happy that we are exterminating the Jewish riff-raff" (quoted in Staub, 1989, p. 158).

Bystander reaction must be early and definitive. The more blood has been shed, the more perpetrators become committed to their deeds. This was the great failure in Argentina. The world had tolerated torture and murder in South America for years. Why shouldn't the Argentine military believe that what they were doing was acceptable? Quite literally it was.

The suggestions I have made regarding the role of bystanders is not new. It is by now part of literature on genocide and its prevention. What I hope I have done is to explain something of the power of bystanders, which stems not only from the perpetrators' fear of being observed but also from the way in which observation has the potential to intervene in two guilty secrets: the pleasures of hatred and destruction and the pleasures of fraternity among the destroyers, a fraternity of those who "hate with a single heart," as Aeschylus put it (*Eumenides*, lines 986–987).

Bystanders need not mention the guilty secret to be effective. They must simply observe what they see publicly and openly, so that the perpetrators are not left alone to cultivate their shared pleasure, which may include the fantasy that the whole world secretly shares their delight in destruction. Perhaps sometimes it does.

CONCLUSION

Once one begins to see hate in terms of its functions, one can see hate everywhere. That is not always a comfort. Consider the myriad functions of hate:

- Hate is a reliable source of attachment, a substitute for love.
- Hate is psychic structure on the cheap, hatred organizing the psyche over time through the narrative of one's hatreds, and thus preventing psychic fragmentation.
- Hate gives meaning to life.
- Nursing one's hatred provides comfort and satisfaction.
- Acting out one's hate is a source of pleasure, that of domination and control. Sadism is the pleasure of hatred. Hate is sadism stretched out over time.
- Hate expresses (or is) its own epistemology, in which knowledge is gained by intrusion and measured by control. Hatred is primordial science.
- Hate envies the self-sufficiency of the good and thus is similar to Milton's Satan.
- "Evil be thou my Good."
- Hatred is a mode of being in the world.
- Hate binds people in a community with others who hate, a community whose intimacy is intensified by the guilty secret that all those who hate share: that there is pleasure in destruction.

If one can bear to know all this, then one shall have learned not only some terrible truths about the world but also something about hate that may from time to time allow one to mitigate its effects. Likely this knowledge will not lessen the sheer amount of hate in the world. Nevertheless, knowing of the secret fraternity of those who hate may allow one to intervene in their guilty pleasures and so short-circuit their satisfaction. The price of this intervention, which will only infrequently be effective, if history is any guide, is that of a terrible knowledge, one that connects the terrible things nations do with the terrible things that each person has at some point done to another person. That connection is hatred, which like Thanatos, to which it is so closely allied, is a principle that connects individual with world history. It is not a connection of which to be proud.

REFERENCES

Classical sources given in the form that is usual in classical studies are not repeated here.

Akhtar, S., Kramer, S., & Parens, H. (Eds.). (1995). *The birth of hatred: Developmental, clinical and technical aspects of intense aggression.* Northvale, NJ: Jason Aronson.

Alford, C. F. (1990). Melanie Klein and the Oresteia complex. *Cultural Critique, 15,* 167–190.

Arendt, H. (1964). *Eichmann in Jerusalem: A report on the banality of evil.* New York: Viking Press.

Chadwick, M. (1925). Über die Würzel der Wissbegierde [The origin of the desire to know]. *Internationale Zeitschrift für Psychoanalyse, 11,* 54–68.

Chasseguet-Smirgel, J. (1994). Brief reflections on the disappearance in Nazi racial theory of the capacity to create symbols. In A. K. Richard & A. Richards (Eds.), *The spectrum of psychoanalysis* (pp. 233–243). Madison, CT: International Universities Press.

Freud, S. (1955). Totem and taboo. In J. Strachey (Ed. & Trans.), *The standard edition of the complete psychological works of Sigmund Freud* (Vol. 13, pp. 1–163). London: Hogarth Press. (Original work published 1913)

Freud, S. (1957). The instincts and their vicissitudes. In J. Strachey (Ed. & Trans.), *The standard edition of the complete psychological works of Sigmund Freud* (Vol. 14, pp. 109–140). London: Hogarth Press. (Original work published 1915)

Freud, S. (1961). *Beyond the pleasure principle* (J. Strachey, Trans.). New York: Norton. (Original work published 1920)

Gay, P. (1993). *The cultivation of hatred.* New York: Norton.

Goldhagen, D. J. (1996). *Hitler's willing executioners: Ordinary Germans and the Holocaust.* New York: Knopf.

Hobbes, T. (1968). *Leviathan* (C. B. Macpherson, Ed.). Harmondsworth, England: Penguin Books. (Original work published 1651)

Kelman, H., & Hamilton, V. L. (1989). *Crimes of obedience.* New Haven, CT: Yale University Press.

Kernberg, O. (1995). Hatred as a core affect of aggression. In S. Akhtar, S. Kramer, & H. Parens, (Eds.), *The birth of hatred: Developmental, clinical and technical aspects of intense aggression* (pp. 53–82). Northvale, NJ: Jason Aronson.

Klein, M. (1975a). Early stages of the Oedipus complex. In R. E. Money-Kyrle (Ed.), *Love, guilt, and reparation and other works 1921–1945* (Vol. 1 of *The Writings of Melanie Klein,* pp. 186–198). New York: Free Press. (Original work published 1928)

Klein, M. (1975b). Envy and gratitude. In R. E. Money-Kyrle (Ed.), *Envy and gratitude and other works 1946–1963* (Vol. 3 of *The Writings of Melanie Klein,* pp. 176–235). New York: Free Press. (Original work published 1957)

Klein, M. (1975c). The importance of symbol-formation in the development of the ego. In R. E. Money-Kyrle (Ed.), *Love, guilt, and reparation and other works, 1921–1945* (Vol. 1 of *The Writings of Melanie Klein*, pp. 219–232). New York: Free Press. (Original work published 1930)

Klein, M. (1975d). Some reflections on 'The Oresteia.' In R. E. Money-Kyrle (Ed.), *Envy and gratitude and other works 1946–1963* (Vol. 3 of *The Writings of Melanie Klein*, pp. 276–299). New York: Free Press. (Original work published 1963)

Kundera, M. (1990). *Immortality.* New York: Grove Weidenfeld.

Lewin, R. (1996). *Compassion.* Northvale, NJ: Jason Aronson.

Machiavelli, N. (1979). The prince (M. Musa, Trans.). In P. Bondanella (Ed.), *The portable Machiavelli* (pp. 77–166). New York: Viking Press.

Marcuse, H. (1962). *Eros and civilization: A philosophical inquiry into Freud.* New York: Vintage Books.

Miller, A. (1983). *For your own good: Hidden cruelty in child-rearing and the roots of violence.* New York: Farrar, Straus & Giroux.

Ogden, T. (1989). *The primitive edge of experience.* Northvale, NJ: Jason Aronson.

Pagels, E. (1995). *The origins of Satan.* New York: Random House.

Petot, J.-M. (1990). *Melanie Klein: First discoveries and first system, 1919–1932* (C. Trollope, Trans., Vol. 1). Madison, CT: International Universities Press.

Phillips, K. (1969). *The emerging Republican majority.* New Rochelle, NY: Arlington House.

Spillius, E. B. (1988). Introduction to 'On thinking.' In E. B. Spillius (Ed.), *Melanie Klein today: Developments in theory and practice* (Vol. 1, pp. 153–159). London: Routledge.

Staub, E. 1989. *The roots of evil: The origins of genocide and other group violence.* Cambridge, England: Cambridge University Press.

Thernstrom, M. (1996, June 3). Diary of a murder. *The New Yorker*, pp. 62–71.

Weininger, O. (1996). *Being and not being: Clinical applications of the death instinct.* Madison, CT: International Universities Press.

INDEX

Adolescent peer relations, 130–135, 139, 140–141
Adorno, T., 105–106, 108–109
Affective functioning
  cognitive–neoassociationistic model, 160–161
  in development of group hate, 160–168
  in hate, 4, 159–160
  in prejudice, 159, 212, 213
  in response amplification, 220, 227
  response to ego threats, 95
  social categorization and, 224–225
  See also Emotion
Alcohol, 174
Allport, G., 106–107
Altruism, 58, 62
Anger
  avoidance behavior and, 14
  cognitive interventions, 82
  cognitive model, 68, 72
  cognitive–neoassociationistic model, 160–161
  environmental conditions in evoking, 163–164
  fear and, 7, 162–163
  hate and, 6, 7–8, 15–18, 19, 21, 125–126
  hostility displacement, 164–165
  as inhibited defiance, 20–21
  intensity, 16
  in legitimization of hateful behavior, 9–10
  meta-descriptive formulations, 13, 15
  popular conceptualization, 15, 16, 21
  power relations and, 17–18
  threat to self-concept as source of, 167–168
  triangular theory of hate, 39
  See also Rage
Anonymity, 172–174
Argentina, 195–198, 251
Aristotle, 4
Assessment of hate
  in groups, 77–78
  in individuals, 75–77
  self-reports in, 75–77

Attack behavior, 4, 14
Authoritarian personality, 105–106, 176–177
Autistic–contiguous experience, 246
Automatic thoughts, 68
Aversive racism
  cognitive component, 215, 219–220
  conceptual basis, 214, 215–216
  emergency intervention and, 217–218
  interventions to combat, 228–230
  response amplification in, 219–223
  sociocultural component, 215–216, 225–226
  subtle manifestations of, 216–219
  transformation into overt racism, 221–226, 227
  in workplace, 218–219
Avoidance behavior, 13–14. *See also* Withdrawal behavior

Baum, L. Frank, 202–203, 205, 206
Beck, A. T., 83
Behavioral aspects of hate, 4, 8–9, 111
  aversive racism theory, 215, 216–223
  cognitive interventions, 78–80
  cognitive model, 71–73
  disinhibitory influences, 171–174
  manifestations of prejudice, 212
  normative judgments, 9–10
  power relations and, 17–18
  in prejudiced persons, 107
  response amplification in prejudice, 219–223
  transformation of bias into overt racism, 221–226
  See also Violence
Bikindi, S., 137, 189–190
Body, 246–247
Byrd, James, Jr., 156–157, 174
Bystander resistance to violence, 250–252

Categorical meta-description, 3–4, 11–22
Causal models of hate, 3–4, 25–28
Character-conditioned hate, 38

Cognitive functioning
    aversive racism theory, 215, 216–217,
        219–220
    categorization of people, 168–171
    disinhibition, 171–174
    group hate and violent behaviors,
        73–75, 159–160, 168–175
    in prejudice, 212
Cognitive–neoassociationistic model of
        anger, 160–161
Cognitive theory and therapy
    assessment of hate, 75–78
    conceptual basis, 68–71, 83
    conceptualization of hate, 67, 71–73,
        82, 84
    empirical studies of hate and violence,
        81–83
    group hate and violent behaviors, 73–75
    interventions to combat hate, 78–81,
        82–83
    research opportunities, 84
Competition for resources, 88–89, 91, 170,
        221–222
Conceptualizations of hate, 11, 37–38,
        121–122, 236
    among adolescents, 131–135, 139,
        140–141
    as attitude, 186
    categorical meta-description in
        formulation of, 3–4, 11–22
    causal models, 3–4, 25–28
    classic formulations, 4
    cognitive perspective, 67, 71–73, 82, 84
    conceptual approaches to, 3–4
    constructive role of hate, 123, 252
    as cool–hot continuum, 6–7, 39–41
    developmental systems model, 103–105,
        111–113
    differences among, 30–31
    duplex theory, 38, 104–105. See also
        Love
    emotion in, 4–6
    folk psychology, 10
    as imitation of love, 236, 239
    as intrapsychic relationship, 236–238,
        239
    as inverse caring, 23–24
    as metaphysics and epistemology,
        241–247
    modern formulations, 6–8
    as negation of intimacy, 38–39, 40, 213
    ostensive formulations, 8–9, 25–28

Platonic, 3–4, 28–30
    post-World War II, 105–108, 110–111
    as psychopathology, 8, 25–26, 107–108
    research base, 87–88
    shortcomings in psychology research,
        122
    stipulative claims, 3–4, 22–24
    triangular theory, 38–39
    true hate, 155
Constructive conflict, 123, 148–149
Constructive role of hate, 123
Contact hypothesis, 229
Contempt, 6
    triangular theory of hate, 39
Cool–hot continuum of hate, 6–7, 39–41,
        72, 73
Courage, 10, 26–27
Crimes, hate, 9–10, 25, 74
    affective functioning in, 160–168
    causes of violence in, 158–159
    cognitive processes in, 159
    common features, 157–158
    definition, 126, 214
    dehumanization and, 174–175
    disinhibiting influences, 171–174
    distinguishing features, 156
    economic stress and, 165–166
    hate killings, 156–157
    justifications, 126–127
    perceived injustice as source of, 167
    personality traits of bigots, 175–178
    prevention, 179
    racial, 214
    as response to ego threat, 92, 177–178,
        221–222
    social acceptance of, 171–172
    threat to self-concept as source of,
        167–168
    trends, 214
    by victims of oppression, 90–91

Darwin, C., 4
Davitz, J., 14–15
Death, 238–239
Decision–commitment in hate, 6, 39,
        213, 223–226
Descartes, R., 4
Destruction of object of hatred, 13, 14,
        40
    bystander resistance to, 250–252
    pleasure in, 249–250

Devaluation of hated people/groups,
    52–54, 169–170, 174–175
  in escalation of group conflict, 223–226
  genocide and, 206–207
  intergenerational transmission, 57
  interventions to prevent, 54
  moral exclusion, 127–130
  origins and development, 59–60
  response of devalued people/groups,
    89–90
  Rwanda ethnic conflict, 136–137,
    139–140, 141, 142–146
Development
  individual–context relations, 110–113
  parent–child relations, 109
  psychoanalytic theories of hate, 124,
    125
  sources of hate, 124–125
  systems theory, 103–105, 113
  See also Socialization
Disgust, 6
  of negation of intimacy, 40
  triangular theory of hate, 39
Disposition to emotion, 5–6
Dozier, R. W., Jr., 7–8
Duplex theory of hate, 38

Economic stress, 165–166, 176
  intergroup competition for resources,
    88–89, 91, 170, 221–222
  racial bias and, 218, 221
Egotism, 92, 93–94
Ekman, P., 6
El Salvador, 198–202
Elster, J., 6
Emergency response, 217–218
Emotion
  cognitive functioning and, 68–71, 82
  in development of hate, 52, 125, 130
  disposition and, 4–6
  emotional attitude, 6
  intensity, 16, 24
  lexical conceptualization, 29–30
  manifestations of prejudice, 212
  meta-descriptive definitions, 14–15
  as moral construct, 19–20
Empathy, 59, 62
Envy, 239
Episodic dispositions/emotions, 5–6
Ethnic violence
  conceptualizations of hate and, 8–9

development of racial supremacist
    groups, 56, 60–61
  hate killings, 156–158
  historical animosities, 124
  process, 27
  in Rwanda, 135–138, 139–140, 141,
    142–146
  Rwandan genocide and, 188–189
  See also Genocide
Evolutionary theory, 91, 123–124

Fascism, 105–106
Fear
  aggression as response to threats to
    identity, 92–97
  anger and, 7
  cognitive–neoassociationistic model,
    160–161
  in concept of courage, 10
  conceptualizations of hate, 4, 6, 7
  in origins and development of hate, 52,
    125, 162–163, 176–177
  trauma experience and, 57
  triangular theory of hate, 39
Fight-or-flight, 6, 40, 162–163
  cognitive–neoassociationistic model,
    160–161
  triangular theory of hate, 39
Fitness, J., 15–16, 19
Fletcher, G. J. O., 15–16, 19
Folk psychological concepts, 10
Freud, S., 238

Gaylin, W., 8, 25–26, 28, 155
Genocide
  Argentinian experience, 195–198
  characteristics of perpetrators, 175–176
  definition, 186
  dehumanization of victims, 206–207
  El Salvador massacre, 198–202
  hatred and, 185–187, 200, 203, 204,
    206–207
  Jedwabne, Poland experience, 157, 158,
    167, 174, 175
  leadership, 205–206
  motivation for, 185–186, 187, 192–194,
    196–198, 200–202, 204–205, 206
  Rwanda experience, 135–138, 139–140,
    141, 142–146, 187–190
  Treblinka, Poland experience, 190–194

in United States, 202–205
See also Ethnic violence; Mass hate
Genovese, Kitty, 217
Gore, A., 115–117
Groups
  affective processes in development of
    group hate, 160–168
  assessment of hate in, 77–78
  cognitive interventions to combat hate
    in, 80–81
  cognitive processes in development of
    group hate, 168–175
  competition for resources, 88–89, 91,
    170, 221–222
  conflict between, 58–59, 61, 88–91,
    124
  constructive conflict between, 148–149
  contact hypothesis, 229
  devaluation of, 52–54, 59–60, 223–226
  development of hate stories about,
    41–45
  genocidal hatred, 186–187
  group identity, 58, 60, 90, 92–97,
    221–222
  human tendency to form, 91
  ideological hate of, 54–55
  individuals and, 73, 74–75
  intergenerational transmission of
    hatred of, 57
  leaders of, in generating hate, 60–61,
    74–75
  moral exclusion, 127–130
  origins and development of hate in, 60,
    73–75, 159–160, 179, 223–226
  realistic group conflict theory, 221
  scope of justice perspective, 127
  selection of target for hate, 161–162
  triangular theory of hate, 39
  victimization of, as cause of hate, 89–91
  See also Ethnic violence; Prejudice;
    Racial attitudes/beliefs

Hate crimes. *See* Crimes, hate
Helplessness, 16–17, 18–19
Holocaust, 249–251
Hostility, 18–19
  as response to victimization, 56–58
Humanism, 81
Hume, D., 4
Humiliation, 18–19, 21, 168
Hysteria, 26

Idealism, 97–99, 100
  genocidal murder and, 201–202
Ideology, 58
  fascist, 105–106
  origins and development of hate, 50,
    60
  social categorization justification, 225
  as source of hate, 54–55, 96–99
Inhibited defiance, 19–21
Inquisition, 98–99
Intensity of emotion, 16, 24
Interpersonal relationships
  adolescent peer conflicts, 130–135,
    139, 140–141
  attachment, 248
  communication to diminish hate,
    147–148
  hateful behaviors in, 13–14
  hate in, 235–236
  humiliation as source of hate in, 168
  violence in, 237, 243–245
Interventions to combat hate, 62–63
  acknowledging one's own hate, 148
  aversive racism theory, 228–230
  cognitive approaches, 78–81, 82–83
  encouraging constructive conflict,
    148–149
  family-centered community building,
    115–117, 118
  group hatred, 61
  hate crime prevention, 179
  individual resistance to hate,
    142–147
  interpersonal communication,
    147–148
  need for, 117–118
  overcoming devaluation of groups, 54
  in prejudiced persons, 109
  promotion of liberty and thriving,
    113–115
  rationale for cognitive approach,
    68–71, 83, 84
  role of bystanders, 250–252
  role of group leaders in, 61
  self-awareness, 58
  triangular theory, 45–47
Intimacy, 6, 7
  hate as negation of, 38–39, 40, 213,
    219
  hateful behavior and degree of, 13–14
Irony, 246
Irrationality of hate, 7–8, 38

Judgment. *See* Normative judgment
Justice, 148
    justification for hate or violence,
        126–127
    perceived injustice as source of group
        hate, 166–167

Klein, M., 238–239, 241, 242
Kressel, N. J., 8–9

Leadership
    in generating hate, 60–61, 74–75
    genocidal murder and, 205–206
Liberty, 113–115
Love, 5, 6
    hate and, 38, 103–105, 236, 237–238,
        239, 241
    prejudice and, 110
    stipulative claims, 23–24
    stories of, 42

Mahr, B., 10
Marital violence, 71, 82
Mass hate, 87
    characteristics of haters, 175–178
    interventions to combat, 45–47
    triangular theory, 41
    See also Ethnic violence; Genocide
Mass media, 135–138
McCandless, B. R., 107–108, 109
McKellar, P., 18–19
Meta-description. *See* Categorical meta-
    description
Mobs, 60, 173–174
Modern racism theory, 214, 215
Monterrosa Barrios, D., 200, 206
Morality
    in devaluation of groups, 52–53
    in development, 115
    emotion and, 19–20
    justification for violence, 59, 122, 123,
        127–130, 142
    moral exclusion, 127–130, 142, 224

Narcissism, 93–94, 177–178
Needs satisfaction, source of hate in,
    55–58
Negative identification, 6, 23

Nietzsche, F., 19
Normative judgment
    in devaluation of groups, 52–53
    disinhibitions to violence, 171–172
    evaluation and, 24
    evolution of hate, 59–60
    expression of racial prejudice, 225–226
    hate as, 4, 9–10
    manifestations of unconscious racism,
        216
    racial attitude trends, 211–212,
        213–214
    See also Categorical meta-description

Object relations, 237, 244–245
Obsessive ideation, 8
Ostensive definitions, 8–9, 25–28
Overgeneralization, 73

Pain, 238
    desire for suffering of object of hatred,
        13
    in development of hostile attitudes,
        18–19
Paradigmatic examples of hate, 25–28
Paranoid ideation, 8
Passion, 6
    triangular theory of hate, 39, 213
Patriotism, 5–6, 249
Personality
    authoritarian, 105–106, 108–109,
        176–177
    racist, 175–178
Phillips, Kevin, 248
Physiological manifestations of hate, 15
Pine, F., 18
Platonic insight, 3–4, 28–30, 246, 247
Pleasure in hatred, 249–250
Poland, 157, 158, 167, 174, 175,
    190–194
Political uses of hate, 42, 126, 248–249
    in Argentine murder of civilians, 197
    in El Salvador civil war, 200–202
    group leadership, 60–61
    ideology in, 54–55
    in Rwandan genocide, 135–138,
        189–190
Positive identification, 6
Power relations, 7
    anger response and, 17–18

cultural determinants of behavior,
21–22
Prejudice and bias, 91
affective processes in, 159, 160–168
cognitive processes in, 159, 168–175
conceptual models, 214–215
as cool hate, 39–40
definition, 212
developmental model, 109
hate and, 38, 103, 106–108, 110, 212,
213, 227
hatred as response to, 89–90
hatred toward prejudiced persons, 99
hostility displacement and, 164–165
love and, 110
manifestations of racism, 212, 213–215
negative *vs.* positive, 106–108
pathological, 109
perceived injustice as source of,
166–167
role of, 211
selection of groups as target for hate,
161–162
social identity and, 212–213
social norms in expression of, 225–226
subtle manifestations, 211–212, 214,
227, 229
symbolic racism, 98
U.S. trends, 211–212, 213–214,
227–228
See also Aversive racism; Racial
attitudes/beliefs; Stereotypes
Prescriptive analysis, 22
Propaganda, 39, 41–42
Psychoanalytic theory, 18, 42, 83,
105–106, 124
of hate, 238–241
Psychopathology
cognitive model, 68–71
hate conceptualized as, 8, 25–26,
107–108, 109

Racial attitudes/beliefs
anxiety in interracial interaction,
219–220
aversive. *See* Aversive racism
categorization process, 168–171
conceptual models of racism, 214–215
dehumanization of hated groups,
174–175
disinhibitions to violence, 171–174

fear in, 163
hate killings, 156–158
hatred toward dominant groups by
oppressed groups, 89–91
ideological justification, 225
manifestations of racism, 212, 213–215
perceived injustice as source of hatred,
166–167
personality of bigots, 175–178
role of bias, 211
supremacist groups, 56, 60–61, 74,
126–127, 166–167, 170–171, 175
symbolic racism, 98
workplace equality and, 218–219, 226
See also Ethnic violence
Radio Television Libre Mille Collines,
135–138, 139–140, 141, 142
Rage, 4, 40
conceptualizations of hate, 8
in hate murders, 158–159
See also Anger
Rational hate, 38
Religion, 52, 59–60, 98–99
conflicts between groups, 124, 158
justification of genocide, 197–198
Repulsion, 39
Resentment, 7, 19
Respect, 7
Revenge, 18, 62
for ego insults, 94–95, 96
Revilement, 40
Revulsion, 40
Robbers Cave study, 222–223
Rusesabagina, Paul, 142–146, 147
Rwanda, 135–138, 139–140, 141,
142–146, 187–190

Sabini, J., 19–20
Sacrifice, to engage in revenge, 94–95, 96
Sadism, 99–100, 241–242, 243
Scapegoating, 53, 58, 225
Scilingo, A. F., 196–198, 206
Self-concept
civic engagement, 113
cognitive model of hate behaviors, 71,
73
deindividuation effects on behavior,
173–174
desire for fusion with other, 236
egotism, 92
group identity, 58, 60, 90

hate as response to threat to, 92–97, 100, 221–222
hate crimes as response to threat to, 167–168
of hater, 41
hate statements as expression of, 135
hate stories in, 42, 52, 239–241
interventions to combat hate, 58
low self-esteem, 92–93, 168, 177–178
prejudice and, 212–213
projection of undesirable traits, 58
stability, 95
stereotyping and, 95–96
of true haters, 176–178
September 11 terrorist attacks, 61–62
Severity of hate, 121–122, 138–142
Shand, A. F., 5–6, 12, 29
Shriver, D. W., 147–148, 149
Silver, M., 19–20
Skin crimes, 242–243
Socialization
civic engagement in, 113–115
development of hate in, 108–109
family-centered community building, 115–117, 118
inculcation of prejudice in, 107–108
interventions to combat hate, 46, 47
perpetuation of hate in, 39, 42
trauma experience in, 56–57
Sociocultural context, 62
aversive racism theory, 215–216
categorical meta-description of hate, 11–12, 21–22
conflict between groups, 124
constructive conflict, 148–149
developmental systems theory, 105, 110–113
disinhibitions to violence, 171–172
economic manifestations of racism, 218
expression of racial prejudice, 225–226
in intergroup conflict, 58–59, 159
interventions to combat hate, 46, 47
origins and development of group hate, 74
perpetuation of devaluation of groups, 53–54
promoting liberty and thriving to diminish hate, 113–115
racial attitude trends, 211–212, 213–214
scapegoating processes, 58

violence in defense of honor, 167–168
See also Economic stress; Socialization
Solomon, R., 7
Spinoza, B., 4
Stangl, F., 192–194, 206
Stereotypes, 91
categorization of people, 168–171
in escalation of group conflict, 223
self-esteem and, 95–96
Sternberg, R., 66–7
Stipulation, 3–4, 22–24
Stories in development of hate
contents, 41–43
duplex theory, 38
self structure and, 239–241
structure of, 43–45
Suffering of object of hatred, 13, 14
Symbolic racism theory, 214–215
Syndrome, hate as, 5, 7

Tadesse, Sinedu, 235–236
Terrorism, 25–26, 60, 73, 117–118
September 11 terrorist attacks, 61–62
triangular theory, 41
Thanatos, 238–239
Trang-Ho, 235–236
Trauma experience, in development of hate, 55–58
Triangular theory of hate, 38–39
interventions based on, 45–47
in psychology of prejudice, 213
True hate, 155, 159, 160, 176–177
Tunnel vision, 73

Uniforms, 172

Victimization
hatred as result of, 89–91
hostility as result of, 56–58
Violence
bystander resistance to, 250–252
childhood traumatization in development of, 56–58
cognitive interventions to prevent, 78–81
cognitive model, 71–75
in defense of honor, 167–168
disinhibitory influences, 171–174

environmental conditions in
evoking, 163–164
fear and, 57
group behaviors, 73–75
hate and, 51, 87–88, 89
hate killings, 156–158
idealism as source of, 97–99, 100
instrumental aggression, 88–91, 100,
158
manifestations of racism, 212
moral exclusion in development of,
128–129, 142
moral justification, 122, 123,
127–130
as response to threats to identity,
92–97, 100
Rwanda ethnic conflict, 136–137,
139–140, 141, 142–146
in sadism, 243
sadistic, 99–100
self-esteem and, 92–93
skin crimes, 242–243
sources of, 88, 100
toward loved ones, 237, 243–245
See also Crimes, hate; Ethnic violence

Wisdom, 47
Withdrawal behavior, 4. See also
Avoidance behavior
Workplace, 218–219, 226
Wounded Knee, 202–205

ABOUT THE EDITOR

Robert J. Sternberg, PhD, is best known for his theory of successful intelligence, investment theory of creativity (developed with Todd Lubart), theory of mental self-government, balance theory of wisdom, triangular theory of love, and theory of love as a story. Dr. Sternberg is the author of more than 900 journal articles, book chapters, and books and has received about $20 million in government grants and contracts for his research. He is past president of the American Psychological Association (APA) and currently is editor of *Contemporary Psychology*. He received his PhD from Stanford University in 1975 and his BA summa cum laude, Phi Beta Kappa, from Yale University in 1972. He has won many awards from APA and other organizations. He has been president of four APA divisions and has served as editor of *Psychological Bulletin*.